On Meat

Modern Recipes for the Home Kitchen

On Meat

Modern Recipes for the Home Kitchen

Jeremy Fox

with Rachael Sheridan
foreword by Paul Bertolli
photographs by Jim Sullivan

7 Foreword by Paul Bertolli

8 Introduction

- 8 On Meat, or How I Learned to Cook Vegetables
- 10 How to Use This Book
- 13 I Don't Love Bacon
- 14 Things You'll Need

19 How To

- 20 Roast a Chicken
- 22 Confit Duck Legs
- 24 Sear a Duck Breast
- 26 Pan Roast a Steak
- 28 Cook a Pork Chop & Make Pan Gravy
- 30 Make & Stuff Sausages
- 32 Make a Terrine
- 34 Torque
- 35 Fold a Cartouche

37 Deli Case

95 Pork

169 Poultry & Rabbit

237 Beef & Lamb

299 The Larder

- 342 Index
- 350 Sources
- 351 Ratios

I met Jeremy Fox in 2007 when he knocked on the door of my *salumi* company, Fra' Mani, to interview for the position of production manager. I didn't recognize him at the time, nor did he identify himself (as I remember it) other than as a chef looking for a job. More than chefs, I needed meatheads. Early on, I discovered that chefs couldn't tolerate the cold of a cut room floor and found the repetition that comes with becoming a craftsman to be a dull exercise. There was no recitation of his creds or details about the fine restaurant he had recently left after four years as Chef de Cuisine. Shortly thereafter, before I was short-sighted enough not to have signed him on, his in-born talent bloomed. Unfortunately, as I was in the midst of my own transition with a newly launched business, I never had the opportunity to eat at Ubuntu restaurant, which established him as a trailblazer in modern vegetable cuisine. In 2024 his first book, *On Vegetables*, was chosen as one of *Food & Wine*'s "Best Cookbooks of All Time." However, after reading his latest work, I am still impressed by his disarming humility and his deference to those who have influenced him. He acknowledges that he is an artist but prefers to keep that to himself, knowing, as I think he does, that every artist channels their medium and that there is no way to bullhorn that anyway. Throughout his about-face in *On Meat*, he shares the details that matter, and his tips are canny. For some readers, certain iconic dishes he presents—bacon, duck confit, roast chicken, and ribs—may seem mundane or obscured by the chaff of social media. Keep reading. There is always something fresh in Jeremy's larder. As if no other poet could write a sonnet after Shakespeare!

At its core, I think Jeremy's cooking is driven by his appetite, which is undoubtedly the best source and also serves as his strong motivation to cook and write about food. Although he describes himself as more of a "thinking chef" than a skilled practitioner, his recipes clearly reflect the practice of lighting up all his senses when he cooks, which is the hallmark of a chef. He recognizes that being an artist means exposing himself to the world rather than siphoning from it. In this book, you encounter Jeremy, generous and candid, offering perhaps only a glimpse of all he has absorbed along his path and of what he is capable of.

Except for certain classics, you might say there is nothing particularly traditional about Jeremy's cooking, yet in each dish you recognize obvious connections, more regularly echoes of culinary history, transformed through his personal style and playful ingenuity. He must have known that one theory of the etymology of the word "mortadella" is attributed to its inclusion of myrtle berries. He must have been reminded of the olive loaf, a staple in American delis and grocery stores in the early mid-twentieth century, a product that time has forgotten but the shelf still remembers. His version is not only a makeover; it's a reinvention. Expect to be surprised.

As I read, I found patterns not so much as organized on the content page but rather as imaginative riffs, cross-cultural references, dishes generated through personal stories of their inspiration, or his use of unusual ingredients and techniques. I've covered my pots with parchment paper but never made a "cartouche." I had to look up what his backyard "makrut" tree leaves are, and "oca" (New Zealand yams), "jaew," and "chili hybrid solids." Take his treatment of "variety meats"—beef tripe and tendon, tongues, pig feet, and trotters seriously. He makes no apologies for these marginal yet richly storied cuts in peasant cooking that find a welcome place among his other mashups and modern improvisations.

As he says, his work reflects "a common search for balance." True to his style, his food and plating are visually stunning. At this stage in his career, he opts for color palettes that "calm the eye." We could all use some calm in these turbulent times, not to mention a warm bowl in tribute to his grandmother's Matzo Ball Soup!

As much as he might scoff at being labeled an artist, I would add, probably to his further chagrin, that he is a philosopher, serving up the Golden Mean with dishes that leave nothing wanting, nothing wasted.

Foreword by Paul Bertolli

The opening to my book *On Vegetables* is long. This won't be. There were pages and pages to write about then. The rise and fall, the comeback, the addiction, the rise again. But that's not me now. Obviously, I want a good opening that's thoughtful, but I don't want to be a poster child for anything anymore. My editor will want you to know my accomplishments, to know my pedigree so I can be trusted as a cookbook author. I'm hoping Jim Sullivan's food photos will be enough to entice you, but in case you need more, here it is in brief: I've won some awards. I've been on some lists. I've won and lost Michelin stars. I've never won a James Beard Award, and I think I've gotten to a place where that's okay.

So, what do I say about a meat book that follows a vegetable book that maybe should have come before that vegetable book? Writing this book has made me realize what I'm good at and what I'm not. I feel like I'm a better cook mentally than I am physically. What I mean is that I think I'm not able to execute at the level that's in my mind. I'm not a great butcher. I'm not the best manager. I'm not a good baker. I'm good at what I'm good at.

On Meat, or How I Learned to Cook Vegetables

How I cook is because of the shortcomings that have gone into establishing my style. People admire the uniqueness of certain styles of art; they think that style is methodical. But in my experience, it's been a product of the skills that I have and the ceiling of those skills. That's why a lot of artists don't think what they do is very good. Why even the best still have imposter syndrome. They know their limitations. And they assume you must see them too. I'm worried this book is trash, even as my wife assures me it isn't. I'm worried because there are fireworks in my head that don't go off in reality.

You'll forgive me for referring to myself as an artist. I am one. But I'm not fully comfortable saying that out loud. I'm practicing on you.

What do I mean when I say that maybe this book should have come before *On Vegetables*? In 2007, when I accepted the job of opening a vegetarian restaurant with a yoga studio on the mezzanine, I truly was an imposter, no syndrome required. I was not a vegetarian, had never practiced yoga, and had zero interest in changing either of those things. Pigs were my muse. I took the job after interviewing with Paul Bertolli for the Head of Production position at Fra'Mani. I was fearless in a way. I couldn't step onto an airplane without panic ensuing (still can't) but leaving the esteemed position of Chef de Cuisine at Manresa to the unknown, and unmapped, Ubuntu just felt right.

I was cooking food the way I saw fit, and that just happened to be vegetarian. There was no awareness of any nutrition that a vegetarian diet should provide. The only thing that mattered was making the ingredients taste as good as my abilities could support. The vegetables were cooked with the same "nose-to-tail" philosophy that I developed to utilize each part of the whole animals we sourced at Manresa. Eventually, I would define this style as "seed-to-stalk." So yes, I cooked vegetables like they were meat. That's it. That's why I got to write a book on vegetables. This brings us back to what I said about shortcomings being interpreted as genius. The fact that I knew nothing about vegetarian cuisine was the very element that connected with people.

This is a book on meat. There are things that are intentionally absent from this book—the kind of information that is well documented elsewhere. You don't need me to teach you to cut up a chicken. At least, not within these pages. If you work for me, I'll gladly show you.

This book truly is my voice. It represents the style of cooking that I have honed over the years in kitchens. My voice wasn't always my job; in the beginning, my job was copying someone else's voice and vision. It may seem odd, but in replicating, you find yourself.

In my kitchens, my chefs learn how to cook like I do. By doing that, they learn what they like and why. The why is important. They learn what they don't like, what they'd do differently, what they'd change, and why. Over time, this data collection becomes the basis of how they cook and express themselves. Every comic starts out sounding like Jerry Seinfeld or Chris Rock, until they don't.

We build larders at the restaurants. They are little puzzle pieces that have been tested and tweaked. On the menu, we put those puzzle pieces together. In the beginning of each new chef's mentorship, I may be the one to decide how those pieces are placed, but I explain my thought process. We taste many things together and discuss specifics. This helps to "calibrate" our palates. How we taste is subjective. It is not possible to know that any two people are tasting something in exactly the same way, but I find that this is the closest thing. Then they take these pieces and hopefully turn them on their head and rework them to present something new, in their own voice, but with the foundational infrastructure that I believe in.

My sincere hope is that this book will give you confidence and encourage your creativity in the kitchen. It contains simple things, complicated things, jumping-off points, and hard and fast truths. When you cook a recipe, I'd love for you to make notes in the margins. What did you love? What would you change? How would you make it yours?

As I grow as a chef, and I hope as a person, the mentoring is the most fun. So, let's get started.

1   For starters, I very rarely put things on high heat, I rarely bring things to a vigorous boil. I like to cook gently, on low heat, barely bubbling. I like to take my time. I coax, I don't rush. As an example, and nothing to do with meat, I roast nuts on low for longer. For almonds, if you toast them on too high a heat, they're still white in the center and not even all the way through. I'm in a constant search for balance.

2   I strive for balance in flavor and balance in presentation. Lately, I've been drawn to monochromatic color palettes on a plate that calm the eye.

3   The sections within each chapter of the book are arranged from easiest to most complicated.

4   You do not need to make all the things from scratch. Just because I'm a maniac doesn't mean you have to be. Buy your own mustard, crème fraîche, and cornichons. The recipes are here if you want to give them a go, but don't feel like you can't try something if you don't personally make all the parts.

How to Use This Book

5 I like to cook the meat from each animal with its corresponding fat. Chicken in schmaltz, pork in lard, beef in tallow. This step, I believe, translates to a much-enhanced flavor profile that diners appreciate, even if they don't necessarily know why. Something that Chef Daniel Patterson said in passing once burrowed into my psyche permanently. I'm paraphrasing here, but the gist was that he wanted people to look at a dish—which in this conversation was, I believe, Lamb with Swiss Chard—and think, "I could make this at home." Then, after they tasted it, to think, "Okay, I couldn't make this at home." This triggered something inside me and was more than a tidbit of culinary wisdom. It was a philosophy to guide a life. It's such a simple premise, right? Make something taste more like what it is, not what it is not. Make something the best version of itself. Make others the best version of themselves. Make ourselves the best version of us.

6 Now, even with all of that said, most of my recipes that call for a specific animal fat will still be delicious if you use vegetable oil in its place. I guess that it comes down to feeling like I'm doing the "right thing" even if nobody is watching.

7 Milk is always whole (full-fat) unless stated. Cream is always heavy (double). Eggs are always large. Herbs are always fresh, unless stated otherwise. Parsley is always flat leaf. Butter is always unsalted. My preferred kosher salt is Diamond Crystal. These things are usually listed in the back of the book where no one sees them. I'm moving them up.

I Don't Love Bacon. But Now, if We Must, a Recipe for Bacon

The consensus is that bacon is tasty. I just don't worship it the same way that many other pork aficionados do. I'm choosy as to what I pair it with. It permeates everything. The smoke seeps in, taking over all the other notes of the food. When striving for balance, bacon can be hard to even out. I especially don't like pairing it with steak, though it's okay with chicken... sometimes.

I understand that bacon can be a gateway meat, and a lot of vegetarians I know still love the smell of bacon. But in the great pantheon of ingredients, it wouldn't be in my top ten.

Makes about 4 pounds (1.8 kg)

pork belly
5 pounds (2.3 kg) skinless pork belly
1 cup (240 ml) bourbon maple syrup
5 tablespoons kosher salt
5 tablespoons maple sugar
1 tablespoon plus 1½ teaspoons black pepper, coarsely ground
1 teaspoon curing salt #1

glaze
6 tablespoons (85 g) unsalted butter
1 cup plus 3 tablespoons (85 g) maple sugar
2 tablespoons sherry vinegar

hickory wood chips or pellets, for your smoker

Maple Smoked Bacon

Because I enjoy a BLT as much as the next guy.

make the pork belly

On a parchment-lined baking sheet, brush the pork belly evenly with the maple syrup. Combine all the dry ingredients and spread evenly over and around the belly, making sure to really press it on.

Place the belly in a brining bag and pour in any maple syrup or residual curing mixture that has fallen to the parchment paper. Seal the bag, pushing out the air, and finagle the syrup to evenly coat the belly.

Refrigerate for 10 days, adjusting the belly daily to distribute the cure and the brine it creates.

After 10 days, remove it from the bag and discard any liquid. Place the belly on a rack-lined sheet tray to drain while you prepare your smoker.

Following your smoker's instructions, heat it to 220°F (104°C) using hickory wood chips or pellets. Place the drained belly inside the smoker on a rack.

make the glaze

Melt the butter with the maple sugar and sherry vinegar and set aside.

When the internal temperature of the belly reaches 130°F (54°C), brush the top with the butter mix. After 20 minutes, flip the belly and brush the other side. Repeat this process until the belly reaches an internal temperature of 150°F (66°C).

Remove and cool on a rack. Wrap and refrigerate for up to 3 weeks.

An Electric Meat Slicer   If you really dig into the Deli Case chapter (page 37), you might want to look into purchasing a meat slicer. Home kitchen versions have gotten better with time and the price tag isn't as shocking as you might suspect. Obviously, there are tricks to slicing meat thin: freeze it for 30 minutes first, use an electric knife, etc. But none of these methods are going to give you the consistently paper-thin slices you want for deli and cured meats.

Coffee Grinder for Spices   Having a dedicated coffee grinder that's just for spices is handy and practical. There are fancy things that you can buy to grind spices, but I find the cheaper, small coffee grinders work just as well, if not better. Just wipe it out with a paper towel after every use.

Knives   Please don't rush out and spend your rent on knives. Start with knives that will cover the most ground: boning, utility, chef's, cleaver.

Things You'll Need

Kitchen Shears	Ideal for spatchcocking and breaking down chicken or cutting frenched lamb rack bones. Once you own a pair, you'll find many other uses for them.
Large, High-Sided Cast-Iron Skillet	At my house, our cast-iron skillet never leaves the stove. It gets used, washed, and put right back. We use it nearly every day. Ours is high sided, seasoned, and 12 inch (30 cm). You'll find yourself using it for anything, and bonus, they're not expensive.
Professional Plastic Wrap (Clingfilm)	Buy your plastic wrap from a restaurant supply store. This plastic wrap is usually called "film" and is thicker and better for wrapping. I know, the roll is huge, and your kitchen might not have room for it, but try to find a place. At our house, we're 12 years in on a 12-inch (30-cm) roll, and at this pace it'll last until I'm 60.
Terrine Mold	One quality 1.5-quart (1.4-liter) terrine mold will get you started and set you up for success. While traveling in Paris years ago I bought my first terrine mold—black cast-iron with a brass handle—but later, when my fortunes turned, I had to sell it to make rent. Try not to do that.
Pullman Loaf Pan	You really only need one, and the 13-inch (33-cm) Pullman loaf pan is it. This size is great for bread and some terrines.
Rondeau	A rondeau is a high-sided pot, somewhere between a sauté pan and a Dutch oven. They're incredibly versatile, perfect for braising, with short handles on the side instead of a long sauté handle. I find them easier to stick in the oven, or into the refrigerator for chilling.

Dutch Ovens	You'll want a round one for stews and an oval one to roast or braise chicken. Don't get caught up in the myriads of sizes, stick to the basics.
Rounded Sauté Pans	I like this style the best because there is less surface area for scorching. Don't rush out and buy new pans, just keep it in mind the next time you need to replace a pan.
Dough Scraper or Bench Knife	Very often these two tools get filed under one name: bench scraper. But they have different uses. A dough scraper is flexible, used for moving dough or vegetables or pushing a purée through a fine-mesh sieve. A bench knife can cut through pasta dough, scrape clean a cutting (chopping) board, level a scoop of flour. Both are things you should have.
Strainers	There are so many, but the soup skimmer, spider, fine-mesh sieve (chinois and China cap) are my favorites. A soup skimmer will help remove foam from the top of stocks or jams. A spider can scoop out eggs or potatoes from boiling water. A fine-mesh sieve will strain your stock or remove bits from sauces. All sizes of fine-mesh sieves do different things, so start with the size that makes the most sense for how you cook at home, and go from there.
Digital Instant-Read Meat Thermometer	Temp your meats, temp your doughs, temp everything. The more you temp your foods and pay attention to the feel and look, the more you'll build the muscle to intuitively know when things are done. But until then, your steak will be perfect. I like the Thermapen ONE.
Delis, Colored Tape, Clicky Permanent Marker	Delis (plastic restaurant containers) are durable, stackable, light-weight, reusable, can be frozen, have airtight lids, and are see-through. You need them for storing your foods. Label them with colored tape that clearly states the food inside and the date it was made. At work, the label also includes the initials of whoever made the item, though I do not require this at home. And always cut your tape. If you don't, I won't be mad, just disappointed. The clicky marker is key. If you go manual here, you'll likely end up with a collection of dots on your index finger.

Rice Bran Oil	I'm throwing a food one in the mix because it doesn't get enough attention. Rice bran oil is perfect for frying, has a high smoke point and cleaner flavor than canola (rapeseed) oil, and, unlike peanut oil, contains no allergens.
Cheesecloth (muslin)	For wrapping cured meats, making herb or spice sachets, further straining of foods, the list goes on. It's inexpensive and a package will last a while in your kitchen.
Butcher's Twine	I like two types: if folks are going to see it, the red and white twisted twine, sometimes called baker's twine, is my go-to. I use this to hang meats that are curing. For cooking applications like making sachets or tying up a pot roast or chicken, I use cotton butcher's twine. Look for the kind where it unspools from the middle, so you don't end up with a tangled mess in your kitchen drawer.
Cast-Iron Grill Pan	Much like the cast-iron skillet, a square cast-iron grill pan is extremely useful for grilling vegetables, meats, even some oily fish. Especially if you live somewhere with no access to an outdoor grill. Heat your oven and pan simultaneously, to replicate a grill surface, at 450°F (230°C). Keep in mind that using this pan will most likely set off your smoke alarm.
Kitchen Scale	When you learn to cook with cups and tablespoons, switching to a scale might seem excessive. But trust me, certain recipes require exact measurements. Especially curing and breadmaking. Look for a kitchen scale that goes up to 11 pounds (5 kg), one you can set a mixing bowl on. The tinier guys are great for weighing the beans for your morning cup of coffee, but we need more heft.
Rimmed Sheet Pans with Racks	Most home ovens can't accommodate a full sheet pan, so stick to half sheet pans and quarter sheet pans. Then find racks that fit inside of them, the grid kind that you can also use to cool cookies and breads.

Parchment Paper	For living that cartouche lifestyle. More on this on page 35.
Cake Tester	Not just for testing the doneness of cakes, a metal cake tester can be inserted into meat to judge the internal temperature. They're thin and don't leave a big hole in the meat, so the juices don't escape. Insert, leave it for a few seconds, remove it, and feel its temperature. If it's cold, the meat is still raw. If it's hot, it's done.
Meat Mallet	Of course, you can use a rolling pin or heavy pot to pound out a chicken breast or pork chop, but if you want to ensure an even thickness, buy a meat mallet. It'll last forever. You can also use it to smash nuts or break down fresh ginger or lemongrass.
Microplane	For zesting citrus to finely grating garlic, nutmeg, chocolate, and cheese.
Kitchen Ruler	Try for 18-inch (45-cm) stainless steel with millimeters, centimeters, and inches for exact measurements on pastries, meat thickness, etc. Eventually you'll train your eye to know most measurements, but in the beginning, double-check yourself. The straight edge of the ruler will also come in handy.
Chef's Press	Incredibly helpful. They stack for weighing things down. Invented by Chef Bruce Hill, one of the longest-tenured chefs in San Francisco.

How to...

How to...

Making a simple roast chicken is something everyone should learn how to do. There are hundreds of methods and classic recipes you can try. The following version just happens to be mine. My hope is that you'll try out a bunch of these methods on your way to learning what you like best and what works best for you. Look to the greats: Judy Rodgers' Zuni Chicken, Marcella Hazan's Roast Chicken with Lemons, Jonathan Waxman's Roasted Chicken with Salsa Verde, and Elizabeth David's Poulet à l'Estragon. Every Sunday, roast a chicken. Flip it over to pull out the chicken oysters, *Amélie* style. Play around with oven temperatures, spice or no spice, some fat or a dry skillet, butter under the skin or olive oil, roasted with vegetables or not.

I'll sound like a broken record here but seek out the best chicken you can afford. Buy local if you can. Save up the feet, necks, and heads and over time you'll have a good amount frozen to add to stock. The same goes for the hearts and livers. Freezer bags are your friends.

After you've enjoyed your roast chicken, make a simple roast chicken stock from the carcass. It won't be as rich as a stock made from uncooked bones, but it'll still be tasty and useful. Barely cover the carcass with water, add a peeled carrot, a stalk of celery, half a peeled onion, a little salt, a few black peppercorns. Let it gently bubble away for a few hours, then strain it. It won't make much, maybe a quart, but that's your stock for the week. For rice, sauces, or a little pastina. These quantities are my estimates. Feel it out, use what seems right.

... roast a chicken

Herb Butter Roast Chicken

Line a half or quarter sheet tray with aluminum foil and put a rack inside. Pat the chicken dry, inside and out, and sprinkle all over with the salt. Using your hands, coat the chicken all over, except for the inside cavity, with the butter. To the inside cavity, add a squeeze of lemon, followed by the rind, another sprinkle of salt, garlic cloves, torn bay leaf, and whole herbs. With butcher's twine, loosely tie the legs together to keep the lemon rind from sneaking out. Sprinkle the buttered chicken all over with the chopped mixed herbs.

Refrigerate the chicken overnight on the prepared tray, uncovered. The butter will harden and encase the bird.

When you're ready to cook, preheat your oven to 500°F (260°C). Put the tray with the cold bird straight into the hot oven and roast it for 15 to 20 minutes, just so it gets some really good color.

Remove the chicken from the oven and lower the temperature to 250°F (120°C). You can keep your oven door ajar a bit to help it lower. After about 20 minutes, once the temperature has set, return the chicken to the oven and slowly roast it until the thigh registers 165°F (75°C). As it slowly roasts, baste the chicken with the melted butter and juices that accumulate at the bottom of the sheet tray.

Remove the chicken from the oven and allow it to rest for 10 minutes. Carve and enjoy with the pan juices on the side.

Serves 4

1 young chicken (3½ to 4 pounds/1.6 to 1.8 kg), head, neck, and feet removed
2 teaspoons kosher salt, plus extra for the cavity
6 tablespoons (85 g) unsalted butter, room temperature
1 small lemon, cut in half
3 to 4 garlic cloves, smashed, skin on
1 bay leaf, torn in half
2 tablespoons mixed chopped herbs, like rosemary and thyme, plus extra herbs still on the stem

How to...

There is something so comforting about making duck confit. It's not the kind of project that requires a lot of active work, though it does take time. Plus, it's such a decadent way to preserve food.

While I was still in culinary school, my first line cook job was at a restaurant called Anson in Charleston, South Carolina. There they made the duck confit in these big roasting plaques; they were giant and full of fat. They'd remove them from the oven and have to walk carefully through the kitchen and toggle them to a counter to cool. It made me so nervous. This big pot of slowly sloshing hot fat. It felt like a scene in a Jim Carrey movie and Jim was surely about to spill the pot, slip in the hot oil, and take down several chefs with him like dominos, all while the duck legs went flying. I would get anxious whenever the ducks were pulled from the oven, but I also wanted to try my hand at it.

These are my measurements for confit duck legs: The amount of poultry cure you need is 1.5 percent the total weight of the duck legs. So, if your duck legs weigh a total of 7 pounds (3.2 kg), you'll use roughly 1.7 ounces (48 g) of poultry cure. And if you're going to go through the work, invest in a bucket of duck fat. The legs, once confit, can last up to six months in your refrigerator submerged in fat. The fat itself can be filtered through a fine-mesh sieve lined with cheesecloth or a coffee filter and stored in the refrigerator or freezer indefinitely until you need it again.

... confit duck legs

Classic Duck Confit

You need a vessel big enough to hold all the legs so that there's space between them. They can't be touching. You also need this vessel to be tall enough that you can cover the legs with the fat by 1 inch (2.5 cm), and it needs to be oven safe. Before you season up your legs, I recommend playing some duck leg Tetris to see what vessel will work best for this purpose. If you've got a roasting pan with a rack, start there, *sans* rack.

To prepare the duck legs, some chefs like to remove the skin on the bone of the drumstick. That's fine and great and classic, but I don't do it. I like to leave whatever is on the little nubbin at the top of the leg bone and I keep all the skin intact around the bone, just like the cover of my late dear friend Chef Naomi Pomeroy's 2016 book, *Taste & Technique*. To my mind, it's just more crispy skin later on. And typically, during the confit process, it shrinks down a bit anyway.

Whatever you choose, pat the legs dry and then evenly distribute the weighed-out cure among them, coating all sides. Transfer the legs to a rack-lined rimmed baking sheet and refrigerate the legs overnight. I don't cover the legs as I do this; I like the cure to pull out as much moisture as possible while the skin dries out a bit.

To confit the legs, preheat your oven to 275°F (135°C).

With the poultry cure recipe at this percentage, I don't rinse the legs after they cure. Simply dry them with paper towels or a clean kitchen towel and load them into your cooking vessel.

In a large saucepan, melt the duck fat. I'm going to make a guess that you'll most likely need 6 to 8 cups (1.4 to 1.9 liters) of duck fat. Use this guess as a guide for buying fat and for how much to warm up. After your first time, you'll know for sure.

Once the fat has reached 200°F (93°C), gently pour it over the duck legs until they're submerged by 1 inch (2.5 cm). Cover the fat with a cartouche (page 35), then heavy aluminum foil, and place in the preheated oven. No convection please. Gently confit the legs for 2½ to 3 hours.

Remove from the oven and allow to cool to room temperature. They'll keep like this, at room temperature, submerged in the fat, overnight. If you want to move them to refrigeration, transfer to a large, lidded container, still submerged in the fat, and store for up to 6 months.

To crisp up, preheat your oven to 400°F (200°C). Remove the duck confit from its fat bath and place skin side up on a baking sheet with a rack, or in a large cast-iron skillet. Bake them until the skin is browned and crisp, 8 to 12 minutes.

Serves 8

8 duck legs
Poultry Cure (page 341)
rendered duck fat

How to...

... sear a duck breast

Much like the Mushroom Carpaccio (page 240), searing duck breasts is more about intuition and feel, with a good dose of repetition, than simply following a recipe. You can absolutely cook a nice duck breast by following these instructions, but an out-of-this-world duck breast will come from these instructions plus time. Really pay attention to your burner and where its sweet spot is, how the duck looks as it reaches the perfect color on its skin, the texture of the meat as you baste, and how it changes. With practice, you'll be able to adjust on the fly, and soon you won't even need to temp to know the meat is done perfectly. This is an incredible skill to foster in the kitchen. I promise you this kind of attention to detail bleeds into other things.

This is my reminder to buy the best meat you can afford. Seek out locally raised duck. Strive for a bird that was humanely raised and is organic.

Seared Duck Breasts

To prepare the duck, start by trimming off any excess fat from around the sides or bottom. It's helpful to do this when the meat is cold. Don't remove any fat or skin from the top, just work to form a uniform piece. If your duck breasts have their tenderloins attached, you have three choices: 1) leave 'em on and cook as directed below; 2) take them off and reserve them for sausage-making or another use later on; or 3) take them off and pop them back in your pan after the breasts are done, rolling them around and cooking for 2 to 3 minutes or so.

Now, score the skin. A crosshatch pattern is typical, but I like to make single straight cuts that line up with where you'll be slicing the duck once it's done. You can use them as a guide. I find that this method, along with pressing the duck while it cooks, helps for evenly cooked meat. To score, use the tip of a sharp knife, only cutting through the skin and fat, not the meat.

Once all the pieces are cleaned and scored, sprinkle all over with salt and pepper, and let sit at room temperature for 20 minutes.

To cook the duck, heat your cast-iron skillet on medium heat until it's hot, but not smoking. Add the duck, skin side down, and cover with a Chef's Press. As the duck renders, tilt the pan and remove spoonfuls of fat to a heat-proof container. We don't want the duck sitting in a pool of fat; if it does, it won't crisp up, it'll be more confit, and we want crispy skin. Keep the temperature mellow. A little sizzle is great, but we're looking for a consistent rendering of the fat.

If at any time your pan starts smoking, turn down the heat. If you stop hearing the sizzle, turn the heat up. Every stove is different, every stove has a sweet spot.

I, very rarely, turn over the breasts. After about 6 to 8 minutes, when you've removed much of the rendered fat, remove the Chef's Press and begin basting. Set a sprig of thyme on top of each piece and add the garlic to the rendered fat. Tilt the pan, then scoop the fat over each breast a few times. Wait a minute. Repeat. Keep basting until the internal temperature reaches 125°F (52°C), remove them from the pan, and let rest for 6 to 8 minutes. Using the score mark as a guide, slice the breasts and serve.

Note: If your duck breasts are very thick and the skin starts to brown before the meat has reached the correct temp, you can slide the pan into a preheated 275°F (135°C) oven for 2 minutes. Then remove, baste, and repeat until the internal temp is reached.

Serves 4

4 boneless, skin-on duck breasts
4 thyme sprigs
1 garlic clove, smashed, skin on
kosher salt
freshly ground black pepper

How to...

I'm positive you've seen this method on TV or social media. Folks love a steak-basting video. Cooking a steak this way is not new or trendy, it's classic. Similar basting methods are used for duck breasts, veal, and pork chops. Quickly basting the meat eliminates that drab gray line that can occur inside a steak with just searing. Plus, adding aromatics like garlic and thyme give the butter even more flavor. The quick basting cooks the steak more evenly, and the hot butter can be directed to spots the hot pan may have missed.

... pan roast a steak

Butter Basted Steak

Season the cold steak all over with kosher salt and black pepper and let stand for 45 minutes at room temperature. This is long enough for the salt to mix with the water the meat releases, creating a makeshift brine. Then the meat reabsorbs the salty brine, seasoning itself.

Heat your cast-iron skillet over medium-high heat until smoking. If the steak you choose has a good fat cap, sear the meat on the cap for 2 to 3 minutes, rendering fat into your dry skillet. If, however, your steak does not have a fat cap, like a filet, add the olive oil to your skillet.

After rendering, or after the oil is hot, turn the heat down to medium and sear the steak on one side until a good crust forms, anywhere from 4 to 6 minutes. Once you've got a good sear, flip to the other side and repeat; after 2 minutes, add the butter, melting it and swirling around the pan.

Add the smashed garlic to the butter in your pan and place a sprig of thyme on top of each steak. With a large spoon, begin to tilt your skillet and baste each steak rapidly. Keep repeating this process every 30 seconds or so, until the juices begin to come to the top of the steak and pool in the fibers of the meat. Once this happens, cook it for 1 more minute, still basting, and then remove it from the pan to rest. You'll have a perfect medium-rare steak.

Now, if your steak is thicker than 1½ inches (4 cm), you'll want to preheat your oven to 275°F (135°C), no convection. After the steak is seared on both sides, move it (still in the pan) to the oven for 3 minutes, then remove it and take the internal temp. If it's not at temp, wait 3 minutes and then move it back to the oven for 3 more minutes. Repeat this process of oven time and rest time until the steak reaches the desired temperature (130-135°F/54-57°C for medium-rare, 140-145°F/60-63°C for medium).

Once the steaks are at the desired doneness, remove from the pan to rest for 5 to 7 minutes before carving. Drizzle with the infused brown butter and sprinkle with finishing salt.

Note: A good rule of thumb for steak is 6 to 8 ounces (170 to 225 g) per portion. Buy the steak of your choice: bone-in ribeye, filet mignon, New York strip, porterhouse, flat iron, etc.

Serves 4

4 steaks of your choice (see Note)
2 tablespoons olive oil (optional)
2 tablespoons (28 g) unsalted butter
2 garlic cloves, smashed, skin on
4 sprigs thyme
kosher salt
freshly ground black pepper
finishing salt

How to...

Being able to cook a piece of meat, make a quick pan sauce, and serve all of that with a vegetable is how dinner gets on the table most nights at my house. Recipes, new methods, all of that is great. I love trying out new things. But nothing beats the tried and true. Learning these basics makes it possible for you to improvise in the kitchen.

... cook a pork chop & make pan gravy

Pork Chops with Pan Sauce

To dry-brine the pork chops, pat the chops dry, salt them all over, and set them on a rack set over a rimmed baking sheet. Let the pork chops sit for at least 45 minutes, or ideally refrigerated overnight, before proceeding. If you refrigerate the chops, don't cover them and let them sit at room temperature for 30 minutes before cooking.

To cook the chops, preheat your oven to 275°F (135°C).

Heat a cast-iron skillet over medium-high heat until smoking. Sear the chops on their fat cap, letting the fat render, about 3 minutes. Swirl the rendered fat around the pan, coating it. You can always supplement the fat with a tablespoon of reserved bacon grease if not enough renders or the chops are lean.

Lower the heat to medium and sear the chops on one side until a crust forms, about 6 minutes. Flip the chops and add the butter. Let the butter melt and add the crushed garlic. Top each pork chop with a fresh thyme sprig. After 2 minutes, begin to baste the chops with the hot rendered fat and butter. Tilt the pan and quickly baste each chop with large spoonfuls of the hot fat. Baste the chops until the internal temperature reaches 135°F (57°C).

If your chops are particularly thick and getting too much color, slide them into the oven at 275°F (135°C) for 5 to 7 minutes until they come to temp.

Remove the chops from the pan to a plate and let them rest for 6 to 7 minutes.

In the meantime, make a quick pan sauce. Keeping your pan on medium heat, guestimate the amount of fat left in the pan. We're looking for roughly 3 tablespoons. If there's not much left, add bacon grease, lard, or olive oil, scraping up the bits of food with a wooden spoon as it melts. Once the fat is hot, sprinkle in the flour and then mix it in with a whisk until a bubbling, thick paste forms. Slowly whisk in the chicken stock, working quickly to avoid lumps. Taste the sauce, add black pepper, and more salt if needed.

Remove from the heat and serve over the pork chops.

Note: You can substitute the chicken broth with cold coffee for a red-eye gravy, or whisk in a tablespoon of mustard at the end for a mustard pan sauce.

Serves 4

4 pork chops (each 12 to 16 ounces/340 to 450 g and 1 to 1½ inches/2.5 to 4 cm thick), bone in, good fat cap
bacon grease, lard, or olive oil (optional)
2 tablespoons unsalted butter
1 garlic clove, smashed, skin on
4 sprigs thyme
2 tablespoons all-purpose (plain) flour
1 cup (240 ml) Rachael's Chicken Stock (page 334)
kosher salt
freshly ground black pepper

How to...

Right off the bat, there are a few things you're going to need

First, a meat grinder
As with everything, buy the best you can afford. Think about how much you'll be using it. If you're a beginner, making small batches, the grinding attachment for your kitchen mixer is probably just fine.

If you think you'll be using it all the time, then you want something that's a bit more heavy duty. When looking at machines, investigate how many pounds of meat they can grind and in what amount of time. Look for a machine that has heavy-duty metal parts, no plastic. Will it fit easily into your kitchen storage? If you hate lugging it out and setting it up, you won't. Get something convenient. What's that saying? Buy once, cry once. Aim for quality, something you'll have forever, within your budget.

And always follow the instructions for cleaning and sanitizing. A lot of these parts cannot go in the dishwasher. We all love to ignore manuals—but don't.

Next, a sausage stuffer
There are machines that can stuff and grind all in one. There are separate machines that only stuff. Again, start with what's readily available to you and go from there.

Other must-haves

Sheet trays for freshly coiled sausage and chilling. Buy the ones that easily fit in your refrigerator.

Large mixing bowls for mixing meat with salt and spices and refrigeration. Again, this needs to fit in your refrigerator.

A kitchen mixer with a large bowl and a paddle attachment, for "kneading" or to paddle the ground meat. I usually do this with a little water, as I'll repeat in each recipe, so the mixture binds cohesively and doesn't become grainy when cooked.

A cake tester for popping air bubbles.

Kitchen shears for separating links of sausage.

... make & stuff sausages

Let's get started

Seasoning the protein
A general rule of thumb for the amount of salt to use is 1.5 percent of the weight of the prepared pork. For the recipes in this book, I've done all the weighing for you. I prefer to marinate the meat once it's cut into chunks, not after its ground. For one, it's much easier to cover the surface area of a chunk of meat than individual grinds of meat. Plus, I find that this prior marination helps with even seasoning, sending the seasoning through the grinder and mixing it all together. Mixing seasoning into ground meat can sometimes lead to pockets of seasoning and we don't want that.

Everything should be cold
Your grinding equipment should be chilled, and the meat should be chilled. If you can freeze the meat for 45 minutes before grinding, even better. It won't freeze solid, but it will be firm and very cold, and the fat will not melt. Heat is the enemy of fat. We want the fat to stay in the sausage, not melt out during cooking. To do this, we keep everything chilly. Under your grinder, set up a bowl over ice to catch the ground meat. Cold, cold, cold.

Add water and paddle
Sometimes people refer to this as "kneading" and the concepts are kind of the same. We want to bring the mix together to make a cohesive and more pliable blend. We're trying to avoid a grainy, dry sausage. Everyone's had one of these, they're a bummer. To do this, we paddle the mixture vigorously while adding a tablespoon or two of cold water. You'll know it's ready when the mixture is tacky.

Testing
Next, test your mix. To do this, take a small amount of the mix, make a small patty, and fry it up in a skillet. Once the tester patty is cooked and cooled, take a bite to test out your seasonings. Here's your chance to add more (less isn't an option at this point, sorry) spice if you like. If you decide to add more spice or salt, make sure it's fully incorporated, and test again.

Casings
Keep your prepared casings in a large deli container filled with cold water. Soak them for at least 30 minutes before beginning. Keeping them wet helps slide them onto the tube. Don't oil the tube—I speak from experience here—just keep your casings in water until you need to remove one to use.

Stuffing the sausage
Chill your mix down again for 30 minutes before stuffing. Remember: the name of the game here is cold. Follow the instructions in the manual for your sausage stuffer. Set up a sheet pan lined with parchment. Leave a space the length of a sausage at the end of your casing, don't stuff it to the very end. Coil the sausage onto the parchment-lined sheet tray. Keep stuffing and coiling the lengths until you're out of mix.

Forming the links
Once everything is stuffed and coiled on your sheet pan, you can create the links. Do this by straightening out one link and tying a knot on the end of the left-hand side. I form links by twisting in opposite directions. To do this, measure out the length of the link, pinch, and twist-twist-twist to the front. Repeat, measure off a length, pinch, and twist-twist-twist to the back. The motion of twisting creates a bit of a spin. Repeat this process to the end of the casing, tying off the end.

Cover the sausage with a dish (tea) towel and refrigerate for 24 hours before cutting them into links. I find this extra time helps the twists dry out and seals in the sausage. Cut through the middle of each twist with kitchen shears, creating the links. The only time I don't cut through the links before poaching is for blood sausage because: liquid blood everywhere.

Finish the links
Inspect the links all over, popping any air bubbles with the tip of a cake tester.

How to...

In general, terrines are fairly easy and turn out beautifully if you follow these two things: 1) Season well. Cold, unseasoned meat? Gross. Get a gram scale and don't look back. 2) Wait. Don't rush it. Weight it down and refrigerate overnight, a full 12 hours, before cutting into it.

What you'll need

Molds

A terrine can generally be made in anything. Glass loaf pan, check. Round cake pans, check. The terrines in this book are made in a more traditional shape, but play around with it. Why not? I recommend buying a 1.5-quart (1.4-liter) terrine mold and a 13-inch (33-cm) Pullman loaf pan. Both pans are versatile and will get you started on your terrine-making journey.

Weights

Whatever pan you use should have a weight. If your terrine came with a weight, great. If not, don't feel bad, not all do, we can fix that. I have never had one, for what it's worth. First, cut a thick piece of cardboard to just rest inside the walls of your terrine. Wrap the cardboard in plastic wrap (clingfilm) and then in aluminum foil. When the time comes, lay the cardboard on top weighed down with heavy cans all of the same weight that fit the width and length of the pan (like soup cans). Make sure to balance them out, as we need equal weight distribution.

... make a terrine

Let's get started.

Lining with plastic wrap (clingfilm)
Have the terrine in front of you and extend the plastic wrap (clingfilm) over it, leaving the long ends. Roll up a kitchen towel and use it to press the plastic wrap into the terrine, paying attention to the corners.

Lining with caul fat
First, clean the caul fat. If your fat was frozen, and it usually is, defrost it in the refrigerator a day before you need to use it. If it feels too hard and not pliable, as it often does, give it a soak in lukewarm water to loosen it up. Caul fat is a web that can tear easily, so be gentle. Rinse it well with water in a colander until the water runs clear. The fat should be bright white, and there should be no smell.

Next, line the terrine. Prepare the terrine mold by spraying it with pan spray and draping the caul fat inside, bringing it up the edges and having it overhang a bit. You want enough overhang so that when you wrap it around the meat it touches in the middle, like wrapping a present. Go slowly. Caul fat loves to stick to itself, which is helpful when wrapping meats like crepinettes and frustrating when lining a terrine. If you have extra caul fat after lining the terrine, it can always be re-frozen.

Tips on water baths
Have a kettle going for the boiling water, something that's easy to pour from. The boiling water should come halfway up the terrine mold. I recommend putting your setup into the oven, and then carefully pouring in the water. Boiling water plus sloshy movement could lead to disaster.

How to...

What I mean is "how to get a tight roll on a food, with no air bubbles, in order to steam, sous vide, or hang it." Think rolled cookie dough. Or a foie gras torchon. Or Lonnie's Quail on page 234. We want an even "log" with no flat side.

For each roll, you'll need plastic wrap (clingfilm) or parchment paper. Each specific recipe will guide you as to what works best. If the product is being vacuum-bagged before poaching, it's most likely plastic wrap. If it's cookie dough or the like, it's most likely parchment paper.

You also need a sturdy, straight, hard edge. This can be a bench scraper, a long kitchen ruler, or (and what I usually use) the edge of a quarter sheet pan.

For the plastic wrap, the big roll from a restaurant supply store will work best. It's thicker and stronger than home rolls. If you don't have access to the chef film, double or triple up on your home plastic wrap, layering it over itself.

Because the box of plastic film we use in the restaurants is large and heavy, I often use it as a counterweight, not tearing the plastic but rolling into the tension of the box.

How to torque with plastic wrap (clingfilm):

1. Roll out the plastic wrap (clingfilm) in front of you on a flat work surface, with the short end facing you. If you have the chef's box of plastic wrap, leave it attached to the roll, and don't tear it off just yet.

2. Following your recipe instructions, load the product onto the plastic wrap.

3. Pick up the edge of the plastic and fold it over so the edges of the food touch. From now on, your dominant hand is in charge of wrapping and rolling. Your nondominant hand is in charge of whatever hard edge you chose.

4. With your nondominant hand, hold your hard edge at a 45-degree angle at the seam of the food. Gently push back as you roll forward. Your dominant hand will roll forward, then you'll push back. Keep repeating this motion as the wrap gets tighter and tighter.

5. At this point, tear off the plastic. Your torque should be tight. Inspect the shape. If it seems off, give it a little roll on the hard surface.

6. Tie off the ends. Starting with one end, twist-twist-twist until it's tight against the end of the log, then tie it off with butcher's twine. Repeat with the other side.

How to torque with parchment paper:

1. Set a long piece of parchment in front of you, with the short end facing you.

2. Following your recipe's instructions, load the product onto the center of the parchment.

3. If it's cookie dough or something that needs to be formed, like ground meat, work it into a rough log that's your desired length and height. You'll want the log to be fairly even to make your job easier later on, so avoid a thick middle or thin ends.

4. Fold the parchment over the food. From now on, your dominant hand is in charge of wrapping and rolling. Your nondominant hand is in charge of whatever hard edge you've chosen.

5. With your nondominant hand, hold your hard edge at a 45-degree angle at the edge of the log. Gently push back as you roll forward. Your dominant hand will roll forward, then you'll push back with the hard edge. Keep repeating this motion as the log gets lighter and more even.

6. With butcher's twine, twist and tie off the ends.

7. To keep the log round while it chills, hang it in your refrigerator using the butcher's twine at the end.

... torque

How to...

I use a cartouche for almost everything. For the kind of slow, delicate cooking that I favor, they're key. A cartouche gently covers food while it cooks, submerging all the components to promote even cooking.

There are two ways to fold, one for a round pot and one for a square or rectangular pan. You don't need to be super precious about it. Like most good things, the learning is in the doing. If yours isn't pristine at first, it'll still work as long as it covers the surface of the food evenly. Think of it as folding snowflakes as a kid. They were trash at first, but your mom still loved them.

I'm numbering these instructions because if I were the one learning, it would help my brain out.

To fold a round cartouche:

1. Cut off a long piece of parchment paper. Make sure it's longer than the width of your pot.

2. Fold it in half, like a book.

3. Fold it in half again.

4. Look at your parchment. You've got one side that's open, and one side that's folded over. The open side should be on your right.

5. Take the top corner of the open side and bring it over to the edge of the folded side, making a triangle. The bottom will look wonky, but that's ok, we're trimming that bit.

6. Take the long right edge of your triangle and fold it over itself again, making a thinner triangle. It'll start to get thick and maybe harder to fold.

7. Keep folding it over, like a fan, until all you have is a slender, pointy triangle with a wonky bottom.

8. Grab a marker or a pencil.

9. Holding your folded paper over your pot, arrange the tip where the center is. Now make a mark on the triangle where it meets the edge of your pan.

10. With scissors, cut across at that mark. Now cut off the tip of the triangle, about 0.5 inches (1 cm), to make the steam hole.

11. Open it up! Cartouche!

To make a square or rectangular cartouche:

1. Cut your piece of parchment to the length of your cooking vessel.

2. Fold it in half, like a book.

3. On the open edge, cut from the corner in at an angle, about 2 inches (5 cm).

4. Repeat with the other corner.

5. Open up the parchment. It will now fit into your cooking vessel. The slits we cut will fold over themselves allowing snug alignment. I don't cut center holes in this version of a cartouche.

... fold a cartouche

POTTED & FORMED	38 → 47
CURED	48 → 55
EMULSIFIED	56 → 63
CUTS	64 → 73
SAUSAGE	74 → 83
SMOKED	84 → 93

Deli Case

Country Pâté

This technique is based on Paul Bertolli's method in *Cooking by Hand*. Through the years, the recipe has morphed and become my own, as things do, but the method remains Paul's. I recommend serving slices with the Apple Cider Mustard (page 318), Pickled Cornichons (page 314), and some crusty bread. One of my favorite things is a simple sandwich of a piece of terrine between whatever bread is handy, along with sliced raw red onion and mustard. Slices can be vacuum-sealed and frozen, or vacuum-sealed and shared. Ratios are listed on page 351, too, which makes preparing different weights easy.

Makes one 1.5-quart (1.4-liter) terrine

1 pound (450 g) pork jowl, cut into 1-inch (2.5-cm) pieces
12 ounces (340 g) chicken livers, rinsed and cleaned
1½ pounds (680 g) pork shoulder, cut into 1-inch (2.5-cm) pieces
3 large eggs
½ cup (120 ml) madeira
½ cup (120 ml) heavy (double) cream
¼ cup (60 g) minced shallots
6 ounces (170 g) Guanciale (page 52), cut into ¼-inch (0.6-cm) dice
¼ cup (15 g) chopped fresh Italian parsley
1 ounce (30 g) kosher salt
2 teaspoons curing salt #1
1 tablespoon coarsely ground black pepper (also known as butcher-ground)
1 teaspoon dextrose
1 teaspoon fresh thyme leaves
1 teaspoon Fox Spice (page 311)
beef caul fat, for lining mold

To prepare the meat mix, you'll need a meat grinder (page 30). For this recipe, you'll need the ³⁄₁₆-inch (4-mm) plate and the ⅜-inch (10-mm) plate, and make sure they're cold. Grind the pork jowl and chicken livers through the ³⁄₁₆-inch (4-mm) plate. Set the mix aside. Switch to the ⅜-inch (10-mm) plate and grind the pork shoulder.

In a mixing bowl, lightly beat the eggs, then whisk in the madeira and cream until well combined. Add the ground meats, and with your hands, gently mix together. Now add the shallots, guanciale, parsley, kosher salt, curing salt, black pepper, dextrose, thyme, and fox spice. Mix well, then test the mix (see page 31).

Clean the caul fat and line a 1.5-quart (1.4-liter) terrine mold (see page 33).

To fill the terrine, start spooning in the meat mixture, knocking the mold on the counter every few inches to burst any air bubbles and compact the meat. Once it's filled to the top, wrap over the sides of caul fat. If your terrine mold has a lid, put it on. If not, cover the terrine with aluminum foil, poking a hole in the top to allow the steam to escape.

Preheat your oven to 350°F (180°C). To set up a water bath, put the kettle on, we need boiling water. Place your terrine in the center of a large oven-safe dish, and place into the oven. Very carefully, pour the boiling water into the dish so that it comes halfway up the sides of the terrine. Close the oven and bake the terrine in the water bath for 1 hour.

Reduce the oven heat to 250°F (120°C) and cook 1 hour more, or until the terrine reaches an internal temperature of 160°F (71°C).

Remove the terrine from the water bath and place it on a cooling rack. Carefully remove the water bath set up from the oven.

While it's still warm, use a terrine weight (see page 32) set over the surface of the pâté to weigh it down. Once it's cool, put the whole setup in the refrigerator overnight. Weight and all.

The next day, invert the terrine onto a cutting (chopping) board. Look how pretty it is! Slice with a sharp knife and serve.

Because there's liver in the mix, it will oxidize within a few days in the refrigerator. I recommend cutting any extra into manageable slices and vacuum-sealing them. Freeze any that you may not get to within a few days.

Wedding Terrine

This is the terrine that I made for my wedding. My wife was extremely excited about it, and our friends demolished the entire thing before we had the chance to even try it. I want to tell you that we were mad about it, but it was so destroyed, so attacked by wild animals, that all we could do was laugh. Somewhere I have photos of the devastation. Word to the wise: If you make this for your wedding, save a piece for yourself before releasing it to the masses.

I live in California where, as of writing this in 2024, it is illegal to serve foie gras. I don't necessarily feel stifled by this, however, I do think it is unfortunate that producers who have committed to humane and sustainable methods do not have access to the fifth-largest economy in the world. Again, ratios are listed on page 351, for ease in preparing different weights of liver.

Makes one 13-inch (33-cm) terrine

foie gras

2 pounds (910 g) fattened duck/goose liver, grade A, cold (see Note)
¼ cup (120 ml) cognac (the expensive stuff, since you only get married, what, a couple of times)
1 tablespoon plus 1½ teaspoons kosher salt
1½ teaspoons granulated sugar
½ teaspoon curing salt #1
½ teaspoon ground white pepper
1 x quantity Schmaltz (page 338) or duck fat

terrine

5 pounds (2.3 kg) pork shoulder, cut into 1-inch (2.5-cm) pieces
1¼ pounds (570 g) pork fatback, cut into 1-inch (2.5-cm) pieces
5 cups (1.2 liters) Rachael's Chicken Stock (page 334)
4 tablespoons plus 1½ teaspoons kosher salt
1 teaspoon curing salt #1
2 tablespoons plus 1½ teaspoons rosemary leaves, coarsely chopped
8 ounces (230 g) black winter truffles, coarsely chopped

Note: For the weight of the liver, if it's a little over or a little under, that's okay.

make the foie gras

Remove the cold liver from the package and place it on a cutting (chopping) board. Cover the liver with a bowl and let sit at room temperature for at least 1 hour. You want the liver to soften up enough to remove the veins.

Separate the large and small lobes by gently pulling apart and remove and discard any hard fat or thin layer of film. With the underside of the liver facing up, use your pinky finger to cleanly tunnel down the center of each lobe, exposing the system of veins branching outward. It will now make sense as to why the liver must be tempered.

Gently slide your finger between the veins and the liver and pull them out into a small container of warm water so they don't stick to your fingers. Once the veins have been removed, transfer each lobe flat to a horizontal and stacked full-sheet-pan-sized sheet of parchment, with the interior against the parchment.

Brush the lobes with a third of the cognac. Then evenly sprinkle over a third of the kosher salt, sugar, curing salt, and white pepper.

Place another sheet of parchment on top. Then invert, remove the parchment, and place under the other sheet. Season the interior of the liver with the rest of the cognac and seasonings. Follow the instructions for torquing in parchment paper on page 34.

The next day, place the log in a container long enough to fit and at least 4 inches (10 cm) taller, and let sit at room temperature for 30 minutes. If you have an extra Pullman loaf pan, this will work perfectly.

Gently warm up enough schmaltz or duck fat to fully submerge the liver, bringing it to 100°F (38°C), pour over the log, and cover with a rectangle cartouche (page 35) to keep it below the fat. Let sit for 30 minutes before moving to the refrigerator to cool overnight. Yes, another night. But don't worry, it'll be at least another night until this baby is ready.

make the terrine

In a wide pot, combine the pork shoulder, fatback, chicken stock, kosher salt, curing salt, and rosemary. Turn the heat to high, stir until it reaches a bubble, reduce to a slow simmer, and cover with a cartouche and lid. Cook for 1½ to 2 hours, stirring occasionally, until the meat is tender enough to just barely be shredable.

Meanwhile, remove the foie gras from the fat, remove the parchment, and freeze for 1 hour. We're multitasking.

Line a 13-inch (33 cm) terrine mold (Pullman loaf pan) with plastic wrap (clingfilm; see page 33).

Drain the pork through a perforated pan or colander, then strain the liquid through a fine-mesh sieve into a tall narrow container. This will make it easier to ladle out the fat while the stock sinks to the bottom.

Transfer the pork to a large mixing bowl and start to break up the meat with your hands, but don't shred it too much. For the fat, just give about half of the pieces a quick squeeze. I've also found that slightly pressing the lot of it with a mallet works well. Work quickly so the meat and fat stay warm.

Ladle in fat until the meat is saturated but not swimming, this is what binds it. Test the seasoning. Add the chopped truffles and mix them in evenly. Spoon the mixture into the prepared terrine mold a tad above halfway.

Remove the foie gras from the fat, unwrap it, and place the log in the center of the pork, nestling it enough that the pork starts coming up the sides of the log. Spoon in the rest of the mixture, close off the plastic wrap, place a light weight on the surface, and weigh down slightly.

Refrigerate overnight before slicing and serving.

Chicken Liver Parfait

Makes about 2 cups (480 ml)

8 ounces (225 g) chicken livers
2¼ cups (600 ml) whole (full-fat) milk
2 teaspoons kosher salt, plus extra to taste
1 teaspoon curing salt #1
1 teaspoon freshly ground black pepper, plus extra to taste
2 tablespoons Schmaltz (page 338)
1 ounce (30 g) shallots, thinly sliced
¾ tablespoon finely grated garlic
1½ teaspoons minced seeded jalapeño chile (chilli)
¼ cup plus 1 tablespoon (75 ml) port
¼ cup plus 1 tablespoon (75 ml) madeira
½ cup plus 1 tablespoon (130 ml) heavy (double) cream
5½ ounces (250 g) unsalted butter, cut into ½-inch (1.3-cm) dice, room temperature

You can of course serve this as it is, all cuddled up to a little toasted bread. Or you can serve it with some roasted grapes on the side, or topped with Date Chutney (page 230), or piped into the center of a roasted apple (page 138) and devoured. Fun fact: Chicken liver is generally made into parfaits, terrines, or pâtés. Think of it like this: Parfait is super smooth, terrine is chunky, and pâté is in the middle of the two. Plus, it's just a fun old-school name for what's basically chicken liver mousse. Feel free to substitute the chicken liver with the liver of a duck or rabbit.

To clean the chicken livers, inspect them one by one and remove any veins, sinew, fat, or green bits (when a little of the gallbladder is still attached). Each liver is composed of two halves connected with a strand of sinew. Get a firm grip on the vein with one hand (index and thumb), and the other hand should cradle one end of the liver, pulling gently to slide the liver loose from the vein. Repeat. All you want is bright red liver. Each liver should be uniform in color.

Add the cleaned livers to a container and run under cold water until the water runs clear, then drain the livers on kitchen towels.

Next, combine the livers and milk in a sealed container to soak for a few hours, or overnight. This will help remove any excess blood and take away any metallic taste.

Drain the milk and run the livers under cold water again until the water runs clear. Dry on kitchen towels and season all over with the kosher salt, curing salt, and black pepper.

To cook the livers, heat a large sauté pan over medium-high heat and add the schmaltz. Once the schmaltz just starts to smoke, add the seasoned livers, spreading evenly apart. Don't overcrowd, which will cool the pan down and result in sad-looking boiled livers.

After achieving caramelization on the first side, flip them to get color on the other side. Cook them until medium rare, 2 to 3 minutes. Remove the livers from the pan onto a room temperature plate or pan.

Add the shallots to the pan and cook until translucent, then add the garlic and jalapeño and cook for an additional minute, trying to not toast the garlic, just to make it fragrant. Deglaze the pan with the port and madeira and reduce it by 75 percent. Add the cream and bring to a boil. Remove from the heat.

To make the mousse, combine the livers and the hot contents of your pan in a blender, filling it no more than halfway, and purée until very smooth. Then, add in the butter in a few stages and purée until the mixture is smooth and creamy like peanut butter.

Adjust your seasoning, if necessary, cool to room temperature, and press the liver mixture through a fine-mesh sieve using a plastic bench scraper. Transfer the sieved liver to a container with a piece of plastic wrap (clingfilm) directly on the surface, tapping the bottom of the container to close up any air pockets, and refrigerate for 2 hours or until ready to serve.

The liver mousse will hold refrigerated for up to 1 week. If the top of the liver in the container turns gray, which it almost certainly will, you can just scoop that off to get to the good stuff. It's just oxygen working against you.

Beef Tendon Terrine

At home in Los Angeles, we're lucky enough to have a makrut lime tree in our yard. We planted a little five-gallon plant when we moved in, and it took off. Los Angeles is incredibly expensive, but the yard citrus is definitely a perk. Here, I added makrut lime leaves to help balance the umami flavors of the coconut aminos, fish sauce, and tamari. The leaves do not take over, only enhance the rest of the flavors. Cut into a thin julienne for Beef Tendon, Tofu, Sweet Chili & Almond (page 244), finely dice into Steak Tartare (page 240), or melt into sauces and soups. If you end up with more cooking liquid than the terrine will hold, it will set up solid in any container. Sliceable liquid.

Makes one 1.5-quart (1.4-liter) terrine

beef tendon
3 tablespoons plus 2 teaspoons kosher salt
1 lemon, quartered
3 pounds (1.4 kg) beef tendon

cuisson
3 cups (710 ml) Beef Stock (page 335)
¼ cup (60 ml) rice wine vinegar
3 tablespoons tamari
2 tablespoons coconut aminos
2 teaspoons fish sauce
4 ounces (110 g) scallions (spring onions), thinly sliced
1 ounce (30 g) fresh ginger, finely minced
3 tablespoons dark brown sugar
4 dried makrut lime leaves

make the tendon

Preheat your oven to 300°F (150°C).

In a large container, combine 3 quarts (2.8 liters) cold water with 3 tablespoons of salt and the lemon. Add the beef tendon and let the mixture sit, covered and refrigerated, for at least 3 hours, or overnight.

Remove the beef tendon from the brine, discard the brine, add the tendon back to the container, and flush under a steady stream of cold running water for 15 to 20 minutes.

Once the tendon is flushed, pat dry and sprinkle all over with the remaining 2 teaspoons of salt. Allow the tendon to sit at room temperature for 30 minutes.

make the cuisson

Combine the cuisson ingredients in a large heavy-bottom pot or Dutch oven and bring to a boil. Add the tendon, bring the mixture back to a boil, cover with cartouche (page 35) and lid, and cook in the oven for 5 hours or until soft and jiggly, like Jello. Skim any fat that has risen to the top.

To assemble your terrine, line a 1.5-quart (1.4-liter) terrine mold with plastic wrap (clingfilm; see page 33) and scoop the tendon into the terrine, removing the ginger and lime leaves as you go, then pour the cuisson liquid over the tendon to just below the rim of the mold. Use a spoon to make sure the tendons are fully submerged.

Fold the plastic wrap over on each side and refrigerate overnight before slicing and serving.

Lardo

I once heard someone refer to lardo as white prosciutto. That's not really accurate, but it is a good way of getting folks that are scared of fat to at least try it. Sliced thin and used to top a perfectly grilled peach is another good way. You can always Hansel and Gretel someone with stone fruit. I love it served on our charcuterie board at the restaurants or wrapped around salty, olive-oily grissini. We sometimes drape it over uni or serve it simply over griddled toast. I could go on and on; it's one of my favorite things.

This is the recipe I use, but I've listed some fun variations you can try once you feel comfortable with the process. Ratios are listed on page 351, too, which makes curing different weights of fatback a breeze.

Makes about 3 pounds (1.4 kg)

5¾ pounds (2.6 kg) pork fatback (see Note)
1 tablespoon black peppercorns
½ cup plus 1 teaspoon (105 g) granulated sugar
½ cup (80 g) kosher salt
1¼ ounces (40 g) rosemary, coarsely chopped
2½ teaspoons curing salt #2

Variations on a theme
To the curing mix you can add:

the zest of 10 yuzu
or
wild fennel pollen and dried orange peel
or
dried rose and ground cardamom

Notes: Try to find fatback that is at least 1 inch, preferably 2 inches thick (2.5 to 5 cm), with the skin removed. It can be hard to find; ask a local butcher or pig farmer. We're not looking for streaky pork here, fatback that has a bit of meat running through it; we want it to be pristine white. If you can find local pork from a nut-finished hog, even better. Stay away from mass-produced pork.

Once prepared, wrap tightly in plastic wrap (clingfilm), or vacuum-seal, and store in the refrigerator for up to 2 months.

To prepare the fatback, using a mortar and pestle, add the peppercorns and start by giving them some firm tap, tap, taps. This helps to bust them open and break them into pieces; it also releases all those good oils. Once you have pieces of various sizes, add the sugar, kosher salt, rosemary, and curing salt to the mortar. Keeping the ingredients in the middle, make firm, circular motions with the pestle, combining and enrobing everything in the oils from the peppercorns.

Over a parchment-lined sheet tray, coat the fatback in the peppercorn mixture. Really get it on there, making sure to coat all sides.

For the next 2 to 3 weeks, depending on the thickness of your fatback, allow it to cure. I find this timeframe works well, even though lardo is traditionally cured for at least 6 months in marble vats. This certainly is more romantic, and I do aspire to cure lardo this way one day.

Ideally, I would use a brining bag or large resealable plastic bag to store the seasoned fatback, but you can also put it in a large container with a lid. Bags work better for me. Seal it in the bag, pushing out all the air as best you can. Make sure to include any cure that doesn't stick to the fatback, just include it in the bag or sprinkle it on the fatback in the container.

I like to store lardo in the darkest corner of the refrigerator, light is your enemy here. You can also tent it with aluminum foil to keep out the light. Restaurant walk-ins and coolers aren't as bright as, say, an at-home refrigerator setup, so foil for home use is your best bet to keep out the light that can turn fat rancid.

If you're using a bag, every few days, check on the lardo, massaging it inside the bag. It will begin to release a bit of moisture, and that's okay, don't drain it. If you decide to use a container, instead of massaging, flip the fatback over every few days. Again, do not drain the liquid.

After curing, the next step is drying the lardo. Remove the lardo from the bag or container and discard any liquid that has accumulated but don't scrape off any of the remaining herbs. If the color bothers you, you can trim it off later.

Next, let's hang the lardo. Using a large, double layer of cheesecloth (muslin), tightly wrap the lardo, and much like when wrapping a roast, use a butcher's knot to secure the cheesecloth. Gather the corners of the cheesecloth at the top and bottom, then twist and tie it with butcher's twine. You'll use that knot at the top to hang it, either from an S hook or a loop of twine.

Before you hang it, weigh it all wrapped up. It will have lost a little weight from losing moisture and gained a tick from the cheesecloth. Write down that number. I promise, you won't remember it later. You can even create a little wax tag with the weight to hang on the piece. We'll need it later when we're trying to confirm that it's done.

With a container set below to catch any drips as it dries, hang the lardo in your refrigerator for 6 to 8 weeks. Again, let's keep the light out. Hang it in a dark corner or make it a loosely fitting foil dress to keep it shielded from the light.

Statistically, cured meats lose 35 to 40 percent of their weight after the drying process, so use this as the barometer.

You'll be sure it's done by texture and color. The lardo will be firm but buttery when thinly sliced, and the color will be bright white.

In case you're making this recipe, and you've just cut into a perfect piece of lardo and there's no one around to tell you, you can picture me standing there sagely. I'm nodding my head. "Nice job, Chef."

Guanciale

Guanciale is one of my absolute favorite things. If a recipe calls for it, I usually double, if not triple, the amount. You won't have to; I took care of it. There are some really fine small producers making excellent versions right now, but with a little time, you can make your own. I use Tellicherry peppercorns in my cure blend, they're the best black peppercorns you can find and they're worth the hunt.

Lardo and guanciale are two sides of the same coin in terms of curing. Different cuts of meat with near identical curing processes. If you can succeed at one, you can succeed at the other. I recommend trying your hand at both. I think you'll be amazed by how different the outcomes are when the methods are so similar. And of course, once your guanciale is done, you have to make Long Bean Amatriciana (page 142). As with lardo, I've listed a few fun variations you can add to the cure once you've got the hang of it. And ratios are listed on page 351, too, which makes curing different weights of jowl easy.

As for the science, I implore you to really dig into Paul Bertolli's *Cooking by Hand*, as I did.

Makes about 6 pounds (2.7 kg)

10 pounds (4.4 kg) pork jowl/cheeks, skinless (see Note)
3 tablespoons black peppercorns
¾ cup plus 2 tablespoons (180 g) granulated sugar
¾ cup plus 2 tablespoons (140 g) kosher salt
4 teaspoons curing salt #2
4 teaspoons dried oregano

Variations on a theme
To the curing mix you can add:

Sichuan pepper and smoked cinnamon
or
crushed dried makrut lime leaves
or
a mix of dried Urfa, Aleppo, and Calabrian chiles

Notes: Quality is key here, so seek out the best pork you can afford. Because jowl is usually 70 percent fat, we want our cut to come from a hog bred for fat, not a commercial variety where all the fat is bred out of it. If you're going to embark on a curing journey, I implore you to learn about the farmers around you. Even in a sprawling city like Los Angeles, I can travel 90 minutes out and find farmers in all directions. As with most of the best things in life, if you're curious, you'll find what you're looking for. Even if you only know of one farmer, ask them. Ask who they recommend and continue like that until you have a nice network of farmers around you.

Once prepared, wrap tightly in plastic wrap (clingfilm), or vacuum-seal, and store in the refrigerator for up to 2 months.

To prepare the jowl, trim off any extra bits or chunks of fat that stick out. We're looking for a uniform piece. Nice bits of fat and meat can be saved for sausage making. Discard any glands you may need to slice away. If you're buying from a proper butcher who can clean it for you, great. Ask them if you can watch how they do it. Pay attention to the knives they use. Curiosity often leads to confidence, in my opinion.

Once the pork jowl is prepped, prepare the cure. Using a mortar and pestle, add the peppercorns and start by giving them some firm tap, tap, taps. This helps to bust them open and break them into pieces; it also releases all those good oils. Peppercorns, next to the quality of the pork, are the stars of the show here. Let's give them the VIP treatment. Once you have pieces of various sizes, add the sugar, kosher salt, curing salt, and oregano to the mortar. Keeping the ingredients in the middle, make firm circular motions with the pestle, combining and enrobing everything in the oils from the peppercorns.

Over a parchment-lined sheet tray, coat the jowl in the peppercorn mixture. Really get it on there, making sure to coat all sides.

Once the jowl is completely coated, I like to cure it in a brining bag or large resealable plastic bag (or you could use a large container with a lid). Add any of the peppercorn mixture that didn't stick into the bag, squeeze out any air, and store it in a dark corner of your refrigerator. This needs to be cured for the next 3 weeks. Every day, EVERY DAY, massage the guanciale inside the bag. This doesn't need to be an hour-long spa treatment, just give it a 15-second massage working around the cure. Over time it will release some liquid, do not drain it.

After 3 weeks on cure, remove the guanciale from the refrigerator and discard any accumulated liquid. Rinse the jowls in cold water to remove excess curing solids, and dry on towels.

Next, let's hang the guanciale. Using a large, double layer of cheesecloth (muslin), tightly wrap the guanciale, and much like when wrapping a roast, use a butcher's knot to secure the cheesecloth. Gather the corners of the cheesecloth at the top and bottom and twist and tie it with butcher's twine. Really swaddle your baby tight, the cheesecloth will naturally loosen as the guanciale shrinks from drying. Use the knot at the top to hang it. Since the shape of the jowl can be wonky, I say the top is the smallest side. You can either hang it from an S hook or use another loop of butcher's twine. While it's not required to use cheesecloth, I find it protects the meat during drying and creates an easier way to hang the product. So, I'm not piercing it with a hole, potentially introducing bacteria and losing a piece where the hole was. I must admit that using the refrigerator for curing and drying is colder than ideal, but it is a safe method that results in a delicious product.

Before you hang it, let's weigh it while it's wrapped. It will have lost a little weight from losing moisture and gained a tick from the cheesecloth. Write down that number. I promise, you won't remember it later. You can even create a little wax tag with the weight to hang on the piece. We'll need it later when we're trying to confirm that it's done.

With a container set below to catch any drips as it dries, hang the guanciale in your refrigerator for 1 month. Again, let's keep the light out. Hang it in a dark corner or make it a loosely fitting aluminum foil dress to keep it shielded from the light.

After 1 month, let's re-weigh it. Cured meats lose 35 to 40 percent of their weight after the drying process. So, as you get to the end of the drying window, weighing again to measure the loss will be a good barometer. If after a month you're not near the 35 to 40 percent loss mark, continue hanging until it achieves that loss of weight.

Smoked Tomato 'Nduja

There was a time not that long ago when you couldn't find 'nduja in the United States. The only way to try it was from food friends who were smuggling it in from Italy in their suitcases. This 'nduja was often the kind packed in oil and sealed in jars—a meaty, spicy, oil-laden spread. 'Nduja dried in the casing was harder still to come by, harder to smuggle in most likely. But we caught up and caught on. I don't claim to be making authentic 'nduja here; this is my take on it, but still, it's very tasty, which is really all it needs to be. The smoked tomatoes can be omitted without any further adjustments to the recipe. And ratios are listed on page 351, which makes preparing different weights of pork belly easy.

Makes about 3 pounds (1.4 kg)

5 pounds (2.3 kg) skinless pork belly, cut into 1-inch (2.5-cm) pieces
¼ cup plus 3 tablespoons (70 g) kosher salt
⅓ cup plus 1 tablespoon (45 g) granulated sugar
2 teaspoons curing salt #2
1 cup plus 2 teaspoons (148 g) sweet Calabrian chili powder
⅔ cup (80 g) hot Calabrian chili powder
½ cup (40 g) fennel seed, ground
¼ cup (113 g) smoked sun-dried tomatoes, coarsely chopped
0.45 g Bactoferm (see Sources, page 350) mixed with ¼ cup (60 ml) water of ambient temperature
1 hog bladder

Note: Once prepared, wrap tightly in plastic wrap (clingfilm), or vacuum-seal, and store in the refrigerator for up to 2 months.

Combine the pork belly with the kosher salt, sugar, curing salt, chili powders, fennel seed, and smoked tomatoes. Mix well.

Follow the instructions on page 30 as you grind and stuff the sausage. Prepare your grinding equipment, taking care that your pork mixture and grinding equipment are very cold. Grind the sausage through a ⅜-inch (10-mm) plate and then through a 3/16-inch (4-mm) plate. Paddle briefly with the Bactoferm and water to form a cohesive mixture.

Stuff the mixture into the hog bladder and tie off, so it's as tightly packed as possible. Record the weight.

To dry the 'nduja, hang the bladder for 4 to 6 weeks, out of direct light, and between 70°F to 78°F (21°C to 26°C) until it has lost 40 percent of its weight.

Rabbit & Myrtle Berry Mortadella

Mortadella really seems to be having a moment, and with good reason, it's delicious. This version, made with rabbit instead of pork, and myrtle berries instead of peppercorns, is just as good as the classic but just different enough to keep things interesting, without being try-too-hard. When springtime hits, make the Rabbit Mortadella, Fava Beans, Pistachios & Mint (page 170) or Anthony Bourdain's mortadella sandwich with melted provolone, Kewpie, and Dijon on a kaiser roll (it feels like a cheffed up version of an Ohio fried bologna sandwich, and it's perfect).

Makes one 3¼- × 14-inch (8.25 × 35-cm) log

2 pounds (910 g) rabbit leg meat, ground with a ³⁄₁₆-inch (4-mm) plate (see page 30)
¼ cup (40 g) kosher salt
¾ teaspoon curing salt #1
2 tablespoons dextrose
1 teaspoon whole mace, ground
1 teaspoon coriander seed, ground
½ teaspoon ground cinnamon
1½ cups (340 g) ice cubes
1 pound 2 ounces (540 g) pork fatback, ground with a ³⁄₁₆-inch (4-mm) plate
10 ounces (285 g) diced Lardo (page 48)
7 ounces (200 g) shelled Sicilian pistachios (see Sources, page 350)
3 ounces (85 g) dried myrtle berries (see Note)
1 sewn hog after-end, double-wall casing (3¼ × 14 inch; 8.25 × 35 cm; optional)

Note: You'll want to gently crack the shell of each myrtle berry to remove the 2 to 3 small "peppercorns" inside. If you'd prefer to go classic, substitute the rabbit leg for pork shoulder and the myrtle berries for whole Tellicherry peppercorns.

Into the bowl of your food processor, add the rabbit, kosher salt, curing salt, dextrose, mace, coriander, cinnamon, and half the ice. Process, occasionally scraping down the sides of the bowl, until the mixture reaches 45°F (7°C) with a meat thermometer. Add in the back fat and remaining ice, and process until the mixture reaches a temperature of 62°F (17°C).

Remove the rabbit mixture to a large bowl and stir in the diced lardo, pistachios, and myrtle berries.

At this point, you can stuff the mixture in the casing or roll it into a large log (see page 34). Then poach the mortadella in water that is less than a simmer until it reaches an internal temperature of 165°F (74°C). Remove from the water, wrap tightly with plastic wrap (clingfilm) to help compress, and immediately chill the mortadella down in an ice bath and refrigerate at least overnight, or up to 10 days. Make sure to remove the casing before serving.

Blutwurst

Yes, there are several recipes inside this recipe, as is the case with a lot of the recipes in this book. Of course, you can buy lardo and pancetta. But half the fun of a project like this is knowing you're responsible for all of the bits. If you're up for it, I recommend trying to make each part yourself. Give yourself the gift of a job well done. And make sure you tell everyone about the amount of work it took and be really tedious about it.

Makes one 3¼- × 14-inch (8.25 × 35-cm) log

13 ounces (370 g) liquid pork blood
2 pounds (910 g) pork shoulder, ground with a 3⁄16-inch (4-mm) plate (see page 30)
¼ cup (40 g) kosher salt
¾ teaspoon curing salt #1
2 tablespoons dextrose
1 teaspoon Hungarian sweet paprika
1 teaspoon whole mace, ground
1 teaspoon coriander pods, ground
1 pound 2 ounces (540 g) pork fatback, ground with a 3⁄16-inch (4-mm) plate
10 ounces (285 g) diced Lardo (page 48)
10 ounces (285 g) diced Pancetta Cotto (page 69)
1 sewn hog after-end, double-wall casing (3¼ × 14 inch; 8.25 × 35 cm)

The day prior to making the blutwurst, fill your ice cube trays with the pork blood and freeze overnight.

The next day, to make the sausage, be sure to keep the shoulder and fatback separate until they take their turn in the food processor. Emulsifying each ingredient with the blood ice cubes to a specific temperature is how we make it nice.

In the bowl of your food processor, combine the ground pork shoulder, salts, spices, and half the blood ice cubes. If your food processor is on the smaller side, divide the ingredients in half and process in two batches. Scraping down the sides of the bowl as you go, process the mixture until it reaches 45 °F (7 °C). Next add the ground fatback and the remaining blood ice cubes to the bowl and process, scraping down the sides when needed, until the mixture is 62°F (17°C).

Remove the mixture to a large bowl and fold in the diced lardo and pancetta cotto.

At this point, you can stuff the meat mix into the hog casing or roll into a large log (see page 34). Then poach the blutwurst in water that is below a simmer until an internal temperature of 165°F (74°C). Chill in an ice bath for 1 hour, then transfer to a sheet tray and refrigerate overnight. It will keep in the refrigerator for 1 week.

Note: Regardless of whether I used casings or not, I like to torque each piece in plastic wrap (clingfilm; see page 34) while still warm, to make sure the interior is compressed. Since the blutwurst is a variation on the Mortadella (page 57) and Olive Loaf (page 61), I like to lightly weigh it down as it cools to give the wurst its own unique and special identity.

Olive Loaf

Anything to do with restaurants is really just an exercise in problem-solving and Hail Marys. I know we want to make it more romantic—and don't get me wrong, at times it very much is—but the day-to-day can be... taxing. Praying that everything is working, the walk-in hasn't broken down, so-and-so is showing up for their shift, plus the ever-present how do we get butts in seats. We conquer, or we try to conquer, these things so we can do the romantic bits. This recipe is from one such Hail Mary: an effort to get more people into Birdie G's the week leading up to the COVID shutdown. Had I known then just how futile this effort would be, had I known that my restaurant and all restaurants across Los Angeles were about to shutter, would I still have thrown this Hail Mary? Probably yes. It's what restaurant people do. We try. We fail. We try again. Even in the face of a historic pandemic.

At the time, we sliced the olive loaf thick and griddled it on each side, much like a fried bologna sandwich, served on Pain de Mie (page 328) with good mustard, fries, and a cold beer for $20. A pretty good deal in my view. I prefer Castelvetrano olives, but play around with what you like. You can either poach the loaf in casings or rolled up like a big meat cookie dough, it's up to you. Adding dextrose here is for sweetness, yes, but it also helps to evenly distribute the salt and keep the color nice.

Makes one 3¼- × 14-inch (8.25 × 35-cm) log

- 2 pounds (910 g) lean pork shoulder
- ¼ cup (40 g) kosher salt
- ¾ teaspoon curing salt #1
- 2 tablespoons dextrose
- 1 teaspoon Hungarian sweet paprika
- 1 teaspoon whole mace, ground
- 1 teaspoon coriander seed, ground
- 1½ cups (340 g) ice cubes
- 1 pound 2 ounces (540 g) pork fatback
- 3 ounces (85 g) diced Lardo (page 48)
- 10 ounces (285 g) green olives, pitted and sliced
- 2½ ounces (70 g) Calabrian Chile Hybrid solids (page 304)
- 1 sewn hog after-end, double-wall casing (3¼ × 14 inch/8.25 × 35 cm; optional)

Into the bowl of your food processor, add the pork shoulder, kosher salt, curing salt, dextrose, paprika, mace, coriander, and half the ice. Process, occasionally scraping down the sides of the bowl, until the mixture reaches 45°F (7°C) with a meat thermometer. Add in the back fat and the remaining ice and process until the mixture reaches a temperature of 62°F (17°C).

Remove the pork mixture to a large bowl and stir in the diced lardo, olives, and chile solids.

At this point, you can stuff the mixture in the casing or roll it in plastic wrap (clingfilm) into large logs (see page 34). Then poach the olive loaf until it reaches an internal temperature of 165°F (74°C). Remove from the water, wrap tightly with plastic wrap to help compress, and immediately chill the loaf down in an ice bath and refrigerate at least overnight, and for up to 10 days. Make sure to remove the casing before serving.

Ohio City Provision's Lamb Shawarma

Makes about 3½ (1.6 kg) pounds

1 pound 6 ounces (625 g) white onion, cut into 1-inch (2.5-cm) dice
3 tablespoons chopped garlic
1 tablespoon extra-virgin olive oil
5 pounds (2.3 kg) lamb shoulder (see Note)
1 pound 4 ounces (570 g) lamb kidney fat (see Note)
5 tablespoons kosher salt, plus extra to taste
4 tablespoons ground black pepper, plus extra to taste
3 tablespoons dried oregano, plus extra to taste

Note: You can also use mixed lamb trim, or vacuum-seal and freeze lamb scraps until you have enough. Same goes for the lamb kidney fat; you can substitute the extra fat trimmed from the cap of a lamb rack, just vacuum-seal and freeze until you have enough.

Ratios are listed on page 351 for ease.

Growing up, I LOVED gyro meat and still do. So, I was sitting in butter when I got a job washing dishes at Gyro Wrap Cafe at Toco Hills in Atlanta near the end of my senior year of high school in 1994. I thought the cooks were so cool because they smoked cigarettes on the line, and one of them had a Camaro. I always wanted to recreate the gyro meat, but chef Adam Lambert, owner of Ohio City Provisions, a most wonderful butcher shop in Cleveland, beat me to it. When I tried his version, cold right out of their deli case, I knew that any effort on my part to make a better version would be in vain. So, I traded the "World-Famous" Rose Petal Pie recipe from Birdie G's for his Shawarma recipe, straight up. Here is Adam's recipe.

In the bowl of your food processor, pulse the onion and garlic until finely minced. Transfer this minced mixture to a fine-mesh sieve set over a bowl and allow the excess water to drain, pushing on the mixture to get as much liquid out as you can. You can save this reserved liquid as a flavoring for your next stew or vegetable broth, or mix with holy water to ward off vampires. You get the idea. Waste not, want not.

Warm the olive oil over medium heat in a large sauté pan and sweat the onion-garlic mixture on medium-low heat until it's translucent. On a parchment-lined sheet tray, spread out the cooked onion/garlic mixture to cool. As a rule, you never want to add a hot mirepoix or hot cooked vegetable to a mince, as the heat will begin to cook the meat.

As your onion/garlic mixture cools, prepare the lamb. Grind your cold lamb meat and fat through a 3/16-inch (4-mm) plate.

In the large bowl of a stand mixer with the paddle attached, mix the ground lamb/fat mixture with the salt, black pepper, and oregano. Next, add in the cooled onion-garlic mixture. Lastly, add in 1 cup (240 ml) cool water and mix until well incorporated.

Adding the cold water as we did above helps to emulsify the mixture and make it more pliable, leading to, in my opinion, a superior texture. We're trying to avoid a grainy, dry sausage. Everyone has had one of these, they're a bummer. You didn't do all this work for bummer sausage.

Next, take out a small amount of the mix, make a small patty, and fry it up in a skillet. Once the tester patty is cooked and cooled, take a bite, we want to test out our seasonings. Here's your chance to add more seasoning if you'd like. If you decide to add more spice or salt, make sure the mix is fully incorporated, and test again.

Let's sous vide. Transfer your lamb mixture to vacuum bags. I used two 8- × 10-inch (20- × 25-cm) bags but use whatever makes sense for your purposes. You'll want as much as will fit in each bag in order to form sliceable "loaves." Seal your bags and cook in a water bath set to 155°F (68°C) for 5 hours. After 5 hours, remove the bags and cool them down in an ice bath, then refrigerate overnight, and up to 1 week.

After being cooked and chilled, the loaves of the shawarmas may have sheets of congealed fat attached to the exterior. This isn't a bad thing. Just pop them off and they might come in handy for warming the meat or adding to other dishes.

Duck Ham

At the restaurants, we source our ducks from Liberty Ducks in Sonoma County, and I am proud to have been working with them for twenty years now, except for a stretch when I cooked vegetarian. They raise a Pekin-style duck that is meatier and tastier than other commercially bred varieties (Pekin is the duck breed). This duck ham pairs well with Skillet Biscuits (page 332), salted butter, and honey. Or draped across hot cornbread. Duck always pairs well with fruit, so try it with the Two-Ingredient Applesauce (page 306).

Makes 4

½ cup (80 g) kosher salt
⅓ cup (70 g) granulated sugar
1 teaspoon curing salt #1
2 teaspoons brown mustard seed
2 teaspoons black peppercorns
8 cloves
3 allspice berries
1 cinnamon stick
2 bay leaves
4 duck breasts (2½ to 3 pounds; 1.1 kg to 1.4 kg)
1 x quantity Fox Spice (page 311)

In a large pot over high heat, combine all ingredients except the duck and fox spice blend with 2 quarts (1.9 liters) water. Bring to a boil, stirring until the salts and sugar are dissolved. Remove from the heat, transfer to a mixing bowl set in a larger bowl of ice, and chill until below 40°F (4°C).

Trim the duck breasts of any excess fat or bone fragments if present. Submerge the duck breasts in the cold brine and refrigerate for 3 days.

After 3 days, remove the duck breasts and pat dry with paper towels.

Preheat your oven to 275°F (135°C). Lightly but evenly dust each duck breast with the spice blend. Place the seasoned duck breasts on a roasting rack. Bake until the duck breasts reach an internal temperature of 145°F (63°C).

Transfer to a rack-lined sheet tray, let cool to room temperature, then refrigerate until cold (the internal temperature should be below 40°F/4°C).

Corned Beef Tongue

Makes 2

2 beef tongues (6 pounds/2.7 kg)
1 x quantity Corn Brine (page 337)
3 cups (720 ml) distilled white vinegar
½ cup (80 g) kosher salt
4 bay leaves

My grandfather Al loved beef tongue. He was the only member of the extended family who would eat it. My grandmother Gladys wouldn't eat it, but she loved him, so she'd make it for him, sliced thick and served pot roast-style with kasha and carrots. I wanted to be just like him, so I tried it with him for the first time at probably age nine or ten. At the time, I was an obnoxiously picky eater, but after one bite I could not understand, objectively, what there was to possibly dislike about it. With the most luxurious texture and clean flavor, beef tongue is right up there with a juicy ribeye as my favorite cut of beef. I think it made him proud of me that I wanted to try it, and he could see that I loved him more than my grandmother, aunts, uncles, and cousins. Winning.

My version here is corned and optimized to make it tender and melting. Like a perfect steak. The corning keeps the color consistent and adds great flavor. The gentle pickling-poaching method keeps it tender. If you can get past the fact that it's tongue, it'll be one of the best things you eat.

To brine the tongues, with a clean skewer, pierce each tongue halfway through (to the center) equidistant along their length 6 times. This will help the brine penetrate through the dense meat. Place the tongues in a large brining bag, pour in the cold brine, and refrigerate on a sheet tray to brine for 10 days.

To poach the tongues, remove them from the brine and dry on paper or kitchen towels. In a large pot big enough to hold both tongues, bring 1½ gallons (3.8 liters) water, the vinegar, salt, and bay leaves to a boil. We're going to poach them in this salted and acidulated water for several hours until tender (like a mild pickling liquid).

Bring the water up to a boil and add the tongues. Bring the pot back up to a boil again and then reduce the heat to a low simmer. Once the simmer is consistent, top with a cartouche (page 35) and a smaller lid to weigh down the tongues, so they stay submerged. Poach for 3 to 4 hours.

Once the tongues are tender, remove them from the poaching liquid, and as soon as they are at a workable temperature, peel their tough outer coating and discard. Yes, I said peel. This outer layer should come off easily when pulled, and you can help it along with your paring or utility knife.

Once peeled, wrap each tongue tightly in plastic wrap (clingfilm) as you go, so they don't dry out. Cool in an ice bath, then refrigerate for up to 1 week.

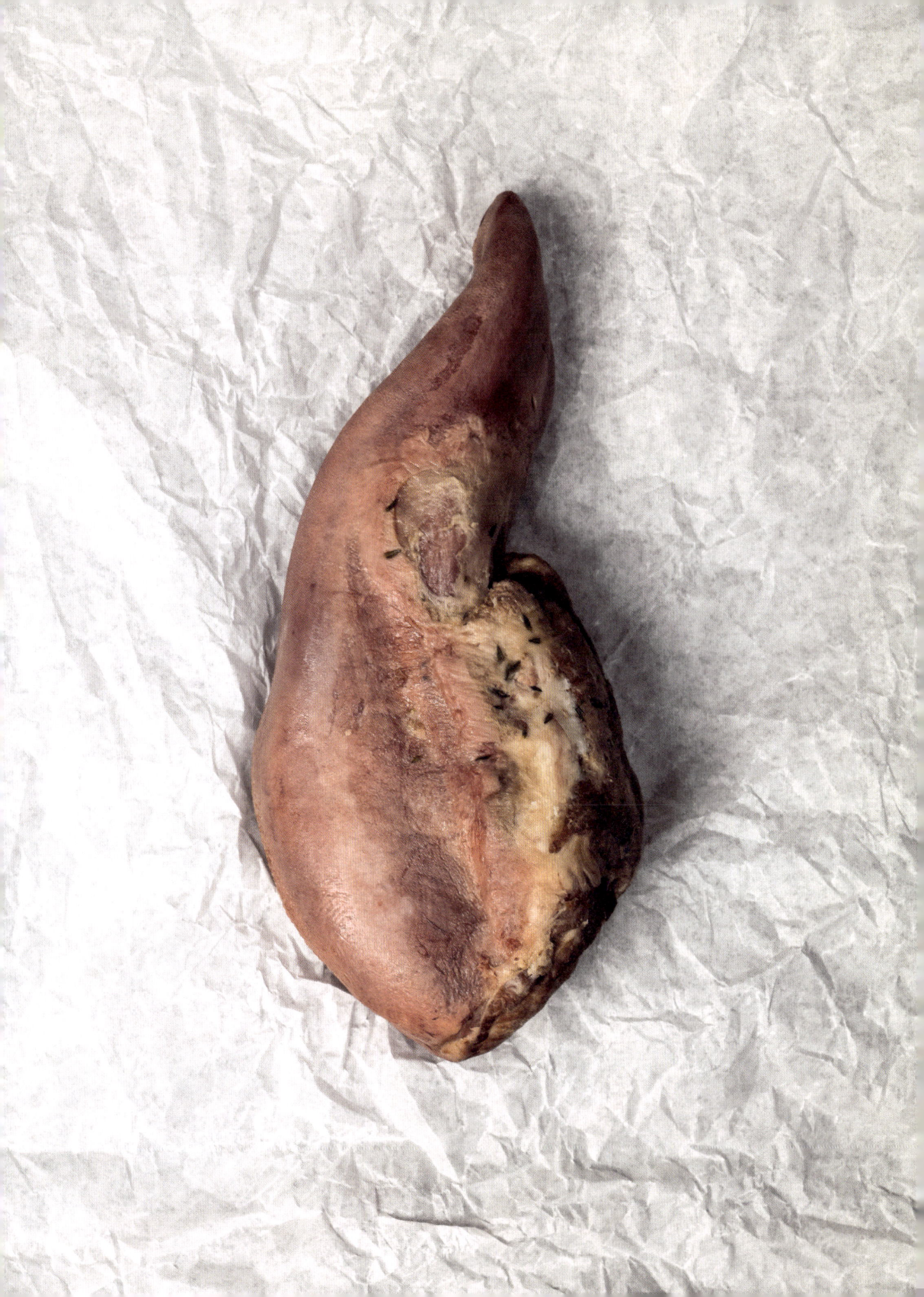

Pancetta Cotto

If you have an immersion circulator and you're deli-meat curious, this is a great way to dip your toes. I love the flavor of traditional cured pancetta, it's one of my favorite things. Real talk: 99 percent of the time, I will easily take pancetta or guanciale over smoked bacon. The versatility of this version makes it a staple for me. It can be sliced thin and wrapped, as is, around Melon with Scallion Jaew (page 112), or diced and crisped up for the Eggs-in-a-Basket Carbonara (page 120). And ratios are listed on page 351, for ease in preparing different weights of pork belly.

Makes about 5 pounds (2.3 kg)

4 garlic cloves, grated
5 pounds (2.3 kg) skinless pork belly
6 tablespoons kosher salt
4 tablespoons black peppercorns, coarsely ground
3 tablespoons juniper berries, smashed
2 tablespoons dark brown sugar
2 teaspoons curing salt #1
1 teaspoon freshly grated nutmeg
4 fresh bay leaves, snipped into small pieces
5 thyme sprigs, stripped

Rub the garlic all over the pork belly. Mix together the kosher salt, peppercorns, juniper berries, brown sugar, curing salt, nutmeg, bay leaves, and thyme leaves in a small bowl, then generously rub the pork belly all over with your spice mixture. Vacuum-seal the seasoned belly. If you don't have bags large enough to contain a 5-pound (2.3-kg) chunk, you can break it down into smaller pieces.

Set up your immersion circulator to 158°F (70°C) and cook the belly for 18 hours.

Remove from the water bath and, still in the bag, put the belly on a sheet tray with another sheet tray set on top to weigh it down, and press it. You could weigh it down with a bag of rice, a bunch of copies of *On Vegetables* (proof that it's useful), a large pot, or a small toddler. You get the idea. Let it cool like this on your kitchen counter before moving the setup to the refrigerator to press overnight.

Rosemary Pork Loin

This pork loin is easy to make and perfect for your next sandwich. Within these pages, you will find it thinly sliced and served with Avocado Tonnato (page 115), as well as in the Chopped Antipasto Salad (page 111). Save any drippings from roasting it and make a warm porky vinaigrette, then serve thin carved slices slathered in said vinaigrette with slices of tomato and peach. You can even cube it up and toss hunks with olives for a nice antipasto. Make sure you get the frilled toothpicks for a really '70s dinner party vibe.

Makes about 7 pounds (3.3 kg)

1 boneless, skinless pork loin (7 to 8-pounds; 3.3 to 3.6 kg)
½ cup plus 2 tablespoons (140 g) kosher salt
1 cup (200 g) granulated sugar
3 teaspoons curing salt #1
3 tablespoons rosemary leaves, plus any stems
1½ teaspoons coriander seed
1 teaspoon black peppercorns
2 bay leaves
1 cup (250 g) Dijon mustard
½ cup (16 g) chopped rosemary leaves

To brine the pork, combine 2 quarts (1.9 liters) water, kosher salt, sugar, curing salt, rosemary, spices, and bay leaves in a pot, bring to a boil, and make sure that the salt and sugar have dissolved. Chill down the brine completely.

In a brining bag, pour the chilled brine over the pork loin. Seal the bag, place on a sheet tray, and refrigerate for 5 days, making sure all sides of the loin are submerged at all times.

To roast the pork, after 5 days, remove the loin from the brine, discarding the brine. Pat dry thoroughly with paper or kitchen towels. Brush the loin evenly with the mustard and cover it with the chopped rosemary; don't forget the ends.

Preheat your oven, with the oven rack set to the center, to 225°F (105°C). Line a half sheet pan with aluminum foil and a rack, place the loin on top, and slowly roast the pork in the oven to an internal temperature of 155°F (68°C).

Let the meat cool to room temperature before wrapping it tightly in plastic wrap (clingfilm) and refrigerating it. As it cools, you're probably going to want to try a slice. Of course you are, it smells of roast pork and rosemary, you're not made of stone. As long as it has rested for 30 minutes, go ahead.

Corned Beef Brisket

Makes about 12 pounds (5.5 kg)

1 whole prime brisket (about 15 pounds/6.75 kg)
2 gallons (7.5 liters) Corn Brine (page 337)
3 carrots, cut into 1-inch (2.5-cm) pieces
6 celery stalks, cut into 1-inch (2.5-cm) pieces
2 white onions, cut into 1-inch (2.5-cm) pieces
distilled white vinegar
kosher salt

Man, I got in my head about brisket. It feels daunting to tackle something that is so iconic within my culture. There was so much noise going on in my brain. As with bagels or smoked fish, everyone has a very set idea on how they think that thing should be, what "the right" way is. And I get it. It's personal.

We first started corning beef tongue (page 66) at Rustic Canyon, but when we finally got into the new kitchen at Birdie G's, we started corning everything—tri tip, short ribs, duck, beef heart. Corned meat has such a special flavor, the tanginess cutting through the fat and bringing balance. That tang reminds me of all the deli things I ate growing up. Eventually, I had to go my own way with brisket. And this is it.

This whole brisket will serve all your friends, unless you're, like, super popular.

Make the Corned Brisket "Steak Frites" on page 285 or literally a thousand other things. Having chunks of this cooked, vacuum-sealed, and frozen will save you on those days when you just don't know what to make.

To brine the brisket, pour the cold brine over the brisket and refrigerate, weighing it down if necessary. Not everyone has a walk-in cooler big enough to accommodate the brining of an entire brisket. My house sure doesn't. You can cut the brisket in half if it's too large. You can also try to use a very large brining bag. Around Thanksgiving, most stores have these for turkeys, so you can try those if you don't have access to the professional kind.

Brine the brisket for 10 days, then drain it and dry it well with paper or kitchen towels. Discard the brine.

To cook the brisket, fill a large pot (I'm talking large) with cold water. Add the carrots, celery, and onions. Next, add the vinegar and salt until it tastes like a mild broth; basically make it taste like something you'd want to eat. That means the cooking liquid is on point. On high heat, bring the liquid to a boil and add the brisket. Cover with a cartouche (see page 35), and what I like to do is add a lid that's just small enough to fit in the pot, in order to keep the brisket submerged. Bring back to a boil, then reduce the heat to a low simmer. Check for doneness after about 2 ½ hours. You're looking for a nice springiness in the meat. A little jiggle. This sounds strange, but you'll just know when it's done. Once it is done, turn off the heat and let it cool in the liquid for an hour before removing. Immediately wrap with plastic wrap (clingfilm) directly against the surface of the meat to prevent drying out. Cool to room temperature before wrapping tightly and refrigerating for up to 10 days.

Italian Sausage

I love Italian sausage cooked simply with peppers and onions and scooped over polenta or mashed potatoes. If you link the sausage, cook it in the oven at 275°F (135°C) until it's at an internal temperature of 150°F (65°C). Let the sausages rest, slice them down the middle to butterfly, then grill them, interior side down, over hot coals to char and get crispy all over. Pair them with the Griddled Potatoes with Fennel Pollen and Lemon (page 141) or use loose in the Italian Sausage Ravioli (page 126).

Makes 4 pounds (1.8 kg)

¾ cup (70 g) fennel seed
1 tablespoon black peppercorns
4 pounds (1.8 kg) pork shoulder, cut into 1-inch (2.5-cm) pieces
2 tablespoons kosher salt
½ teaspoon curing salt #1
1 tablespoon plus 1½ teaspoons hot Calabrian chili powder
1 tablespoon plus 1½ teaspoons sweet Calabrian chili powder
1½ teaspoons smoked paprika
1 tablespoon grated garlic
hog casings (about 1½ inches/38 to 42 mm in diameter)

In a dry cast-iron skillet, toast the fennel seed and black peppercorns until fragrant, cool to room temperature, then grind in a spice grinder.

In a large bowl, combine the pork with the kosher salt, curing salt, fennel seed, black peppercorns, both Calabrian chili powders, paprika, and garlic. Mix well. Let this mixture sit and chill and marinate in the refrigerator for at least 2 hours.

Next, follow the instructions on page 30 as you grind and stuff the sausage. Prepare your grinding equipment, taking care that your pork mixture and grinding equipment are very cold. Grind the sausage through a ⅜-inch (10-mm) plate. Transfer to a stand mixer with a paddle attachment, add ¾ cup (180 ml) cold water, and paddle it gently and briefly to combine.

Adding the cold water as we did above helps to emulsify the mixture and make it more pliable. Then test the mix as directed. Once you're happy with the seasoning, stuff the mixture into the casings. Or you can leave it in bulk as for the Italian Sausage Ravioli (page 126). It will keep in the refrigerator for 2 days.

Merguez Sausage

When we opened in late 2019, I put this sausage on the menu at Birdie G's, my restaurant in Los Angeles named for my daughter Birdie and my grandmother Gladys. On the menu, we called it Mouradian Lamb Sausage in honor of my dear friend Chef Mourad Lahlou, who hails from Marrakesh. He has lots of tattoos and is eternally bothered by having to wear a shirt. Anyway, soon after opening, a family came in and was very tickled because their last name just happened to be Mouradian. They took home copies of the menu to show their friends and family. In a restaurant named after two women who are the dearest to me, with a menu full of references to family and friends, this coincidence wasn't lost on me. Sometimes, most times, I hope, it's the care we show, not just in food or service, but our shared existence, that lasts long after the taste of the food has faded.

Makes about 6 pounds (2.7 kg)

1 tablespoon plus 1½ teaspoons coriander seed
2¼ teaspoons cumin seed
2¼ teaspoons caraway seed
1½ teaspoons nigella seed
1½ teaspoons fennel seed
¾ teaspoon black peppercorns
¼ teaspoon ground allspice
10 ounces (285 g) dried guajillo chiles, seeded
1 tablespoon plus 1½ teaspoons sweet Hungarian paprika
6½ pounds (3 kg) lamb shoulder, cut into 1-inch (2.5-cm) pieces
¼ cup (40 g) kosher salt
½ cup (120 g) chopped garlic
lamb casings (about 1 inch/22 to 28 mm in diameter)

Toast the coriander, cumin, caraway, nigella, and fennel seeds with the peppercorns and allspice in a dry pan until fragrant. Cool to room temperature, and grind to a powder.

Soak the guajillo chiles for 1 hour in enough hot water to cover. Blend the chiles with the paprika and just enough of the soaking water to facilitate a smooth purée. Chill.

In a large bowl, combine the lamb with the salt, ground spices, guajillo purée, and garlic. Marinate, covered, in the refrigerator for 2 hours, or ideally, overnight.

Next, follow the instructions on page 30 as you grind and stuff the sausage. Prepare your grinding equipment, taking care that your lamb mixture and grinding equipment are very cold. Grind the sausage through a 3/16-inch (4-mm) plate. Transfer to a stand mixer with a paddle attachment, add 1 cup (240 ml) water, and paddle it gently and briefly to combine.

Adding the cold water as we did above helps to emulsify the mixture and make it more pliable.

Then test the mix as directed. Once you're happy with the seasoning, stuff the mixture into the lamb casings, and refrigerate for up to 2 days.

Wild Ramp Cotechino

I had never had cotechino until about ten years ago, when Chef Lachlan Mackinnon-Patterson and Master Sommelier Bobby Stuckey from Frasca Food & Wine in Boulder, Colorado, held a private wine lunch at Rustic Canyon. Lachlan made cotechino formed into meatballs, each secured tightly in plastic wrap (clingfilm), then poached and served them with risotto. I ate way too many that day and set out to work on my own version. It should come as no surprise that Paul Bertolli's *Cooking by Hand* was an indispensable resource.

Ramps are only in season for a short time, early spring for a month, a month and a half if you're lucky. So, we stock up at the restaurants. Cotechino is fatty and sticky, and the ramps add some brightness. Of course, if it's off season, or you can't get your hands on ramps, you can omit them or use scallions (spring onions) or garlic scapes.

Makes about 5 pounds (2.3 kg)

12 ounces (340 g) pork skin
3 pounds (1.43 kg) pork shoulder, cut into 1-inch (2.5-cm) pieces
1 pound 6 ounces (625 g) pork fatback, cut into 1-inch (2.5-cm) pieces
3 tablespoons plus 1½ teaspoons kosher salt
2¼ teaspoons granulated sugar
¾ teaspoon curing salt #1
1 tablespoon black peppercorns, ground
1½ teaspoons coriander seed, ground
4 cloves, ground
½ teaspoon sweet Hungarian paprika
½ teaspoon ground mace
4 ounces (120 g) wild ramps, coarsely chopped
pork casings (about 2 inches/55 to 60 mm in diameter)

With kitchen shears, cut your pork skin into manageable squares, 3 × 3 inches (7.6 × 7.6 cm) is usually good. It needs to be a size you can easily grab onto and scrape later. Get a large pot of unseasoned water boiling, add the skin pieces, and lightly simmer for 45 to 60 minutes until soft.

Drain the skin pieces; once they're cool enough to handle, scrape any fat and meat with a bench scraper or utility knife, and chill them down. Once chilled, cut them into 1-inch (2.5-cm) pieces.

Combine the pork shoulder, fatback, skin pieces, kosher salt, sugar, curing salt, peppercorns, coriander seed, cloves, paprika, mace, and ramps and mix well. Marinate, covered, overnight in the refrigerator.

Next, follow the instructions on page 30 as you grind and stuff the sausage. Prepare your grinding equipment, taking care that your pork mixture and grinding equipment are very cold. Grind half through a 3/16-inch (4-mm) plate, switch to a 3/8-inch (10-mm) plate, and grind the rest. Transfer to a stand mixer with a paddle attachment, add ¾ cup (180 ml) cold water, then paddle gently and briefly to combine.

Adding the cold water as we did above helps to emulsify the mixture and make it more pliable.

Test the mix as directed. Once you're happy with the seasoning level, stuff the mixture into the casings.

Poach the cotechino at 175°F (79°C) until it reaches an internal temperature of 160°F (71°C).

Immediately, shock in ice water for 30 minutes until cooled down, then transfer to a sheet tray lined with paper or kitchen towels to refrigerate overnight, and up to 1 week.

Apple & Black Rice Morcilla

This blood sausage recipe is the product of years and years of trial and error. I first attempted morcilla as a line cook at Manresa back in the mid-2000s. Quite often, after service, at the end of the night, after the kitchen was all cleaned down, someone would make nachos and we young cooks would tackle a project as an extracurricular activity. This was fun for us, more than going out drinking or doing who knows what. Morcilla was my project and something I was eager to master. That first attempt, however, was a disaster. For starters, we didn't have the right stuffer at the time, one that could handle liquid. We could have used pastry (piping) bags, but none of us were remotely familiar enough with sausage-making to realize that was an option. It made a huge mess, as if a grisly murder had taken place, as we tried, and failed, and tried again to get the mix stuffed into the casings. Finally, we got them stuffed as best we could—all lined up on a sheet tray, covered with towels, and put into the walk-in to be poached the next morning. We were triumphant, we had figured it out.

When we arrived the next morning, blood was seeping out from under the walk-in door. The towels covering the sausage were soaked in blood. And because the corners of the towels were hanging off the sheet tray, the absorbed blood had begun a slow drip-drip-drip onto the floor, creating a puddle that ran out from under the door. Good times.

As our attempts went on, we got cleaner and faster and never had a horror night incident again.

Makes about 6 pounds (2.7 kg)

pork mix
4 pounds (1.8 kg) pork fatback, cut into 1-inch (2.5-cm) pieces
3 pounds (1.4 kg) white onion, cut into ¼-inch (0.6 cm) dice
1 cup (60 g) finely chopped fresh Italian parsley
3 tablespoons fresh thyme leaves
3 tablespoons Fox Spice (page 311)
3 tablespoons smoked paprika
2 tablespoons sweet Calabrian chili powder
2 tablespoons Korean chili powder (gochugaru)
½ cup (80 g) kosher salt
½ cup (100 g) granulated sugar
1½ teaspoons curing salt #1

sausage
10½ ounces (300 g) black rice
2 quarts (1.9 liters) liquid pork blood (see Note)
1 cup (240 ml) heavy (double) cream
2 pounds (910 g) pork fatback, cut into small dice
1 pound (455 g) Granny Smith apples, peeled
pork casings (about ½ inch/38-mm to 42-mm in diameter)

Note: Fresh pork blood usually comes in liquid or coagulated form. I prefer liquid; it's easier to work with and the color is better. If all you can find is coagulated, you can blend it to loosen it up. To source pork blood, you can ask your local butcher, but sometimes the best bet is an Asian market. Call ahead.

make the pork mix

In a large mixing bowl, mix together the fatback pieces, diced onion, parsley, thyme, fox spice, paprika, both chili powders, the kosher salt, sugar, and curing salt. Cover and refrigerate for at least 2 hours.

make the sausage

While the pork mix is refrigerating, in a large saucepan, boil the rice in plenty of water until it's tender. Drain the rice and cool it down on a baking sheet. Keep the cooked rice refrigerated until you're ready to mix the sausage.

Follow the instructions on page 30 as you grind and stuff the sausage. Prepare your grinding equipment, taking care that your fatback mixture and grinding equipment are very cold. Grind the pork mix through a 3⁄16-inch (4-mm) plate. Transfer to a stand mixer with a paddle attachment, add the pork blood, cream, small-diced fatback, and cooked rice. Now dice the apple, adding it in as you go. Mix well, making sure all the components are evenly distributed.

Stuff the mixture into pork casings. Due to the loose nature of these sausages when raw, I cook them in lengths of still-connected links, not individually.

To poach, start the sausages in a large pot covered with cold water. Slowly bring the water up to 180°F (82°C) and hold it there until the sausages reach an internal temperature of 165°F (74°C), 1 to 1½ hours. Remove the sausages from the pot and place into a large container filled with lukewarm water. Use your hands to agitate the surface of the casings and remove any caked-on blood. Then place on a rack set inside a sheet pan to cool and refrigerate. Once chilled, you can separate the links with scissors. They will hold under refrigeration for up to 5 days, or in vacuum bags in the freezer for several months.

Pork Blood & Buckwheat Kishka

Much of Birdie G's identity has been tied to my Ashkenazi Jewish and Eastern European roots: Hungary on my dad's side and Ukraine on my mom's. This has introduced me to a vast world of comfort food beyond what I have been exposed to throughout my life. Kishka was something that really jumped out and spoke to me. The best way that I can describe it is as a "Thanksgiving stuffing sausage." Further research steered me in another direction. It seems that pretty much every culture has their own blood sausage: *morcilla* in Spain, *sundae* in Korea, *boudin noir* in France, *sanguinaccio* in Italy, and *hurka* in Hungary. This variation is inspired by both *kishka* and *hurka*, bound with buckwheat kasha and matzo meal. Cooked in a large casing, you're able to sear puck-like slices to maximize the sweet and crispy caramelization.

Makes one 4-inch (10-cm) log

pork belly mix
- 9 pounds (4 kg) pork belly, cut into 1-inch (2.5-cm) dice (see Notes)
- 7 pounds (3.2 kg) white onion, cut into 1-inch (2.5-cm) dice
- 2 cups (120 g) finely chopped fresh Italian parsley
- 3 tablespoons fresh thyme leaves
- 5 tablespoons Fox Spice (page 311)
- 3 tablespoons sweet Hungarian paprika
- 2 tablespoons Korean chili powder (gochugaru)
- 1 tablespoon sweet Calabrian chili powder
- 1 cup (160 g) kosher salt
- 1¼ cups (240 g) granulated sugar
- 1 tablespoon curing salt #1

sausage
- 1 to 2 beef bungs
- 1 lemon
- 1 gallon (3.8 liters) liquid pork blood (see Note, page 81)
- 3 pounds (1.4 kg) pork fatback, cut into ¼-inch (0.6-cm) dice
- 2¼ pounds (1 kg) Crispy Kasha (page 329)
- 11¼ ounces (320 g) Matzo Ball Mix (see Sources, page 350)

make the pork belly mix

To marinate the pork, in a large mixing bowl, combine the pork belly, diced onion, parsley, thyme, fox spice, paprika, both chili powders, kosher salt, sugar, and curing salt. Cover and refrigerate overnight to meld the flavors.

make the sausage

To prepare the casings, rinse any salt from the outside of the beef bungs and flush the insides by filling with cold water and draining a few times. Submerge the cleaned casings in a container of water with 1 squeezed lemon and refrigerate overnight. When ready to stuff, drain and dry on paper or kitchen towels.

Follow the instructions on page 30 as you grind and stuff the sausage. Prepare your grinding equipment, taking care that your pork belly mixture and grinding equipment are very cold. Grind the pork belly through a ⅜-inch (10-mm) plate. To this mixture, add the pork blood, fatback, kasha, and matzo meal. Mix well, making sure all the components are evenly distributed.

Stuff the mixture into the prepared beef bungs. Tie the end off with twine and use a cake tester or sausage pricker to release any air pockets.

To poach, bring a large pot of water to 180°F (82°C) and poach the kishka until it reaches an internal temperature of 165°F (74°C), approximately 1½ hours. Remove from the pot and into a large container or sink filled with lukewarm water. Use your hands to agitate the surface of the casing(s) and remove any cake-on blood. Next, plunge into an ice bath. Hang in the refrigerator by S hooks to dry overnight. I like to slice into 1-inch (2-cm) rounds, snip off the casing, and fry up in clarified butter (page 323).

Smoked Ham Hocks

Makes about 5 pounds (2.3 kg)

5 pounds (2.3 kg) pork hocks, also called pork knuckle
3 quarts (2.8 liters) Smoke Brine (page 337)

Note: You'll need wood chips or pellets for your smoker; apple or cherry wood is nice here.

A great thing to have around for so many applications. Split pea soup, need I say more? Also, several uses that are actually in this book. When you go to buy pork hocks, make sure you're buying raw pork hocks and not already cured and smoked ham hocks. That's what we're doing here! Don't rob yourself of the fun.

To brine the pork, in a brining bag or large container with a lid, cover the pork hocks with the cold smoke brine and refrigerate, covered, for 10 days. Make sure to adjust them daily to evenly distribute the brine.

Remove the hocks from the brine, dry on paper or kitchen towels, and discard the brine. Transfer the hocks to a sheet pan with a rack while you prepare your smoker.

To smoke the pork, set your smoker up at 200°F (93°C). Place the pork hocks on the racks. Smoke until they reach an internal temperature of 155°F (68°C).

Cool to room temperature, then refrigerate until cold. The hocks will hold in vacuum sealed bags inside your freezer for several months.

Polska Kielbasa

Polish sausage. The iconic horseshoe/teardrop shaped sausages that I grew up eating. Sometimes I would just snack on them cold, right out of the package. But I never ever had a homemade version until these. The biggest compliment I can give this recipe is that they're at least as good as the stuff in your grocer's case.

Due to a mathematical error, I found that this recipe can easily pass for andouille sausage. Simply double the amount of cayenne. Dried milk works as a binder here, but also leads to a juicier sausage.

Makes about 6 pounds (2.7 kg)

1½ cups (325 g) white onion, ¼ inch (0.6 cm) dice
¼ cup (45 g) grated garlic
1 tablespoon Leaf Lard (page 339)
¼ cup (40 g) kosher salt, plus a pinch
6¼ pounds (3 kg) pork shoulder, cut into 1-inch (2.5-cm) pieces
1 teaspoon curing salt #1
5 tablespoons powdered milk
2 tablespoons sweet Hungarian paprika
2 tablespoons Korean chili powder (gochugaru)
1 tablespoon cayenne pepper
1 tablespoon yellow mustard seed, ground
1 cup (240 ml) beer
pork casings (about ½ inch/38 mm to 42 mm in diameter)

Note: You'll need wood chips or pellets for your smoker; apple or cherry wood is nice here.

In a large sauté pan, cook the diced onion and garlic in the leaf lard with a pinch of kosher salt until it's fragrant and lightly caramelized. Spread it out evenly on a sheet tray and refrigerate until cold.

Mix the cubed pork with the remaining kosher salt, the curing salt, powdered milk, paprika, chili powder, cayenne, and mustard seed. Now, mix in the chilled-down onion and garlic, and combine well. Cover and let the mixture marinate overnight, refrigerated.

Follow the instructions on page 30 as you grind and stuff your sausage. Prepare your grinding equipment, taking care that your pork mixture and grinding equipment are very cold. Grind the sausage through a ⅜-inch (10-mm) plate. Transfer to a stand mixer with a paddle attachment, add the beer, and paddle it gently to combine. Test the mix as directed.

Once you're happy with the seasoning level, stuff the mixture into the casings. We're stuffing to a length of 16 inches (40 cm), leaving a couple inches of casing at each end. Tie both ends of the casings together so the sausage holds its iconic shape. Make sure to remove any air pockets/bubbles.

Ideally, allow the sausages to dry in the refrigerator for a few hours or up to overnight, either on a sheet tray fitted with a rack or by hanging.

To smoke the sausages, prepare your smoker to a temperature of 175°F (79°C). Be careful not to let the smoker get too hot or you'll end up with wrinkly kielbasa, and nobody wants that. Smoke the sausages until they reach an internal temperature of 150°F (66°C). Cool down and refrigerate. It will keep chilled for 3–4 days.

Beef Brisket Pastrami

This style of brisket takes the corning method of Corned Beef Brisket (page 73) and then subs out the oven and Manischewitz for a smoker and a spice rub. Think of this as your go-to brisket for sandwiches, like a killer reuben, and a friend to all things cabbage.

Serves 10 to 15

1 whole prime brisket (about 15 pounds/6.8 kg)
2 to 3 gallons (7.5 to 11.25 liters) Corn Brine (page 337)
½ cup (120 g) Dijon mustard
¼ cup (60 g) black peppercorns, coarsely ground
¼ cup (60 g) coriander seed, coarsely ground
2 tablespoons brown mustard seed, finely ground

Note: You'll need wood chips or pellets for your smoker; apple wood is nice here.

To brine the brisket, pour the cold corn brine over the brisket, cover, and refrigerate, weighing it down if necessary. Not everyone has a walk-in cooler big enough to accommodate the brining of an entire brisket. My house sure doesn't. You can cut the brisket in half if it's too large. You can also try to use a very large brining bag. Around Thanksgiving, most stores have these for turkeys, so you can try those if you don't have access to the professional kind.

Brine the brisket for 10 days, then drain it and dry it well with paper or kitchen towels. Discard the brine.

To smoke the brisket, set your smoker up at 200°F (93°C). Brush the brisket with the mustard. In a small bowl, combine the black peppercorns, coriander, and mustard seed. Lightly but evenly coat the brisket with the spice rub.

Smoke the brisket on a rack until it reaches an internal temperature of 160°F (71°C).

Remove from the smoker, wrap with aluminum foil, place on a sheet tray, and transfer to a 275°F (135°C) oven. Continue to cook to an internal temperature of 203°F (95°C). Remove from the oven and cool slightly. If you won't be serving the brisket right away, wrap it tightly in plastic wrap (clingfilm) while the brisket is still warm, and allow it to cool to room temperature before refrigerating for up to 1 week.

Duck Pastrami

This is a smoked variation on the Duck Ham from page 65. Enjoy slices on a charcuterie platter (page 166) or grilled on skewers with Duck Ham & Heart Skewers with Grapes (page 218).

Not a ton of fireworks here, so your final product will only be as good as the quality of the ducks you use. When in doubt, choose local.

Makes 4

brine
½ cup (80 g) kosher salt
⅓ cup (65 g) granulated sugar
1 teaspoon curing salt #1
2 teaspoons brown mustard seed
2 teaspoons whole black peppercorns, plus 1 tablespoon, coarsely ground
8 cloves
3 allspice berries
1 cinnamon stick
2 bay leaves

duck
4 duck breasts (2½ to 3 pounds / 1.1 kg to 1.4 kg)
2 tablespoons Dijon mustard
1 tablespoon coriander seed, coarsely ground
1 teaspoon brown mustard seed, finely ground

Note: You'll need wood chips or pellets for your smoker; apple or cherry wood is nice here.

make the brine

In a large pot over high heat, combine 2 quarts (1.9 liters) cold water, the kosher salt, granulated sugar, curing salt, mustard seed, whole peppercorns, cloves, allspice, cinnamon, and bay leaves. Bring to a boil, stirring until the salts and sugar are dissolved. Remove from the heat and let cool to room temperature.

Transfer the brine to a nonreactive container, cover, and refrigerate until well chilled, at least 2 hours or overnight.

make the duck

Trim the duck breasts of any excess fat or bone fragments if present. Remove any silver skin. Submerge the duck breasts in the cold brine, cover, and refrigerate for 3 days.

After 3 days, remove the duck breasts and pat dry with paper or kitchen towels.

To smoke the duck, set your smoker up at 200°F (93°C). Brush the duck breasts with the mustard. In a small bowl, combine the ground black pepper, coriander, and mustard seed. Lightly but evenly coat each duck breast with the spice rub (you may not use it all).

Place the seasoned duck breasts on a rack. Smoke until the duck breasts reach an internal temperature of 145°F (63°C).

Transfer to a rack-lined sheet tray, let cool to room temperature, then refrigerate until fully chilled. They will keep in the refrigerator for 1 week.

Black Sugar Tri-Tip

Tri-tip is one of my favorite slow-roasting meats. It's not as expensive as other tender cuts and can be served warm or chilled for sandwiches. It makes an excellent French dip, or serve it simply with Nasturtium Salsa (page 305). Please note that this recipe is based on my love for supermarket versions of Montreal-style steak blends, not so much authentic Montreal smoked beef... only because I have not yet traveled to Montreal.

Serves 4 to 6

1 beef tri-tip (about 2½ pounds/1 kg)
¼ cup (60 ml) tamari
¼ cup (60 ml) balsamic vinegar
2 tablespoons fish sauce
¼ cup (40 g) rice flour
½ cup (110 g) Okinawan Black Sugar (see Sources, page 350)
½ cup (120 ml) Sweet Chili Sauce (page 303)
1 tablespoon Worcestershire sauce
¼ cup (40 g) Montreal Steak Rub (page 308)

Note: You'll need wood chips or pellets for your smoker; apple wood is nice here.

In a mixing bowl, add the tamari, balsamic vinegar, fish sauce, and rice flour. Whisk until smooth. Next, add the black sugar and sweet chili sauce and mix well.

Add the marinade to a large ziptop bag, add the tri-tip, and make sure it's fully-coated. Refrigerate overnight.

The next day, transfer the tri-tip to a sheet pan with a rack, and sprinkle generously with the Montreal steak rub.

To smoke the tri-tip, set your smoker up at 225°F (107°C). Place the tri-tip on a rack and smoke until it reaches an internal of 135°F (57°C) at the thickest area of the cut.

Transfer to a rack-lined sheet tray, let rest for 30 minutes, then either slice and serve or chill completely to slice later for sandwiches. It will keep in the refrigerator for 1 week.

SNACKS	96 → 105
STARTERS	106 → 117
HOT PLATES	118 → 137
ACCENTUATIONS	138 → 147
ENTRÉES & LARGE FORMAT	148 → 167

Pork

'Nduja & Saffron Pizzelle Sandwiches

Makes 6

2 teaspoons saffron threads
2 teaspoons champagne vinegar
3 large eggs
¾ cup (150 g) granulated sugar
¼ cup (60 ml) extra-virgin olive oil
1 tablespoon fennel pollen
1 teaspoon baking powder
1¾ cups (215 g) all-purpose (plain) flour
8 ounces (230 g) Smoked Tomato 'Nduja (page 54)

My wife Rachael has a vintage pizzelle iron—a wedding present from 1973—that her mom gifted to her. It's well seasoned and missing one leg. She props it up on a crème brûlée dish to steady it, and there's a worrisome plug that sparks a little when you unplug it. This is one of her most cherished belongings. There are companies in Burbank, California, that will refurbish, clean, and update the plug. Rachael has investigated this but has never taken it in. I think she's worried the iron won't be the same after; that all the love that's been churning out perfect pizzelles over the last 50 years will wash away.

I took the maker into Birdie G's one Saturday; I was hell-bent on making pizzelles. This recipe had been knocking around in my head for a while, and we finally made it for the tasting menu at the chef's counter in 2023. It's a delicious bite and makes perfect hors d'oeuvres.

To make the pizzelles, mix the saffron and vinegar in a small bowl and microwave for 10 to 20 seconds to heat and help the saffron infuse, then let cool to room temperature.

In a mixing bowl, lightly beat the eggs and sugar for 2 to 3 minutes until light in color. Add the olive oil, vinegar-saffron mix, fennel pollen, baking powder, and flour. Mix to combine.

Preheat your pizzelle iron and cook the pizzelles according to the manufacturer's directions. Remove from the iron and let cool on a rack. Make sure you cool completely so they remain nice and crispy.

To put the sandwiches together, divide the 'nduja among half the pizzelles, spread into an even layer, and top each one with another pizzelle to make a sandwich.

Whipped Lardo with Flowers

Like Funfetti frosting but it's pork fat with flowers! While the title of the recipe could be considered misleading, since it doesn't actually contain lardo, I promise it will be worth it. The "octopus"-inspired cuts on the radishes make what was already a great dipping vessel even more enjoyable.

Serves 6 to 8

2 cups (410 g) Leaf Lard (page 339), cold
2 tablespoons grated garlic
1 tablespoon chopped fresh rosemary
3 tablespoons white wine vinegar
zest of 2 lemons
kosher salt
2 cups (60 g) assorted edible flower petals, such as zinnia, calendula, marigold, bachelor button, and nasturtium
24 French breakfast radishes, washed
flaky sea salt

Take 3 tablespoons of the leaf lard and melt it in a small saucepan. Add the garlic and rosemary and sweat them down. We don't want them to color at all, so keep the temperature moderate.

Meanwhile, boil the vinegar in a small saucepan and reduce by half, then chill.

Add the lard, cold vinegar reduction, and lemon zest to your food processor. Give it a good whip until it has nearly doubled in volume and is light and fluffy (but as it warms up it will lose that quality). Season to taste with kosher salt and fold in the flowers.

For the radishes, take a utility knife and make 3 incisions lengthwise from the tip to just shy of the stem, then rotate 45 degrees and make 3 more incisions from just below the stem all the way through the tip. Let sit in ice water for 30 minutes, then dry on paper or kitchen towels.

Serve the whipped lardo with the radishes for dipping, on a charcuterie board, or simply with crackers. Sprinkle the surface of the lardo with flaky salt.

Bacon-Wrapped Oca

Serves 8 to 12

1½ pounds (1 kg) oca or New Zealand yams, cut into 1- to 1½-inch (2.5- to 3.8-cm) pieces
1 x Maple Smoked Bacon (page 13), sliced ⅛-inch (0.3 cm) thick in 5- to 6-inch (13- to 15-cm) lengths (1 slice per piece of oca)
1½ cups (350 ml) Tiki Sauce (page 303)

My wife's family has an hors d'oeuvre they bust out at Christmas and that she makes whenever we go to a potluck: it's water chestnuts, wrapped in bacon, topped in a sweet chili sauce, and baked. People often scoff at it until they try it. When I did some digging, I realized this was a variation on rumaki, minus the chicken livers, a dish popularized in the 1950s at Trader Vic's in Los Angeles. Trader Vic's of Tiki fame. I'm sure the copycat rumaki recipe came about in an effort to sell Heinz Chili Sauce, cans of water chestnuts, and mayonnaise. You know those old recipe ads that folks would cut out of magazines or special fliers. Buy an old recipe box at any flea market and it'll be full of them. I am never not impressed by what these corporate chefs come up with using only their company's products.

When I set out to make my own version, I turned to oca. Sometimes called New Zealand yams, oca are not potatoes or yams, rather a starchy tuber that you can eat baked or raw. Here they fill in nicely for that water chestnut crunch. The Tiki Sauce fills in for Heinz, but honestly, I wouldn't kick Heinz outta bed for stealing the covers. Aaron Choi, the owner of Girl & Dug Farm in San Marcos, has kept us stocked with oca for years, as well as fun stuff like true Pickled Cornichons (page 314) and French ice plant.

Preheat your oven to 350°F (180°C).

Wrap each piece of oca in a slice of bacon. The bacon should meet on the bottom and overlap slightly. Drive a toothpick down the center of each oca, piercing the overlap of bacon on the bottom and holding the bacon in place. Arrange the oca in a baking dish, seam side down.

Bake the wrapped oca for 12 minutes, remove from the oven, and carefully drain the rendered fat. Save the fat for another use.

Smother the wrapped oca evenly with the tiki sauce. Some will inevitably get on the toothpicks, it's okay. Return to the oven to continue cooking until the sauce reduces and gets a little sticky, 20 to 30 minutes.

Remove from the oven and serve in the casserole on a trivet (you can skim any egregious rendered fat or say heck with it and leave it, it's up to you).

Creole Pig Ears & Okra

I didn't learn to cook pig ears until my time at Manresa, when I became obsessed with all things pork. As I taught myself to cook different parts, pig ears were a surprise because they were relatively easy. This dish has some prep involved, but overall comes together quickly. It'll be a fun snack for you and your friends, and, like a lot of this book, I hope it gives you the confidence and courage to branch out to more complex preparations.

The pre-toasted flour saves some time in front of the stove, and this is a great item to have around to help bang out a Wednesday étouffée swiftly.

Serves 4

simmered pig ears
3 tablespoons kosher salt
1 pound (455 g) fresh pig ears (about 20 ears) (see Notes)
1 quart (0.9 liter) Ham Hock Stock (page 336)

Creole sauce
3 tablespoons all-purpose (plain) flour
1 tablespoon Leaf Lard (page 339)
¼ cup (100 g) onion, cut into ¼-inch (0.6-cm) dice
¼ cup (100 g) celery, cut into ¼-inch (0.6-cm) dice
¼ cup (100 g) green bell pepper, cut into ¼-inch (0.6-cm) dice
1 tablespoon plus 1½ teaspoons Creole Spice (page 311)

fried pig ears and okra
3 cups (710 ml) buttermilk
1 large egg, lightly beaten
12 ounces (340 g) fresh okra, sliced ¼-inch (0.6-cm) thick (see Notes)
oil, for frying (I like rice bran oil)
2 cups (300 g) fine cornmeal
¼ cup (28 g) cornstarch (cornflour)
2 teaspoons Creole Spice (page 311)
1 teaspoon kosher salt

Notes: Pig ears should be cleaned of any hair before brining. To do this, run a cooking torch over the hair to burn it off. Or use clean steel wool to scrape it off.

When choosing okra, you want to squeeze a little pinch to the middle to feel if there's a "skeleton" inside. This is the woody inside of old okra. We don't want that. It'll be tough and unpleasant when cooked. Young pods will be smooth, bright green, and no more than 3 to 4 inches (7.5 to 10 cm) long. Not to be ageist but pick the young pods.

make the simmered pig ears

Make a simple brine of 3 quarts (2.8 liters) cold water and 3 tablespoons salt. Stir together until the salt has dissolved, add the pig ears, cover, and brine the ears overnight in the refrigerator.

The next day, drain the ears. To a pot, add the ham hock stock, ears, and enough water to cover. Bring the pot to a boil, skimming any foam that comes to the top. Reduce the heat to a simmer, add a cartouche (page 35), cover, and slow-simmer for 1½ to 2 hours.

Cool the ears to room temp in liquid, remove, and dry with paper or kitchen towels on the top and bottom. Reserve 2¼ cups (530 ml) of the cooking liquid, i.e. ham hock stock, for the sauce. Refrigerate the ears until completely chilled, then slice them quite thin, about ⅛ inch (0.3 cm).

[...]

[...]

make the Creole sauce

Preheat your oven to 325°F (165°C).

Spread the flour out on a sheet tray and toast it for 15 to 20 minutes, stirring it every few minutes. It'll start to form a skin as it dries out, and you want to break that up. It's done when it's a caramel color and smells toasty. DO NOT use the fan in your oven. You'll create a flour windstorm and there will be tears as you clean it up. You'll curse my name, and I don't need that negativity floating around.

Melt the leaf lard in a medium saucepan, add the onion, celery, bell pepper, and spice mix and sauté on medium heat until the vegetables are caramelized. Add half of the reserved ham stock and bring to a boil. Add the toasted flour to a small mixing bowl and ladle in some of the other half of the stock, whisking vigorously so there are no lumps and adding a ladle at a time until the mixture has reached a pourable viscosity. Then, drizzle it back into the pot, whisking to incorporate. This is called making a slurry. It can be done with flour or cornstarch (cornflour), here we're using flour. Add the remaining stock to the pot and bring it to a simmer. Gently simmer to thicken and reduce to a nice, dipping-sauce thickness.

make the fried pig ears and okra

In a bowl, mix the buttermilk and egg until well incorporated. Now add the sliced pig ears and okra and let it all sit at room temperature for 1 hour.

Heat the oil to fry at 350°F (180°C).

Mix the cornmeal, cornstarch (corn flour), spice mix, and salt together in a wide bowl. Pull the ear pieces and okra from the buttermilk, letting them drain above the bowl slightly, and dredge them through the cornmeal mixture.

Carefully add the dredged pieces to the oil, working in batches. Once they're golden all over, remove them from the oil to drain on paper towels, and sprinkle with a little salt. Serve warm and crispy with the Creole sauce.

Blutwurst & Raclette

This is such a nice dish for a hungry group. Serve it on a large platter and then cover everything with the melted cheese. If you can find a raw milk raclette, even better. I love a cheese called Reading, a raclette-style cheese from Spring Brook Farm in Vermont.

Serves 4

2 large eggs
10 thumb-sized fingerling potatoes (your thumb, not mine)
pinch of kosher salt
12 ounces (340 g) Blutwurst (page 58), sliced ⅛-inch (0.3-cm) thick or thinner
10 thumbprint-sized French breakfast radishes, washed and halved
24 Pickled Cornichons (page 314)
fresh Italian parsley leaves, to garnish
flaky sea salt
freshly ground black pepper
1 pound (455 g) slab raclette cheese
3 tablespoons Smoky Honey Mustard (page 302)

To soft-boil the eggs, bring a small saucepan of water to a boil. Poke the oblong end of each egg with a straight pin. With a small skimmer/spider/strainer or ladle, gently lower the cold eggs into the simmering water. Cook for 6 minutes.

Set up an ice bath while the eggs cook. After 6 minutes, plunge the hot eggs into the ice bath and let them sit for 30 minutes. Peel the eggs under cool running water and then dry them on paper or kitchen towels.

Meanwhile, to boil the potatoes, refill your saucepan with cold water and add a good pinch of kosher salt. Add the potatoes, making sure they're covered by the water by at least an inch (2.5 cm), and bring the water to a boil. Lower to a simmer and cook until tender, 10 to 15 minutes, depending on the size of the potatoes. Pierce one with a paring knife to make sure they're tender, then drain and allow the potatoes to cool. Once cool, cut each potato in half lengthwise.

To assemble, cut the eggs in half lengthwise, arrange them with the blutwurst, potatoes, radishes, cornichons, and parsley leaves on a platter. Season with flaky sea salt and black pepper.

In a toaster oven, a preheated 400°F (200°C) oven, or one of a multitude of raclette melters, bake the cheese until melty, then immediately spoon it over the platter. Serve with a side bowl of smoked honey mustard.

Endive Doty

This recipe is named for Shaun Doty, the chef I worked under for almost three years at the restaurant Mumbo Jumbo. I credit Shaun, along with Anne Quatrano and Michael Touhy, with being Atlanta's biggest proponents of local ingredients, and he really solidified the true "farm to table" foundation that Michael Lata passed along to me in Charleston, South Carolina. Chef Shaun had a way of translating the memory of a singular dish he may have had at a truck stop in Rome into something new and exciting. The flavors of this recipe are inspired by a pasta dish he taught me while running the Hot Apps station. I was so gung-ho; I shaved my arms so the long pasta sheets would be free of hair. I can still taste it. The pasta, not the hair. And picture it. Sicily, Italy, 1922. (Atlanta, Georgia, 2000, in reality.) Handmade tagliatelle pasta cooked fresh to order, sauced with aged balsamic and butter, twirled over a dollop of soft goat cheese, and topped with toasted pine nuts and crispy slices of pancetta.

Serves 4 to 6

8 ounces (225 g) Pancetta Cotto (page 69), cut into ½-inch (1.3-cm) dice
1 ripe avocado, cut into ½-inch (1.3-cm) chunks
¼ cup (30 g) blue cheese, crumbled
2 tablespoons toasted pine nuts
2 heads red Belgian endive
1 teaspoon Dijon mustard
¼ cup (60 ml) plus 2 tablespoons balsamic vinegar
2 tablespoons olive oil
kosher salt

Render the fat from the pancetta in a dry cast-iron skillet. Really crowd the pan at first, so the pancetta starts to confit in its own fat. Once it's crispy, drain the pancetta on paper towels and pour off and reserve ¼ cup (60 g) rendered fat.

Once the rendered pancetta is lukewarm, combine it with the avocado, blue cheese, and pine nuts. Don't mash it, leave chunks, just make it a cohesive mixture.

Separate the leaves of the endive by cutting off the root end, cutting the endive in half, and removing the leaves one by one. Stuff the endive leaves with the pancetta-avocado mixture. Arrange the loaded leaves on a platter.

To make the vinaigrette, whisk together the mustard and balsamic vinegar, then slowly add the olive oil and warm reserved pancetta fat until emulsified. Check the seasoning and add salt to taste.

Spoon the vinaigrette over the endive and serve.

Chopped Antipasto Salad

If you don't like a chopped salad, of any kind, I don't know how to relate to you. I mean, it's a chopped salad. It's all the best things cut into bite-sized pieces for easy shoveling into your face. It's the perfect balance of crunch, acid, fat, meat, cheese, and more crunch. I could eat this every day. Switch up any of the meats and cheese to your liking. Just make sure the lettuce has a bite. Butter lettuce and the like aren't right here. The judges will accept iceberg.

Serves 6 to 8

dressing
1 cup (240 ml) extra-virgin olive oil
⅓ cup (80 ml) Calabrian Chile Hybrid oil (page 304)
½ cup (120 ml) red wine vinegar
1½ teaspoons garlic powder
1½ teaspoons dried oregano, plus extra for sprinkling
1 teaspoon fennel seed, crushed with a mortar and pestle

salad
1 head romaine lettuce, leaves washed, dried, and coarsely chopped
1 head radicchio, leaves washed, dried, and coarsely chopped
1 bunch Tuscan kale, leaves washed, stemmed, and coarsely chopped
1 pound (455 g) mixed meats, such as Mortadella (page 57), Olive Loaf (page 61), Rosemary Pork Loin (page 70), Pancetta Cotto (page 69), and Corned Beef Tongue (page 66), cut into ½-inch (1.3-cm) dice
8 ounces (225 g) provolone, cut into ½-inch (1.3-cm) dice
1 cup (165 g) cooked chickpeas
¼ cup (40 g) sliced cucumbers
¼ cup (40 g) Ohio Peppers (page 317)
¼ cup (45 g) torn pitted olives, such as castelvetrano, kalamata, or niçoise)
¼ cup (40 g) red onion, cut into thin julienne

to serve
kosher salt
freshly ground black pepper
Garlic Bread Croutons (page 326)
Parmigiano-reggiano cheese, for grating

make the dressing — In a mason jar with a lid, combine the olive oil, chile oil, vinegar, garlic powder, oregano, and fennel seed and give it a really good shake-shake-shake to emulsify. Pretend you're a bespoke bartender. Really get into it. Make awkward eye contact with someone, the whole bit.

make the salad — In a large bowl, combine all the salad ingredients and give them a good toss to combine. Add half of the dressing, tossing to coat. Try a leaf. If it needs more dressing, add more and toss to combine again.

to serve — Season with salt and pepper to taste. Pile the salad high into wide bowls or plates, and top with the croutons and grated Parmigiano.

Pancetta-Wrapped Melon with Scallion Jaew

A little play on prosciutto and melon, a perfect summer dish. If I didn't already mention it, jaew (page 304) is just good on everything, especially raw, fresh melon. When picking out a great melon, feel for it to be lighter than it looks, smell for fresh melon, and give it a little squeeze—there should be the slightest give.

Serves 4

8 ounces (225 g) Pancetta Cotto (page 69)
1 ripe orange melon, such as Crenshaw, Sugarcube, or Cavaillon
1 cup (250 g) Scallion Jaew (page 304)
extra-virgin olive oil, for drizzling
flaky salt
freshly cracked black pepper
fresh basil and mint, for sprinkling

Slice the pancetta cotto, ideally on a meat slicer; you want it to be thin enough so it's still pliable, around $1/8$ inch (about 0.3 cm). This thinness equals soft, pliable, melty.

If you're not serving it immediately, arrange the slices on parchment paper, but don't overlap them as they will stick, and refrigerate.

Everyone has their way to cut a melon, here's mine: cut just a bit off each end of the melon so it stands flat. With a long knife, peel carefully, not digging into the meat. Start at the top as it stands, and shave down with the knife, taking off a long strip all the way to the bottom. Try and do this in one motion; don't saw at it. This strip should be the entire rind and just the thinnest layer of outer melon. Take its jacket off.

Once you've worked all the way around and the melon is "naked," check the bottom end for any bits you might have missed, and cut those off too. Slice the melon in half from top to bottom, exposing the seeds inside. Scoop the seeds out of each cavity with a spoon, and push through a fine-mesh sieve to capture any juice. You can use this reserved melon juice to make a round of melon gin and tonics. Discard the solids.

Once you have your halves of melon, cut them into thin slices from end to end, making a "smile slice."

To serve, wrap each piece of melon with a slice of pancetta. Spoon the jaew on the base of each plate or a platter. Nestle the wrapped melon pieces on top of the jaew, drizzle with olive oil, and sprinkle with flaky salt, cracked pepper, and the basil and mint.

Rosemary Pork Loin, Avocado Tonnato & Capers

Vitello tonnato is one of my favorite things. I order it whenever I see it on a menu, in any iteration. At Bestia in Los Angeles, Chef Ori Menashe makes a veal tartare with tonnato that I crave. This version is me putting a California spin on the dish. The pork fills in for the veal for those who are squeamish, and it also happens to be much more affordable. Use the avocado tonnato to dress fresh tomatoes, or on grilled bread with anchovies on top.

Serves 6

avocado tonnato
2 ripe avocados
7 tinned, oil-packed anchovy fillets
3 garlic cloves
2 tablespoons caper brine
1 cup (240 ml) Aioli (page 321)
kosher salt

to assemble
18 ounces (510 g) Rosemary Pork Loin (page 70)
3 lemons
extra-virgin olive oil, for drizzling
4 teaspoons capers
fresh Italian parsley leaves, for serving
6 caper leaves (optional)

make the avocado tonnato	In a blender, purée the avocados, anchovies, garlic, caper brine, and ½ cup (120 ml) cold water until smooth. Add to a mixing bowl and gently fold in the aioli; go slow, you want it nice and whippy. We don't want the air to escape by mixing it too hard or too fast. Taste for seasoning and adjust if necessary.
to assemble	Slice the pork loin about ⅛-inch (0.3-cm) thick. If you have a meat slicer, now is the time to bust it out. If not, sharpen your knife and get the slices as thin as possible.
	Cut the lemons in half along their equator. Pick the seeds out with either tweezers, a cake tester, or a skewer. Or get fancy and wrap in nice official lemon wraps (see page 154).
	Arrange the sliced pork loin on a plate with a good dollop of the tonnato, a glug of olive oil, and the capers along with the parsley and caper leaves, if using, and a halved lemon per person.

Red Pea Farinata, Olive Loaf & Calabrian Chile

During the pandemic, I became obsessed with perfecting farinata. I bought a 19-inch (48-cm) copper farinata pan from Agnelli and set to work testing recipes and methods. We all had our thing, or things, to attempt to remain sane at that time, and this was one of mine. My sourdough.

I've made a lot of panisse, French chickpea flour fritters, in my career, but the classic Italian farinata was new for me. This version takes a detour and uses Sea Island red pea flour, instead of the traditional chickpea. Anything to utilize Anson Mills products. I'm not a guy for kitchen gadgets, but if there's a traditional or proper pan for something, I want it. If you're able, I recommend treating yourself to the Agnelli Copper Farinata Pan, but a high-sided cast-iron skillet will work, too.

Serves 6 to 8

8 ounces (225 g) Sea Island red pea flour
1½ teaspoons kosher salt, plus extra to taste
½ cup (60 g) finely grated Parmigiano-reggiano cheese
3 tablespoons rosemary leaves, coarsely chopped
3 tablespoons plus 1½ teaspoons extra-virgin olive oil
¼ cup Calabrian Chile Hybrid solids (page 304)
flaky sea salt
12 ounces (340 g) Olive Loaf (page 61), sliced ⅛-inch (0.3-cm) thick

Note: If you can't find red pea flour, you can substitute chickpea flour, which is the traditional choice when making farinata.

In a large mixing bowl, whisk to combine 2¾ cups (650 ml) water, red pea flour, and kosher salt. Cover the mixture and let it sit at room temperature for 6 hours. Check it periodically, scooping off any foam that forms.

To cook the farinata, set your oven rack to the middle position and preheat your oven to 500°F (260°C). Add the Parmigiano and rosemary to the red pea flour mixture and double-check the seasoning, adding more salt if needed.

Place your farinata (or cast-iron) pan in the oven to preheat; no vent fan should be running. After 5 minutes, once the pan is hot, remove it from the oven and add the olive oil, carefully and gently swirling it around. Then return it to the oven for another 2 minutes.

Remove the pan from the oven, add 1 quart (0.9 liter) of batter without agitating the pan. Return to the oven and cook for 10 minutes. Next rotate the pan 45 degrees to help it cook evenly. Then, every 5 minutes, rotate it another 45 degrees. Everyone's oven has hot and cool spots, even the fancy ones. When it's done, you'll see the edges have pulled away from the sides and look crisped. Check the center with a cake tester, it should come out clean.

Remove from the oven and allow the farinata to cool in the pan for about 5 minutes. Then cover the pan with a cutting (chopping) board or plate and turn it upside down, showing off the crispy bottom.

Lightly spread the Calabrian chile solids over the top. Depending on how spicy you like it is how much you should add, then sprinkle with a little flaky sea salt. Shingle the olive loaf over the top to completely cover the surface. Make it nice. Cut into triangles or squares or six-pointed hexagons. I'm kidding, triangles are fine. Enjoy immediately.

Johnnycakes with Smoked Ham Hock

Serves 8

4 large eggs
2⅓ cups (565 g) buttermilk
2 cups plus 1 tablespoon (250 g) all-purpose (plain) flour
1¾ cups (250 g) fine cornmeal
¼ cup (50 g) granulated sugar
2 tablespoons baking powder
2 teaspoons kosher salt
1 pound (455 g) Smoked Ham Hock, meat picked (page 85)
4 tablespoons (56 g) unsalted butter

The first time I ever had johnnycakes was in fifth grade on a field trip in Cleveland, Ohio. I don't remember exactly where we went on that field trip, somewhere outdoors, but I clearly remember the johnnycakes. Crispy around the edges with a sweet corncake middle. There are some foods that just open a door in your brain. In fifth grade, johnnycakes did that for me. Here, I'm folding in some pulled ham hock for smoke and fat, and just all-around goodness.

Add the eggs to a mixing bowl and lightly beat to liquify, now add the buttermilk and whisk again to combine. Add the flour, cornmeal, sugar, baking powder, and kosher salt and mix well. Fold in the picked smoked ham hock.

In a cast-iron skillet on medium heat, melt the butter. When the butter stops foaming, swirl the pan to coat it in the butter. Add the batter, ¼ cup (60 ml) at a time. When bubbles start to come to the surface of the cake and pop, flip the cake over using a spatula. Cook 1 more minute on the flipped side. Transfer the cooked johnnycakes to a warm platter as you finish the rest of the batter.

Serve the johnnycakes as part of your Sunday breakfast spread, or I'd suggest something acidic like a cherry tomato bruschetta situation.

Egg-in-a-Basket Carbonara

My grandmother Gladys made me eggs-in-a-basket growing up, and I looked forward to mornings because of this. Who can resist a runny yolk oozing over crispy bread? When we started getting fresh peas a few Februarys ago (it's California, our seasons host seasons inside of other seasons), I quickly started playing around with a pea-studded carbonara, and that's how this dish was born. So many times, these mashups just come from me wanting to eat one thing with another thing and wondering in real time if it'll work. It did. It's truly one of my favorite things that has appeared on the Birdie G's menu.

Serves 4

2 cups (280 g) shucked English peas (see Note)
kosher salt
1 pound (455 g), Guanciale (page 52), cut into ¼-inch (0.3-cm) dice
1½ cups (355 ml) Béchamel (page 322)
4 slices Pain de Mie (page 328), cut 1½ inches (3.8 cm) thick
1 tablespoon minced shallots
1 tablespoon plus 1½ teaspoons banyuls vinegar
freshly cracked black pepper
4 large egg yolks
flaky sea salt
block of good Parmigiano-reggiano cheese, for grating

Note: Keep in mind while you're shopping: as a rule of thumb, 1 pound (455 g) of whole English peas yields 1 cup (280 g) of shucked peas. Also keep in mind that frozen (shucked) peas are delicious.

Blanch the shucked peas in heavily salted boiling water for 90 seconds, then shock in ice water and drain on paper or kitchen towels.

Put the diced guanciale in a small sauté pan on medium heat, crowding the pan; the fat will begin to render. Bring up to a bubble on medium heat then reduce to low. Stir as you go until nicely crisped but still chewy. Drain the guanciale on paper towels, reserving the rendered fat.

Warm the béchamel in a small saucepan, remove from the heat, and set aside.

Brush the pain de mie lightly with some of the rendered fat and sprinkle with a pinch of kosher salt.

Cook the bread in a toaster oven or in a cast-iron skillet on medium heat until golden on both sides and warmed all the way through. With a biscuit cutter, punch out a circle from each piece of bread.

In a large pan, combine the drained guanciale, peas, shallots, vinegar, and a good amount of cracked black pepper. Slowly warm everything and season with kosher salt.

Plate the toast slices in the center of each warmed plate, saving the punched-out circles for last.

Place an egg yolk in each hole, sprinkle with a few grains of flaky sea salt, spoon the warm béchamel over each egg yolk to fill the hole, and smother the bread with more sauce.

Spoon the peas and guanciale mixture over the top. Grate Parmigiano over the dish and finish with the toast circle.

Hangtown Brei

My elementary school years were spent with a lot of other Jewish kids. I thought back then that most people were Jewish. My friend circle at Cross Keys High School in Atlanta, Georgia, however, was a virtual Benetton advertisement, and I think we relished in it. Coming of age in the American South, we became acutely aware of the stereotypes attached to our own heritage, and we learned to exchange jokes to take the sting away from their bite. Even so, I had to become accustomed to a life that was not built for me, watching every fall as the city decorated itself for Christmas… for everyone else. And when I started going through kitchens, I was the Jewish guy. But eventually, I was the Jewish guy who was obsessing over how to cook every single part of a pig.

Cut to many years later: I'm thinking about the Birdie G's menu and all these different parts of my life are swirling around in my head, coming together in one dish: Hangtown Brei. I have loved Hangtown Fry since the first time I tried it, the classic San Francisco dish consisting of an omelet with bacon and oysters. And my grandmother Gladys's matzo brei was a childhood staple. Pairing them felt like a bolt of, albeit potentially blasphemous, inspiration. The hot sauce represented the South, while the hollandaise harked on the sauce I was unable to properly replicate during the final exam of my first class in culinary school. It was San Francisco, Judaism, my childhood, and the South connecting through one single plate of food. An homage on a plate. Which really, if we're being honest, is all most chefs are trying to accomplish. To be known, really known, through their food.

Serves 4

hot sauce hollandaise
4¼ ounces (120 g); about 7 large egg yolks
1 cup (120 g) Clarified Butter (page 323), melted and cooled slightly
4 teaspoons Dijon mustard
3 tablespoons hot sauce (Mama raised a Crystal boy)
1 tablespoon fresh lemon juice
kosher salt

fried oysters
1 cup (120 g) all-purpose (plain) flour
3 large eggs, whisked together
1 cup (120 g) seasoned matzo meal (I use Matzo Project, see Sources, page 350)
oil, for frying
4 medium shucked oysters

pork belly
1 pound (455 g) Pancetta Cotto (page 69)

matzo brei
10 large eggs
1½ teaspoons kosher salt
5½ ounces (160 g) matzo (6 to 7 sheets)
3 tablespoons sliced scallions (spring onions)
2 tablespoons (28 g) unsalted butter

to serve
fresh Italian parsley leaves, to garnish

---

make the hollandaise | Making hollandaise at home in a blender couldn't be easier. Make this first and then hold it in a warm water bath to keep it warm. In the jar of your blender, add the egg yolks and zip to combine for a few seconds. Now, through the opening at the top of the blender, add the clarified butter in a slow stream while processing the yolks. Add the mustard, hot sauce, and lemon juice, and process again to combine. Check the seasoning, adding salt to taste.

make the fried oysters | Set up a frying station with one bowl of the flour, one with the whisked eggs, and one with the matzo meal. Heat the oil in a medium saucepan to 350°F (180°C). Bread the oysters by coating them in the flour, then the egg, then the matzo meal. Fry in the hot oil until crispy, 4 to 5 minutes. Remove to a rack set over paper towels to catch the oil.

make the pork belly	Slice the pancetta cotto into 4 equal "steaks" and fry in a dry cast-iron skillet. Let it crisp up and then flip and crisp on the other side. Set aside.
make the matzo brei	Crack all your eggs into a large bowl and whisk them well with the salt. Next, hold the matzo under gently running water, wet it briefly, just long enough that the matzo can no longer shatter, and then drain. Break up the wet matzo and fold into the eggs with the scallions (spring onions).
	In a large saucepan over low heat, melt the butter. Once it's melted and has stopped foaming, add the egg mixture. Using a silicone spatula, stir the eggs as they cook, breaking up curds and bringing the cooked edges to the center. Once the eggs are nearly all set, with a thin layer of liquid eggs on the top, remove the pan from the heat.
to serve	Divide the matzo brei among 4 warmed plates, nestle the crispy pork belly up to the eggs, top everything with a fried oyster, and smother the plate with the hollandaise sauce. Garnish with the parsley leaves and serve immediately.

Italian Sausage Ravioli

Serves 8

pasta dough
4 cups (480 g) "00" flour
11 ounces (300 g) whole egg (about 6 large eggs)
2 tablespoons extra-virgin olive oil
4 teaspoons kosher salt

filling
1¾ pounds (800 g) loose Italian Sausage (page 74)
1 pound (455 g) fresh ricotta cheese, squeezed dry
½ cup (60 g) finely grated Parmigiano-reggiano cheese
½ cup (60 g) breadcrumbs, crushed Garlic Bread Croutons (page 326) work nicely
1 large egg

ravioli shapes
semolina, for dusting

sauce
1½ cups (355 ml) Easy Tomato Sauce (page 306)
1¼ cups (300 ml) Rachael's Chicken Stock (page 334)
4 ounces (115 g) Calabrian Chile Hybrid solids (page 304)
2 tablespoons fennel seed, crushed
2 tablespoons (28 g) unsalted butter

to serve
kosher salt
2 tablespoons chopped fennel fronds
2 teaspoons fennel pollen

For a time, between the ages of eight and eleven, I lived with a gangster. Maybe mobster is more appropriate. Appropriate seems a strange word here regardless. But it happened. My late mother's boyfriend was in the mob. He was not a good man. He was violent with my mother. He once shot a gun in our home during one of their fights, lodging a bullet in a wall. He was giant. Maybe six feet five inches and 300 pounds. My mother was five feet three inches, maybe 105 pounds. I was told he was a bookie, but I had no idea what that meant, I was eight. Sometimes he would take me along on his runs, where he picked up envelopes all over Cleveland.

The only upside of this chaos was the food he brought home from his "bookie" runs: veal parmesan, chicken marsala, loaves of garlic bread. Cleveland, Ohio, along with a hundred small towns dotted all around the state, has a large population of Italian-American immigrants. If you go to Ohio now, you'll still find family-run, "red-sauce Italian" restaurants. The kind with the red-check tablecloths, spaghetti that comes with a side of spaghetti, sides of escarole soaked in garlicky olive oil, their house version of Hungarian Wax Peppers (page 317), and bottles of Lambrusco.

A not-so-secret secret dream of mine is to move back to Ohio and own one of these places. The kind of place where you know your regulars, where they celebrate their milestones and mourn their losses with you. The kind of place that sponsors the local little league team. The kind of place where an eight-year-old, out of his depth, could feel like a place is a hug, and food is safety. If you too are from a town like this, I think you know what I mean.

This dish was on the opening menu of Birdie G's. It's still one of my favorites. Serve it with the Chopped Antipasto Salad (page 111) and a glass of dry Lambrusco. Serve it to the people you love most.

make the pasta dough

Gather all your ingredients (if you have a kitchen scale, I highly recommend using one). On a large wooden cutting (chopping) board, pour the flour into a large mound and, with your fist, make a shallow well in the middle, flattening out the mound. To the well, add the eggs, olive oil, and salt. Using a fork, whisk the eggs inside the well, gathering up small bits of flour as you go. Keep whisking, adding more and more flour from the inside of the well border. Once it starts to look like a thick batter, switch to a bench scraper. Using the scraper, mix in the rest of the flour, scraping up the sides and cutting it in. You'll start to see a more unified dough at this point; keep scraping and cutting, turning the dough over, until you have an albeit shaggy mass.

Next, knead the dough for 10 minutes. To knead, push the dough down and forward with the heel of your hand, rotating it to the right as you pull back. The rotation can be slight, we're just working the dough slowly in a circle and pulling back. We're looking for the dough to be uniform with no creases, pleats, or folds. After 10 minutes, it should be glossy with a nice sheen. Flatten the ball of dough slightly and wrap it tightly with plastic wrap (clingfilm), then refrigerate the dough for 1 hour to rest.

After the dough has rested, remove it from the refrigerator and allow it to stand at room temperature for 30 minutes.

make the filling

We want loose sausage, not links, for this recipe. So if you've stuffed the sausage, cut them open and bust up the meat inside for cooking.

In a large sauté pan, cook the Italian sausage over medium heat, using a wooden spoon to break up any lumps. Once any sign of pink is gone, remove the pan from the heat and drain the sausage. Reserve the fat for another use. Cool the sausage to room temperature, then refrigerate until cold. Once cold, mix in the ricotta, Parmigiano, breadcrumbs, and egg. Give it a good stir, breaking up any lumps. We're looking for a uniform mix. Now you have a few choices: a pastry (piping) bag makes for easy work of filling ravioli, but you can also use a small cookie-dough scoop or, if all else fails, a spoon. Depending on which way you want to go, either transfer the filling to a large pastry bag or cover the filling with plastic wrap and refrigerate.

make the ravioli shapes

Set your pasta rolling machine to its widest setting, dusting it with a little semolina.

Now, using your bench scraper, cut the ball of dough into quarters, wrapping 3 of the pieces back up in the plastic wrap so they don't dry out. For the other piece, dust your cutting (chopping) board with some semolina and flatten the dough lengthwise with a rolling pin, so we can begin to feed it through the machine.

Run the dough through the widest setting a few times as the pasta adjusts to being flattened and squeezed. Fold the sides of the piece to create a uniform shape and run it through the widest setting again. Adjust your pasta machine, lowering the setting, and repeat the previous steps, folding to keep the shape and adjusting the setting lower and lower until you've achieved a thin, long strip. Dust your wood board or workstation with a thin layer of semolina, lay out the long pasta strip, and cover it with plastic wrap or damp dish (tea) towels so it doesn't dry out. Repeat the process with the other 3 pieces of dough.

On your work surface, dust a little semolina, a whisper if you will, and lay out one sheet of your pasta with no pleats or wrinkles. Starting from one end and working down the center until you reach the other side, place approximately 2 tablespoons of the filling in even intervals, leaving about 2 fingers of space between the filling and on each end of the sheet.

Carefully top the filled sheet with another sheet of pasta, like a big pasta hoagie, gently pushing around the filling and being careful not to flatten it out. Use your fingers to smooth it from top to bottom, going slowly so as not to create pleats or wrinkles while working out any air bubbles.

With a fluted pastry cutter or a sharp knife, cut the ravioli into 3 × 3-inch (7.6 × 7.6-cm) squares.

Set the finished ravioli onto a tray dusted with, you guessed it, more semolina flour. Cover with a kitchen towel while you repeat the process with the remaining 2 sheets of pasta until you've cut all your ravioli. Cover the whole ravioli-laden tray with the kitchen towel to rest as you finish the sauce and boil the water.

make the sauce

In a medium saucepan, add the tomato sauce, chicken stock, Calabrian chile solids, and crushed fennel seed. Gently simmer the sauce for 20 minutes as it thickens and the flavor deepens.

to serve

Bring a pot of heavily salted water to a boil, "salty like the sea" as they say. Once it boils, tenderly add your ravioli and simmer them gently for 4 to 6 minutes. Once they float to the top, they typically have only 1 minute of cooking left.

As the pasta cooks, finish the sauce by mounting it with the butter. I typically do this right before I'm ready to serve it. The butter gives it good flavor and a nice gloss, and binds the sauce so the water in the sauce doesn't seep and separate away in the bowl. Lastly, mix in the fennel fronds.

Remove the ravioli from the water with a strainer to warm pasta bowls. Spoon the sauce over them and sprinkle with the fennel pollen.

Borlotti Bean, Sauerkraut & Kielbasa Stew

Ever since discovering Lidia Bastianich's recipe for a Trieste-inspired soup called *jota*, I have looked for any opportunity to combine smoked pork, beans, and sauerkraut. Some chefs have been able to travel the world, trying out first-hand the many regional specialties. While I have been fortunate to stage in Bruges and London, I never had the means to do much more than work. So random recipes, such as the one referenced here, are the gateways for many of us to experience whatever we can extract. During my twenties, most of any expendable income was spent on cookbooks, which exposed me to as much as was humanly possible. Fifty dollars spent on a cookbook could provide much more "mileage" than putting it towards a meal or a plane ticket. With that, make this stew.

Serves 4 to 6

beans
8 ounces (230 g) dried borlotti beans, soaked overnight, drained, and rinsed
2 cups (475 ml) Ham Hock Stock (page 336)
2 cups (475 ml) Rachael's Chicken Stock (page 334)
1 teaspoon baking soda (bicarbonate of soda)
1 onion, cut into 1-inch (2.5-cm) pieces
4 celery stalks, cut into 1-inch (2.5-cm) pieces
1 tablespoon caraway seed

stew
12 ounces (340 g) drained Sauerkraut (page 320)
2 pounds (910 g) Polska Kielbasa (page 86), sliced ¼-inch (0.3-cm) thick
3 tablespoons (42 g) unsalted butter
kosher salt
freshly ground black pepper

to serve
extra-virgin olive oil
¼ cup (60 g) Pickled Mustard Seeds (page 318)
celery heart leaves, to garnish
freshly ground black pepper
Parmigiano-reggiano cheese, for shaving

make the beans — Preheat your oven to 300°F (150°C). In a large Dutch oven, add the beans, stocks, 1 cup (240 ml) cold water, and baking soda (bicarbonate of soda). Bring the pot to a boil and skim any foam that rises.

Add the onion, celery, and caraway seed, top with a cartouche (see page 35) and lid, and cook in the oven until the beans are soft and creamy, about 4 hours.

make the stew — Return the Dutch oven to a burner on low heat and stir in the sauerkraut and kielbasa. Let steep for 30 minutes, turn off the heat, adjust the seasoning with salt and pepper, and stir in the butter.

to serve — Divide among warmed bowls and top off with a glug of good olive oil and a scattering of pickled mustard seeds, celery leaves, black pepper, and shaved Parmigiano.

Spareribs with Peach BBQ

We source much of our stone fruit from Andy's Orchard, located in Morgan Hill, California (see Sources, page 350). They grow some of the most delicious fruit I've ever tasted. Folks line up at the Wednesday Santa Monica Farmer's Market just trying to get a few peaches. They make the best jam and tarts, and when they get really soft and juicy, I make this barbecue sauce. The recipe is perfect for summer and great for entertaining. Everything can be done ahead of time and finished when your guests arrive. If you have a few peaches on the firmer side, grill up a few halves to serve alongside the ribs.

Pro-tip: Since recipes such as this sauce or jams and the like call for soft fruit, ask your local farmers if they have "seconds" available. It helps your pocketbook and theirs.

Serves 6 to 8

spice-rubbed ribs
2 tablespoons brown sugar
4 teaspoons kosher salt
1 tablespoon plus 1½ teaspoons smoked paprika
2 teaspoons Aleppo pepper
2 teaspoons freshly ground black pepper
1 teaspoon garlic powder
5 pounds (2.3 kg) pork spareribs

sauce
5 ounces (140 g) white onion, cut into ½-inch (1.3-cm) dice
2 tablespoons Leaf Lard (page 339) or oil of your choice
2 pounds (900 g) peaches or other stone fruit, pitted
½ cup (120 ml) sherry vinegar
¼ cup plus 2 tablespoons dark brown sugar
2 tablespoons grated garlic
2 tablespoons grated peeled ginger
1 tablespoon kosher salt

make the spice-rubbed ribs

In a small bowl, combine the brown sugar, salt, paprika, Aleppo pepper, black pepper, and garlic powder and stir to combine.

Pat the ribs dry and season all over with the spice rub. Vacuum-seal in a large bag and refrigerate at least 4 hours, or overnight.

Set your immersion circulator to 165°F (74°C) and poach the ribs for 12 hours. If you're not serving them immediately, chill the ribs down in the bag.

make the sauce

While the ribs cook, in a large sauté pan, sweat the onion down in the lard until soft, then add the peaches, vinegar, brown sugar, garlic, ginger, and salt and continue to cook until the released liquid has reduced to a syrup. Remove from the heat and allow to cool for a few minutes.

Purée the sauce in your food processor or blender, then push the mixture through a fine-mesh sieve with a bench press.

When you're ready to finish the ribs, set up your grill for direct heat. Brush the ribs with the sauce and place them, sauce side down, on the grill, allowing the sauce to caramelize, before brushing the top side with sauce and then flipping the ribs. Repeat the process 3 more times, basting and flipping so each side gets 2 layers of sauce. It'll get sticky and charred and delicious.

Fried Pork Trotter, Ginger Shoots & Yuzu

Chef Josef Centeno, of Orsa & Winston and Bar Ama, showed me how to prepare stuffed trotters—aka pork shanks with the foot attached—when he was chef de cuisine and I was a line cook at Manresa back in the early 2000s. It's been one of my favorite things to cook ever since, and through the years I've experimented with dozens of flavor combinations. The crispy rounds of trotter lend themselves well to whatever your creativity can come up with.

Yuzu seems to pair well with most anything, and if you come across myoga (young ginger shoots), pounce on them.

Serves 8 to 12

poached trotters
- 2 pork shanks with foot attached (each about 3 pounds/1.4 kg)
- 2 onions, quartered (about 10 ounces/280 g)
- 3 celery stalks, cut into 2-inch (5-cm) lengths (about 4 ounces/115 g)
- 2 carrots, halved lengthwise, and cut into 2-inch (5-cm) lengths (about 4 ounces/115 g)
- 1 head garlic, halved
- 2 bay leaves
- 2 quarts (1.9 liters) Ham Hock Stock (page 336)

quick-pickled ginger shoots
- 8 ounces (240 g) myoga or ginger shoots
- ¾ cup (300 g) granulated sugar
- ¾ cup (180 ml) rice wine vinegar
- 2 teaspoons kosher salt

yuzu sauce
- 2 cups (440 g) Aioli (page 321)
- 2 tablespoons white soy sauce
- 1 tablespoon yuzu juice
- 1 teaspoon fish sauce

stuffed trotters
- ¼ cup (60 g) finely diced red onion
- 3 tablespoons fresh Italian parsley, finely chopped
- 1 tablespoon Dijon mustard
- kosher salt (optional)

to serve
- 2 cups (240 g) all-purpose (plain) flour
- 6 large eggs, whisked with 2 tablespoons cold water
- 2 cups (160 g) panko breadcrumbs, ground very fine in a food processor
- oil of your choosing (I prefer rice bran, peanut, or canola)
- flaky sea salt
- cilantro (coriander) flowers, to garnish (optional)

make the poached trotters

Preheat your oven to 275°F (135°C).

Using a large, double layer of cheesecloth (muslin), tightly wrap each trotter and, much like when wrapping a roast, use a butcher's knot to secure the cheesecloth. Gather the corners of the cheesecloth at the top and bottom, and twist and tie it with butcher's twine. Really swaddle your baby tight.

In a Dutch oven large enough to accommodate the trotters, combine the onions, celery, carrots, garlic, bay leaves, ham hock stock, and 2 quarts (1.9 liters) cold water. Warm the pot over low heat to melt the ham hock stock if it's still cold and solid. Add the wrapped trotters, making sure they're submerged, and bring the pot to a boil.

Cover the surface with a cartouche (see page 35) before wrapping with aluminum foil; this is a good rule of thumb so that whatever you're cooking doesn't rise and stick to the foil.

Place the whole setup in the oven until the skin of the trotters is soft and you can tell that the meat has softened as well, 2 to 3 hours. Let the trotters cool to room temperature in the liquid until it's workable with your hands. Don't burn yourself.

make the quick-pickled ginger shoots

Separate the myoga into petals and transfer them to a container that holds about twice their volume. In a small saucepan, bring ¾ cup (180 ml) water, the sugar, vinegar, and kosher salt to a boil and stir to make sure the salt and sugar dissolve completely. Pour the hot brine over the ginger shoots, fully submerging them. Cover the container with either a lid or plastic wrap (clingfilm), cool to room temperature, then refrigerate indefinitely.

make the yuzu sauce

In a small mixing bowl, combine the aioli, white soy, yuzu juice, and fish sauce. Gently mix to combine. Store, covered, in the refrigerator until you're ready to use it.

make the stuffed trotters

Set up a sheet pan on which to pick the trotters. In addition, set up a container with enough poaching liquid to cover the meat as you pick it, we don't want it to dry out.

Gently remove the trotters from the cooking liquid, one at a time. You want to remove the trotters from the cheesecloth immediately after leaving the cooking liquid. If not, due to the extreme amount of natural gelatin, the skins will stick to the cheesecloth and make it difficult to roll the picked meat in the skin as described below. (Should this happen, it's not the end of the world. Just chop up the skin and add it to the meat. But try to avoid the mess if you can.)

Snip the end strings and slowly unroll the cheesecloth to remove the trotters onto the sheet pan. Using a paring knife, make an incision running from the top of the shank to where the toe bones begin. Without tearing the skin, pick the meat and tendon, careful to leave behind any bones (there will be many bones of various sizes, some as small as a pebble). Don't rush. Give the tendon a rough chop.

Once the meat and bones have been picked, cut straight across the skin just above the toe bones, and carefully transfer the skin to a nice length of plastic wrap.

For mixing and stuffing the meat, it's important to work with warm meat and cuisson (French for poaching liquid; use this word to make you sound very cheffy).

[…]

[...]

Add the picked meat, tendon, red onion, parsley, mustard, and enough cuisson (there it is again, look at us, so professional) to saturate the ingredients (about 1 cup/240 ml liquid). The cuisson (now I'm just putting suspenders on a belt) is what binds the meat; once chilled, it sets solid. Adjust the seasoning with kosher salt if necessary.

To stuff the trotters, divide the mixture between the 2 squares of skin, arranging it in one long strip along the edge of the skin closest to you. Lift the edge of the plastic wrap closest to you and start rolling it over the meat, tightening as you go. Once you've made 2 cylinders, tie off each end with twine, leaving a few inches of extra twine at one end so you can hang them in the refrigerator to chill and set overnight.

Bring the remaining cuisson (I couldn't help myself) to a boil, strain, and decant to remove any fat. Reserve for the sauce.

to serve

You want to slice and bread the trotters when they are very cold, so they don't get misshapen.

Set up your breading station with flour, whisked eggs, and breadcrumbs in separate bowls or pans. Line a sheet pan with baking parchment.

Slice the trotters into 1-inch (2.5-cm) slices.

If you're a righty, use your left hand to lightly coat the trotter slices in flour (no bare spots!); still with your left hand, transfer to the eggs to completely coat the flour. (If you're a lefty, reverse the order of your hands).

Now use your right hand to transfer to the breadcrumbs and coat completely. Remove from the breadcrumbs with your left hand and chill on the parchment-lined sheet pan.

When ready to fry, rest the breaded trotters at room temperature for 30 to 60 minutes.

Fill a large pot with oil no more than halfway and heat on medium-high heat to 325°F (165°C).

Carefully add the breaded trotters to the oil, careful not to splash yourself, or anyone really.

Fry for 3 to 4 minutes, until lightly golden brown. Using a cake tester as a "probe," make sure the interior is hot. If the trotter stays too long in the oil, it will burst due to the jellied cuisson (ha ha!) melting.

Remove the fried trotters to paper towels and sprinkle with a few grains of flaky sea salt.

Serve on room temperature plates with the yuzu sauce, pickled ginger shoots, and cilantro (coriander) flowers if available.

Pork Blood Kishka, Hoshigaki & Persimmon Mustard

Serves 4

1 very ripe Hachiya persimmon
1 tablespoon Dijon mustard
1 teaspoon extra-virgin olive oil
4 slices Pork Blood & Buckwheat Kishka (page 82), sliced 1-inch (2.5-cm) thick, casing removed
½ cup (120 g) Leaf Lard (page 339)
flaky sea salt
4 persimmon hoshigaki, sliced ⅛-inch (0.3-cm) thick (see Sources, page 350)

This recipe combines what have probably been my two biggest obsessions of the last few years: *kishka* and *hoshigaki* (a Japanese snack made from dried Hachiya persimmons). For years during late fall, I would scroll through numerous social media posts of people hanging persimmons in the air and massaging them. Finally, in 2020, we experimented with peeling and hanging about 120 unripe Fuyu persimmons from hooks I attached to the rafters at Birdie G's. They turned out great, and the next year we upped that amount to over 1,000, followed by over 2,000 the next year. We've since slowed to less than 1,000 per year. If you happen to walk into Birdie G's between October and January, you will see them everywhere. I especially love the ones hanging not far above the tables in the center of the main dining room. As I hold these squishy fruits so close to my heart, it didn't feel like a book of 150 meat recipes was the proper venue to dive into all the little details and idiosyncrasies that *hoshigaki* deserves. Maybe for the next book. You can source *hoshigaki* online if you'd rather not make your own.

Squeeze the meat from the skins of the persimmon into a blender. Blend with the mustard and olive oil and transfer to a small container.

Let the slices of kishka rest at room temperature for 1 hour.

Heat up your cast-iron skillet on high heat and add the leaf lard. When just smoking, add the kishka carefully so as to not splash the hot fat. Cook on both sides so they're crisp and the burgundy hue has become black. Using a cake tester, make sure the interior is hot. Dab on paper towels to absorb the fat and sprinkle the presentation side with flaky sea salt.

Place in the center of a plate and arrange the sliced persimmon hoshigaki as a crown on top of the kishka, leaving the center empty to spoon in the mustard sauce.

Apples Roasted in Bacon Fat

Serves 4

4 apples, such as Fuji, Pink Lady, or Honeycrisp
1 lemon, halved
¼ cup (60 g) rendered bacon fat or Leaf Lard (page 339)
1 tablespoon fresh rosemary leaves
1 teaspoon kosher salt

In my opinion this is an A-plus side dish. Roasted apples are loved by everyone but they're rarely made anymore, like a baked grapefruit. Let's bring them back. Pair with roast pork or serve warm with a nice triple cream cheese and toasted bread. They'll make a great addition to your holiday table as well.

Preheat your oven to 350°F (180°C).

Halve each apple, scoop out the core with a melon baller, and "vein" with a utility knife. Make a tiny, angular cut along that little line you see running from the seeds to the top and bottom of the apple. Then make a small angular cut and pop out that tiny piece. It's edible, just a little fibrous. Rub the meat side of the apples with the lemon as you go.

In a small saucepan, melt the bacon fat with the rosemary and kosher salt until lukewarm.

In a large bowl, toss the apples with the lukewarm fat mixture. The fat should start to congeal pretty quickly and encase the apples.

Transfer to a parchment-lined sheet tray or a casserole dish, making sure to press any extra goodies (like the rosemary) onto the apples. They'll actually hold in this state overnight in the refrigerator without browning, covered tightly with plastic wrap (clingfilm), so feel free to prep them ahead of time. If you do refrigerate them, allow them to come to room temperature before you bake them.

Bake for 12 to 15 minutes until the apples are tender. If they split, don't worry about it. We're, like, totally rustic here.

Griddled Potatoes with Fennel Pollen & Lemon

Serves 4 to 6

2 pounds (900 g) medium-sized potatoes, such as Yukon gold creamers
1–1½ cups (235–355 ml) rendered Leaf Lard (page 339)
2 tablespoons fennel pollen
zest of 1 lemon
kosher salt
flaky sea salt
freshly ground black pepper

This is the recipe of my mother-in-law Debbie—and her brother Den and mother Lillian before her. Now my wife Rachael makes these potatoes. This is the kind of recipe that a lot of families have, the passed-down kind; the kind you just "do," when there isn't a recipe tucked away. If I asked my wife for quantities, she would most likely just squint her eyes at me. Rachael's family will only use the microwave to cook these potatoes, though usually they use extra roasted or boiled potatoes tucked away in the refrigerator for just this purpose. Debbie, Rachael, and Den and Lillian before them, all use leftover bacon grease, and I've substituted rendered lard. Usually, they add sliced onions or shallots, and peppers frozen from summer. I'm adding lemon zest and fennel pollen. I'm sure you will come up with your own way, too.

I'm recommending the microwaving method for this specific recipe, and for good reason. We want the potatoes to slowly caramelize and create a delicious crust, and we don't want them sticking to the pan. So, this dry method of cooking is perfectly suited here.

To microwave the potatoes, wash them well, we're leaving the skins on. Fork the potatoes a few times, this will allow some steam to release as they cook. Place them on a plate or paper towel and microwave for 4 to 6 minutes. Check the potatoes. If a knife can be inserted easily, they're done. If not, microwave for an additional 2 minutes. Remove the potatoes and allow them to cool slightly.

To griddle the potatoes, halve each one; if they're larger potatoes, slice them into ½-inch- (1.3-cm-) thick slabs, and season with a little kosher salt. Add the lard to a seasoned cast-iron skillet and melt it over medium-high heat.

Add the potatoes, meat side down, to the hot, but not smoking, fat. Don't overcrowd the pan and cool the fat down, and don't shake the potatoes too early and disrupt the aforementioned crust production. You want to almost shallow-fry these puppies, so the fat should come nearly halfway up the sides of the potatoes.

Cast iron is a great conductor of heat, so once it's hot, you don't need to keep the flame as high. The goal is to cook the potatoes completely on the meat side, then there's this sweet little happy place where fried potato meets boiled potato. After a few minutes of the potatoes sizzling away, check one. Use kitchen tongs or a fork to try and nudge the bottom. If it sticks, don't force it, it still needs a few moments, it will release when ready.

Once your potatoes are golden, flip them. If you've cut them in half, allow the skins to crisp up a bit, though not as golden as their meat sides. If you've cut slices, turn them over and crisp the other side. Slices tend to fall apart some, this is my wife's favorite part. All the little broken bits tend to get extra crispy and salty.

Once everything is golden and perfect, remove from the skillet to a large bowl. Sprinkle flaky sea salt and black pepper over the potatoes while they're still hot to help the seasonings stick. Taste one and add more flaky salt if necessary. Now add the fennel pollen and lemon zest and give it a gentle toss. Serve immediately with basically anything.

Long Beans Amatriciana

I had been kicking this recipe around in my mind for a while. Every time I cooked long beans, I just kept thinking that they could be "pasta"-like; who needs zoodles, these are right here! So finally, I stopped thinking about it and made it happen. I've done it a few ways, carbonara over potato purée being one, but I always come back to the amatriciana version. I cannot get enough guanciale, so I like to render more and spoon the meat and fat over the finished dish. I've listed a conservative amount here, but you have my permission to go nuts and double it.

Serves 6 to 8

amatriciana
1 pound (455 g) Guanciale (page 52), cut into ¼-inch (0.7-cm) dice
1 pound (455 g) white onion, cut into ¼-inch (0.7-cm) dice
3 ounces (85 g) green garlic, sliced thin (or 1½ ounces (45 g) conventional garlic, grated)
1 cup (240 ml) dry white wine
4 cups (about 1 liter) good-quality canned tomatoes; if tomatoes are whole, break them up or blend gently with an immersion blender

long beans
2 pounds (900 g) long beans
kosher salt

to serve
3 ounces (90 g) unsalted butter
pecorino toscano cheese, for grating

---

make the amatriciana

In a large, high-sided skillet, render the guanciale over medium heat until nicely browned and crisped. This is one occasion where I support crowding the pan, as the guanciale will basically confit in its own fat while crisping up, instead of drying out or burning. Remove the crispy guanciale bits to a plate and set aside, while leaving the rendered fat in the pan. No need for a paper towel to soak up the crispy guanciale... you want all that fat!

Return the skillet to medium heat and add the onion and garlic, cooking until just slightly caramelized, being careful not to burn the garlic. Deglaze the pan with the white wine and reduce by 75 percent. Add the tomatoes and reduce the heat to medium-low, and cook until the sauce is thickened to your liking, or 30 to 40 percent reduced. Make sure to stir as you go to avoid scorching.

make the long beans

While your amatriciana gently bubbles away, let's cook the beans. We're going to blanch until tender, so they swirl like pasta. I can't stand the "squeak" of an undercooked green bean, but Rachael loves that. (Edit from Rachael to include that "his mentioning of this is moot because they have to be soft for this dish. Don't yuck my yum, Fox.")

To prepare the beans, wash and then trim the ends. Make sure to leave them long so that they mimic a long noodle.

To blanch, fill a large pot with salted water and bring to a boil. When I say salted water, I mean salty like the sea. Don't be stingy with the salt. Unless bland is your thing. Add the long beans, but not enough so the water drops below a boil for more than a few seconds. If you must do this in batches, so be it. Blanch until tender.

If you're prepping ahead or working in batches, shock in ice water until fully chilled, then spread out on paper or kitchen towels to dry. You can even twist them into portions like you would actual pasta.

to serve

If serving right away, drain off the long beans and add directly to the sauce.

Once you're pleased with your sauce, turn off the heat and add the butter, tossing very well but gently so as not to break up the beans. Transfer to a large platter or individual dishes and finish with the grated cheese (and extra crispy guanciale if you, like me, can't get enough).

Salt-Baked Daikon, Lardo & Bottarga

Daikon is such a versatile vegetable. It's wonderful in raw applications, sliced thin with apple in a simple salad, or just dipped into salt and crunched on. Of course, you can cut it into batons and sauté it in animal fat, or roast it in chunks with rutabaga (swede), carrot, and beet (beetroot). Salt-baked is a very gentle way of cooking it while still getting seasoning into it. It's always fun to crack the salt crust, I don't care how long you've been cooking. The lardo and bottarga give the dish richness in two different ways: sweet porkiness and an umami tang, making it very well balanced and tasty.

Serves 4 to 6

3 daikon (about 1½ pounds/680 g)
4 cups (640 g) kosher salt
1 tablespoon black peppercorns
2 teaspoons fennel seed
2 teaspoons coriander seed
½ teaspoon red pepper flakes
8 large egg whites
2 to 3 tablespoons Yuzu Kosho Sauce (page 302)
4 ounces (115 g) Lardo (page 48), sliced as thin as you can in 2-inch (5-cm) lengths
1 ounce (30 g) Parmesan, for grating
1 ounce (30 g) mullet bottarga, for grating
freshly cracked black pepper

Give the daikon a quick rinse, and remove the leaves and stems if present.

Preheat your oven to 300°F (150°C).

To prepare the salt crust, combine the salt, peppercorns, fennel seed, coriander seed, and red pepper flakes in a small bowl, stirring to combine. In the bowl of your kitchen mixer, with the whisk attachment at the ready, beat the egg whites to soft peaks. You'll see soft peaks when the egg whites look fluffy and when you lift out the whisk, the little peaks turn down. Boop.

[...]

[...]

Now, fold the egg whites into the salt mixture in stages. Gently mix until it's pliable like a dough, and you may not need all the egg whites. Do a scoop, fold, check consistency, and repeat until the salt "dough" is formed.

To cook the daikon, line the bottom of a long casserole dish with some of the salt mixture. Pierce the daikon about a dozen times with a cake tester. Using your hands, form the salt mixture around the daikon, and gently set it into the baking dish. If cooking multiple daikon, make sure there's space between them in the dish.

Bake for 45 to 60 minutes, or until the daikon offer no resistance when a cake tester is poked through the crust into the center.

To serve, here's where it gets fun; if you can do this in front of someone or your dinner party, do that. Absorb their validation, let it make you stronger. Crack the crust open with a butter knife or tap it open with a spoon (like what posh people do to 6-minute eggs in the movies), and gently remove the daikon to a cutting (chopping) board.

Slice the daikon 2.5 mm thick. Lightly brush each slice with the yuzu kosho sauce and arrange on plates. Drape the lardo over each slice, finish with cracked black pepper, and finely grate some bottarga and Parmesan directly over the plate.

Blackened Pork Tenderloin with Chow-Chow

At my first prep cook job at Sonoma Cafe in Charleston, South Carolina, chow-chow was on the menu, and it was my job to prep it. That version was corn-based, but it still hit the sweet and sour notes of a classic Southern recipe. Some chow-chows can be spicy, some sweet, all are delicious in their own way. This is my favorite. The green tomatoes lend good acid and bright notes, the cabbage comes through unexpectedly assertive, and the spices hold everything together. Pork is a classic combo, but I think you'll soon be putting it on many things. Paired with a fried saltine cracker with Chicken Liver Parfait (page 44) is epic.

Serves 4 to 6

chow-chow
14 ounces (400 g) unripe green tomatoes, cut into 1-inch (2.5-cm) pieces
12 ounces (340 g) green cabbage, cut into 1-inch (2.5-cm) pieces
7 ounces (200 g) red bell pepper, seeded and cut into 1-inch (2.5-cm) pieces
3 ounces (90 g) white onion, cut into 1-inch (2.5-cm) pieces
1 tablespoon grated garlic
1 tablespoon kosher salt
1 cup (240 ml) distilled white vinegar
1 cup (240 ml) apple cider vinegar
1 cup (200 g) granulated sugar
1 tablespoon Dijon mustard
2 tablespoons brown mustard seed
2 teaspoons celery seed
1 teaspoon ground ginger
1 teaspoon ground turmeric
1 teaspoon cayenne pepper
¼ teaspoon ground allspice

pork tenderloin
3 pounds (1.4 kg) pork tenderloin (about 2 pieces)
3 tablespoons Creole Spice (page 311)
1 tablespoon kosher salt
¼ cup (60 g) Leaf Lard (page 339), or bacon fat

make the chow-chow

Combine the green tomatoes, cabbage, bell pepper, onion, and garlic with the salt. Let the mixture sit for 2 to 4 hours. This will help pull a lot of the water from the vegetables.

Meanwhile, you'll have time to prep the rest of the chow-chow and marinate the pork.

Add the vinegars, sugar, Dijon mustard, mustard seed, celery seed, ginger, turmeric, cayenne, and allspice to a wide pot, bring it to a boil, then turn the heat down to a light simmer until it reduces by 50 percent.

Drain the salted vegetables very well and discard the liquid. Squeeze out more liquid by hand. Push the drained vegetables through the ⅜-inch (10-mm) plate of your meat grinder. Add the ground vegetables and any liquid to the reduced vinegar mixture, bring it all to a boil, then simmer until the liquid has reduced by 90 percent. It should resemble a relish.

make the pork tenderloin

Remove any fat and silver skin from the tenderloins and pat them dry. Mix together the Creole spice and salt and season the pork generously. Let the pork sit in the refrigerator, uncovered, for 2 to 3 hours as it marinates.

Remove the pork from the refrigerator 30 minutes prior to cooking.

Preheat your oven to 350°F (180°C). Heat a large cast-iron skillet over medium heat. Add the lard, swirling it around the skillet as it melts. Once it glistens, it's ready. Sear the pork on all sides, about 3 minutes per side; this will impart the blackening effect we want. Once the pork is seared on all sides, slide the skillet into the oven and slow-roast to an internal temp of 145°F (63°C). Let the meat rest for 10 minutes, slice against the grain, and serve with the chow-chow.

Pork Chops with Sauce Charcutière

How do you not want porky fat cut through with vinegary pickles? Sauce charcutière is one of those classic French sauces that just makes so much sense and is so very tasty. I'll follow that up by saying this is my take on the sauce, and by no means authentic. I recommend serving this dish with Potato Purée (page 166). Or boiled potatoes. Or Griddled Potatoes with Fennel Pollen and Lemon (page 141). I'm sorry for the repetition but it just screams POTATOES. Or polenta. It could also scream POLENTA. Or SPAETZLE. There's a lot of screaming going on. Welcome to my brain. Serve the extra sauce on the side in a warmed gravy boat.

Serves 4

pork chops
4 bone-in pork chops (each about 1 pound/455 g)
1 quart (0.9 liter) All-Purpose Meat Brine (page 337)
2 tablespoons lard
kosher salt

sauce charcutière
4 ounces (120 g) shallots, minced
½ cup (120 ml) cognac
2 cups (475 ml) Ham Hock Stock (page 336)
½ cup (120 ml) heavy (double) cream
3 tablespoons brine from Pickled Cornichons (page 314) or Dill Pickles (page 312)
3 tablespoons Dijon mustard
2 tablespoons (28 g) unsalted butter

to serve:
Pickled Cornichons (page 314), whole, sliced, or chopped. Dealer's choice.

make the pork chops

In a large ziptop bag, combine the pork chops and brine. Massage the chops with the brine, seal the bag, really pushing out the air, and refrigerate for at least 8 hours, or overnight.

After brining, remove the pork chops from the bag and pat them dry on paper or kitchen towels. Discard the used brine. Let the pork chops sit at room temperature for at least 30 minutes before you cook them.

Preheat your oven to 275°F (135°C), with the oven rack set to the middle position. Set up a sheet pan with a rack and hold it off to the side as you sear the meat. I prefer to cook the chops in the oven on this setup, rather than putting the entire cast-iron skillet into the oven, because I want to slow the cooking process. I don't want them to cook too much on one side, as they could in the hot cast-iron pan. But I digress, first things first…

In a large cast-iron skillet on medium-high heat, add the lard, swirling the pan to coat as the lard melts. Season your towel-dried chops with a little kosher salt, and begin by searing the fat cap first to render more fat into the pan and color the cap. It can help to stand the chops up against the side of the pan as the fat cap cooks. If they won't stand, you may have to hold them in place with kitchen tongs, or your hands if they no longer feel pain. I find that 3 to 4 minutes usually works well. Next, sear each side of the chop, again around 3 minutes per side, we're looking to get them some nice golden color.

Once seared, transfer the chops to your sheet pan set with the rack, and then transfer that whole number to your preheated oven. Cook until the chops reach an internal temperature of 130°F (54°C). Remove the chops to a plate or cutting (chopping) board to rest for 10 minutes. As your chops rest, let's make the sauce.

make the sauce charcutière

Reuse that cast iron where we seared our chops, as well as the remaining fat. Over medium-high heat, add the shallots, sweating them down until tender. Let them caramelize a little bit, doing a maintenance stir as you go. Deglaze the pan with the cognac and reduce by three-quarters. Stir in the ham hock stock and bring it to a boil, simmering for a few minutes to meld the flavors. Then add the cream and bring it up to a simmer for a few minutes. Add the cornichon brine and bring that to a boil. Now, remove the pan from the heat and whisk in the butter and mustard. Strain through a fine-mesh sieve.

to serve

Once the pork chops have had time to rest, you can carve them up or serve them whole. On warmed plates, spoon the sauce charcutière over the bottom, floating the pork chops on top. Cover the pork chops with the pickled cornichons and serve.

Shrimp-Crusted Pork Cutlets with Newburg Sauce

I really enjoy working with the shrimp (prawns) from TransparentSea Farm, a sustainable indoor shrimp farm in Downey, California. I had been thinking about making a shrimp toast and then a little voice inside my head said, "What if the toast was pork?" Pounding a pork chop on the bone is always a winner, and the Newburg sauce makes it even more decadent.

Serves 4

pork chops
4 bone-in pork chops (each about 1 pound/455 g)
3 cups (700 ml) All-Purpose Meat Brine (page 337)

shrimp crust
1½ pounds (680 g) peeled and deveined shrimp (prawns), coarsely chopped, tails and shells reserved
2 tablespoons (30 g) large egg whites
3 tablespoons tamari, or soy sauce
3 ounces (90 g) Tokyo negi, coarsely chopped (see Notes)
1 ounce (30 g) fresh cilantro (coriander), coarsely chopped
1 ounce (30 g) fresh basil, coarsely chopped
1 ounce (30 g) fresh mint, coarsely chopped
2 tablespoons cornstarch (cornflour)
¼ cup plus 2 tablespoons (90 ml) sesame oil
kosher salt

Newburg sauce
1 tablespoon (14 g) unsalted butter
2 ounces (60 g) shallots, sliced
1 tablespoon tomato paste (purée)
2 tablespoons madeira
3 cups (710 ml) Rachael's Chicken Stock (page 334)
2 teaspoons dried porcini powder
¼ cup (60 ml) heavy (double) cream
kosher salt

to finish
¼ cup (35 g) benne or white sesame seeds (untoasted)
1 cup (120 ml) Clarified Butter (page 323)
all-purpose (plain) flour, for testing oil temperature
2 lemons, halved, each half in a wrap (see Notes)

Notes: Tokyo negi are Japanese white onions, similar to scallions (spring onions) or leeks, which can be substituted, if needed.

Listen, I know it's old school, but I love a lemon wrap. Those yellow, mini shower caps that fit on a lemon half so that when you squeeze it, no seeds get in your food. They're easy to find at most restaurant supply stores and online. And they're fun.

make the pork chops	In a lidded container or large ziptop bag, combine the pork chops and the brine. Make sure the chops are fully submerged, forcing out any air if using a bag. Seal and refrigerate for 8 hours, or overnight.
	Rinse the chops in cold water and dry on paper or kitchen towels. Using the flat side of a meat mallet, pound the pork between layers of greased parchment paper or plastic wrap (clingfilm) to a thickness of ½ inch (1.3 cm). I recommend starting from the center and working out, being mindful of the bone so the meat doesn't tear from the bone.
make the shrimp crust	Combine the shrimp (prawns), egg whites, tamari, Tokyo negi, cilantro (coriander), basil, mint, cornstarch (cornflour), and sesame oil in a food processor. Pulse just until semi-coarsely chopped and homogenized. Taste and adjust the seasoning with salt.
make the Newburg sauce	Toast the reserved shrimp shells and tails in the butter. Add the shallots and sweat until translucent. Add the tomato paste (purée) and stir to incorporate, then toast for about 2 minutes, scraping up any fond. Deglaze your pan with the madeira and reduce by half. Add the chicken stock and porcini powder, bring to a boil, and simmer until reduced by half. Add the cream, bring to a boil, and simmer for 5 minutes. Adjust the seasoning with salt and strain through a fine-mesh sieve.
to finish	Evenly coat each chop on one side with the shrimp mixture, really pat it on there. Sprinkle the shrimp mixture with benne or sesame seeds.
	We're going to shallow-fry the chops; a large, high-sided cast-iron skillet works well for this. Heat the cast iron dry over medium heat; after a few minutes, add enough clarified butter to your skillet so that the melted depth is ½ inch (1.3 cm). Heat the butter over medium heat. The clarified butter is hot enough to add the chops when a tiny bit of flour added to it sizzles. So, just add a small pinch of flour; if it sizzles, you're good to go. If not, give it a few moments and try again.
	Cook the pork "toasts", shrimp side down, until the crust and benne seeds are nice and golden, about 3 minutes. Carefully flip the chops to cook the meat side. Continue to cook the chops to an internal temperature of 140°F (60°C) near the bone. Transfer the chops to paper towels to soak up excess oil.
	Serve up one chop per person, with the Newburg sauce passed around in a gravy or cream boat or spooned on the base of the plate, and an old-school wrapped lemon on the side.

Vernors "Old School" Pork Collar Roast

I've loved Vernors ginger ale ever since I stayed home for two weeks with the chicken pox in the fourth grade and practically lived off the stuff. I grew up in Cleveland, Ohio, and our relatively close proximity to Michigan meant we were very familiar with, in my opinion, the best ginger ale. It might just be my favorite soda, next to Dr. Brown's black cherry. When planning the menu for Birdie G's, I knew I wanted some fun sodas on the menu and came across an old ad for Vernors ham with the classic pineapple rings and cherries. Pork collar is an underutilized, tough cut that slow-roasts up nicely. I've decorated it here with fresh pineapple rings and Luxardo cherries, but no one in the Midwest would mind if you used canned pineapple and the bright-red kind of maraschino cherries. But don't dare substitute another ginger ale.

Serves 4–6

brine
1 teaspoon black peppercorns
1 teaspoon coriander seed
1 teaspoon cloves
4 star anise
1 cinnamon stick
1 cup (200 g) granulated sugar
1 cup (160 g) kosher salt
3 teaspoons curing salt #1
2 teaspoons ground ginger
2 teaspoons fresh rosemary leaves
3 ounces (90 g) fresh ginger, sliced ¼-inch (0.6-cm) thick

pork collar
1 whole pork collar (about 4 pounds/1.8 kg)
4 × 12-ounce (355-ml) cans Vernors ginger soda
1 pineapple, cut into rings
about 25 Luxardo maraschino cherries

make the brine

In a dry pan over medium heat, combine the black peppercorns, coriander seed, cloves, star anise, and cinnamon stick and toast until fragrant. We're not looking for color here, just for the oils in the spices to begin to release. You'll know this has happened when you start to smell the spices, around 5 to 7 minutes. Add the toasted spices to 8½ cups (2 liters) water along with the sugar, kosher salt, curing salt, ground ginger, rosemary, and fresh ginger. Bring everything to a boil, making sure the salt and sugar have dissolved completely, cool, then refrigerate until cold.

make the pork collar

Once the brine has cooled completely, cover the pork collar, making sure it's completely submerged, and refrigerate it for 10 days.

After 10 days, remove the collar from the brine and discard the brine.

To bake the collar, preheat your oven to 250°F (120°C). Place the collar in a deep roasting pan set on a rack and add the ginger ale slowly so it doesn't bubble up everywhere.

Cook until the internal collar temperature reaches 155°F (68°C). Remove the collar from the oven, reserving the cooking liquid, wrap tightly in plastic wrap (clingfilm) so it doesn't dry out, and cool to room temperature. You can continue on here or refrigerate the collar (and cooking liquid, covered) for up to 5 days to finish on the day you plan to serve it.

To make the glaze, strain the cooking liquid through a fine-mesh sieve and skim off any excess fat. In a saucepan over medium heat, reduce the liquid until glossy and the consistency of maple syrup. Be careful with the temperature; reducing it too fast can cause the glaze to burn.

To finish, if you've had your pork collar wrapped and refrigerated, remove it 45 minutes before you're ready to cook, so it can come up to room temperature.

Preheat your oven to 400°F (200°C), with the oven rack set to the middle position. Place the collar in a baking dish and, using a pastry brush, coat it generously with the glaze. We're going to warm the collar through to an internal temperature of 155°F (68°C), which should take 20 to 25 minutes. Every 5 to 7 minutes, reglaze the collar and rotate the pan.

During the final 10 minutes of cooking, remove the collar from the oven and arrange the pineapple rings and cherries in a pretty pattern on top, giving the meat and fruit a final glaze as you go. Continue baking.

Present your masterpiece to anybody you can find and let the positive reinforcement pour in. Be a real ham about it. Sorry, dad jokes are my thing now.

Pig Head Pozole

I can't think of pig head without thinking of Judy Rodgers' seminal book, *The Zuni Cafe Cookbook*. In it, she makes a pig-head stock and describes how someone, walking past the open back door of the Zuni kitchen, saw the head bobbing along in the stock pot, snuck into the kitchen, and grabbed it right out of the hot pot. They then ran with it down the alley. Football style, I imagine. While making this at my restaurant, Rustic Canyon, I often glance at our back kitchen door and wonder if today will be the day I get a great story like that. Alas, not yet.

This recipe makes a feast. There's really no way around it (okay, you could freeze some, but where's the fun in that?). So make it when you're ready to feed a group. If you're someone who doesn't enjoy traditional American Thanksgiving fare, this would be a wonderful replacement. Or make it and drop containers off on friends' porches. Personally, I like a fold-out table, a potluck invite, paper plates and bowls, a backyard, string lights, a good playlist, and even better, friends. Food like this is meant to be shared.

Serves 20-plus

pig head
1 pig head (15 to 20 pounds/7 to 9 kg; see Notes)
6 quarts (5.7 liters) Ham Hock Stock (page 336)
8 carrots, cut into 2-inch (5-cm) pieces
6 onions, cut into 2-inch (5-cm) pieces
1 bunch celery, cut into 2-inch (5-cm) pieces
½ cup (25 g) dried oregano
6 bay leaves
⅓ cup (50 g) kosher salt

green purée
2 pounds (900 g) poblano peppers, seeded, stemmed, and cut into ¾-inch (2-cm) dice
4 ounces (120 g) jalapeño chiles, stemmed and sliced ⅛-inch (0.3-cm) thick
2 ounces (60 g) garlic, smashed
¼ cup (40 g) kosher salt
10 ounces (285 g) fresh cilantro (coriander) leaves and stems, coarsely chopped

hominy
¼ cup (45 g) pickling lime (aka calcium hydroxide or cal) (see Notes)
3¼ pounds (1.5 kg) dried hominy (I like Rancho Gordo)

pozole
⅓ cup (80 ml) Leaf Lard (page 339)
2 pounds (900 g) poblano peppers, seeded and cut into 1-inch (2.5-cm) dice
2 pounds (900 g) onions, cut into 1-inch (2.5-cm) dice
2 jalapeño chiles, stemmed and sliced
kosher salt
3 to 4 tablespoons fresh lime juice (optional)
1 cup (60 g) coarsely chopped fresh cilantro (coriander) leaves and stems

to serve (optional)
warm corn tortillas
tostada bases (toasted or fried)
tortilla chips
sliced red radishes
picked fresh cilantro (coriander) leaves
grated green cabbage dressed with lime and salt
diced onion
hunks of avocado
dried Mexican oregano
lime wedges
chicharrónes
crema or queso fresco

Notes: You're looking for a fresh pig head that has all its parts intact: eyes, tongue, brain, etc. Ask around, your local butcher will know where to go if they don't carry or can't get you one.

Pickling lime can be caustic to some and cause skin irritation, so use caution and wear gloves when handling the hominy until it goes into the pozole to finish.

make the pig head

This is an example of a fortified or compound stock. Usually, you'd find this in French cooking when making a game or duck stock, for example. Here we're adding ham stock for flavor and water to pull out more flavor from the head so the resulting broth is rich and complex. If we did all ham stock it wouldn't pull out as much goodness from the head because it's already saturated, hence the water. If we used all water, too much flavor could be pulled from the meat and leave it flavorless. Balance is always key.

You'll want to go with an extra-extra-large, commercial-size stock pot, so get thee to a restaurant supply shop. In said pot, cover the pig head with the ham stock and 6 quarts (5.7 liters) water. Allow it to come to a boil over medium heat, this may take some time. Once it starts to bubble and foam, use a mesh skimmer or large spoon to skim the foam from the surface, then keep skimming until no more foam comes up. Add the carrots, onions, celery, oregano, bay leaves, and salt and bring it back up to a boil. Give it one good last stir, tucking down all of the vegetables, and then turn down the heat so it reaches just a bare simmer; every few seconds you should see a bubble escape to the surface. A slow blub, blub, blub. Now leave it alone. Don't disturb the head and vegetables as they gently cook. Allow the head to cook like this for the next 6 hours, or until the meat comes off of the bone easily.

Remove the head from the pot using a large spider strainer. Set the head aside to cool so you can pick the meat. Cool the stock and vegetables to a temperature that won't scald you and then discard the vegetables to your compost pile. Once the stock is cool, refrigerate it, covered, until you're ready to assemble the pozole.

To pick the meat from the pig's head, start by removing all the skin. This gets chopped up and added to the pulled meat. Remove the tongue, peel it, and chop it up. The ears are removed and sliced thin. Pull all the meat and shred it into spoon-size pieces. The eyes and brain are pretty spent in the cooking process, so they are not used. Refrigerate all the meat and bits, covered, until you're ready to assemble the pozole.

make the green purée

In a blender, combine the poblanos, jalapeños, garlic, salt, and 1 cup (240 ml) water and process until smooth. Next, add the cilantro (coriander) and continue to blend until smooth. Refrigerate the green purée, covered, until ready to use, up to 1 day; after that, it will start to lose its vibrancy.

make the hominy

In a medium pot, bring 2 gallons (7.5 liters) water to a boil. Stir in the pickling lime (see Notes), then add the dried hominy and reduce the heat to a slow boil. Cook until the kernels puff up and become tender. Remove from the heat, cover, and let sit at room temperature overnight. After sitting, drain and discard the cooking liquid. Transfer the hominy to a container of fresh, cool water and agitate it with your hands. Drain and repeat until the water is clear. Reserve in the refrigerator until ready to add to the pozole.

make the pozole

In a very large stock pot, melt the lard over medium-high heat. Once hot, add in the picked pig's head meat and bits and allow them to crisp up, getting a good color on all sides. Now add to the pot your reserved pig head stock, the diced poblanos and onions, and sliced jalapeños. Cook this mixture at a gentle boil until the vegetables are tender. Then add the prepared hominy and green purée and bring it back to a boil. Check your seasonings, adding salt and a few tablespoons of lime juice if it needs it. We're looking for balance: good salt, good acid. Finish with the chopped cilantro.

to serve

If you can, bring the big pot right to the table. Set out warm corn tortillas to mop up the broth, crispy tostada bases or tortilla chips, and a mixture of savory and crunchy bits for toppings: sliced radish, picked cilantro leaves, grated green cabbage dressed with lime and salt, diced onion, hunks of avocado, dried Mexican oregano, more lime wedges, chicharrónes, and crema or queso fresco if you like. Encourage your guests to top their pozole however they choose; sometimes I like to top the tostada and then dunk that in the pozole. Experiment and enjoy.

Manresa Staff Gumbo "YaYa" by David Kinch

I got a job at Manresa through luck and failure.

I'll back up.

I had been the executive chef at a hotel and bar/lounge in Aspen, Colorado, and I hated it. After about six months, I put in my notice, but I was let go before it ended because of my attitude. They were not wrong. I would have fired me, too. My own expectations of where this job would take me were far removed from the reality of the situation. I thought I was going to turn that bar/lounge into the best restaurant in the country. They just wanted it to be successfully operated. I knew my thinking was misguided. Have you ever been aware that you don't know what you don't know? That's where I was headed. On my way to clear, but not clear yet. My fault, not theirs, and a good lesson learned.

So, I moved back to Sunnyvale, California, where my first wife Deanie's family lived, tail between my legs. Angry. Blaming everyone else, but knowing I was the problem. What I did know was that I needed to start over. I needed a career reset. I wasn't the chef I wanted to be yet. Temperament-wise, skill set-wise. I needed to find someplace where I could start at the bottom and work my way up again.

And then a review of Manresa was featured in *San Francisco* magazine.

It looked so different from any kitchen I had worked in. The kitchen had windows! A French stove! The food was modern (I had always done casual). The way the review was written made Chef Kinch sound like the iconoclast he is. And obviously, I thought that was cool. He was doing things his way, kind of different. That's how I wanted to be, but I was failing.

I staged a few times, and through the luck of someone not showing up for their shift, I got a job. At first, I worked the entry level amuse station. I cleaned the walk-in, made staff meals, and was very happy with all of it. I could see all this cool stuff going on around me. I was inspired and content in a way I hadn't been for a long time.

And then one day, David made gumbo for the family meal. I was blown away. He made it again weeks later and I watched him, trying to figure out why it was so good. I needed more intel. So, I devised a manipulation. I told him the new cook wanted to make gumbo for the family meal, and could I order him the proteins he wanted for it? He squinted, "They're not making gumbo. I'll make the gumbo." I tried a few more times before he caught on to me and slyly asked, "Are you fucking with me?"

Serves 10

chicken thighs
10 bone-in, skin-on chicken thighs
3 tablespoons kosher salt
1 teaspoon freshly cracked black pepper
1 teaspoon cayenne pepper
3 tablespoons Crystal hot sauce

roux
2 cups (475 ml) duck fat or canola (rapeseed) oil
2½ cups (300 g) all-purpose (plain) flour

gumbo
5 pounds—yes, 5 pounds—(2.5 kg) white onions, cut into ½-inch (1.3-cm) dice
1 cup (120 g) diced celery (½-inch/1.3-cm dice)
1 cup (120 g) diced seeded green bell peppers (½-inch/1.3-cm dice)
6 garlic cloves, chopped
5 bay leaves
6 quarts (5.5 liters) Rachael's Chicken Stock (page 334; see Note)
2 pounds (910 g) Andouille Sausage (page 86), sliced into thick coins
1½ pounds (680 g) peeled shrimp (prawns), heads removed, cleaned
½ cup (120 ml) fresh orange juice
kosher salt

Note: Duck and chicken stock are great here. If a few pork bones and shrimp (prawn) shells/heads find their way in, okay. You can always fortify the stock with these things, straining them out and then proceeding.

Working for David Kinch changed my life. Not only was Manresa a seminal learning experience for me, but my time there also made me a better person. I met friends and colleagues I still count on and value. David was more than a mentor to me.

This gumbo reminds me of David. It is purely him. He was kind enough to put it into a recipe and share it with me specifically for this page you're reading.

It reminds me that we can start over. Do better. Be better. I'm not perfect, I'm still learning these lessons. I try my best, I fail, I try again. I've had more than one career restart. But my time at Manresa, with Kinch and those chefs, in that kitchen, changed my DNA and I will forever be grateful.

Now go make some gumbo, this pot serves a family.

And from David, "You can serve the gumbo with rice, but I love it with potato salad or macaroni salad instead. Garnish with sliced green onions if you wish."

make the chicken thighs	Marinate the chicken thighs in the salt, black pepper, cayenne, and hot sauce. Set aside at room temperature for about 1 hour.
make the roux	Preheat your oven to 350°F (180°C).
	In a large cast-iron skillet over medium heat, add the duck fat and sprinkle in the flour, which should sizzle, then whisk quickly to combine. Stir with a wooden spoon until the roux starts to bubble and turn a bit blonde, the color of coffee with a lot of milk. Place the skillet in the oven and stir every 10 minutes until the roux reaches the color of milk chocolate. This gumbo does not want a very dark roux.
make the gumbo	When the roux is ready, pour it into a heavy-bottom pot big enough to hold all the ingredients. Put the pot on a medium flame and add the onions. Stir the onions, being careful as the roux can spatter. Stir continuously until the onions are golden brown, about 30 minutes.
	Add the celery, bell peppers, garlic, and bay leaves, and stir well.
	Turn the heat down to low, cover with a lid, and cook the mixture for 15–20 minutes until everything is very soft. Stir it occasionally to prevent scorching, and so you can spy on it.
	Push the vegetables to the side, add the chicken pieces to the room left, and cook until browned on all sides.
	Add 1 cup (240 ml) of the chicken stock to deglaze the bottom of the pot. Cover the pot again and cook slowly until the chicken starts to kick out its juices, about 15 minutes.
	Slowly add the rest of the stock, raise the heat, and gently simmer until the chicken starts to fall off the bone, about 25 minutes, adding the andouille about halfway through.
	Add the shrimp (prawns) at the last moment followed by the orange juice, and adjust the seasoning with more salt if needed.
	The gumbo is finished when the shrimp are cooked through, about 3 or 4 minutes.

Choucroute Royale

This recipe is very loosely based on the classic French dish *vol-au-vent*, but with a bent that's been knocking around in my head for at least ten years. It's an epic dish of all the things I love most: kraut, mashed potatoes, gravy, a buttery crust, and all the meats. She's a real showstopper, perfect for the winter months. Serve on a large platter or cutting (chopping) board that you bring right to the table, then dig in. It's the perfect recipe for when you have a few days to spare.

Serves 8 or more

vol-au-vent shell
all-purpose (plain) flour, for dusting
1 x Puff Pastry (page 330) or two 14-ounce (400 g) packages premade puff pastry
1 large egg yolk
2 teaspoons milk
pinch of kosher salt

braised meats and kraut
4 ounces (115 g) Guanciale (page 52), cut into ¼-inch (0.7-cm) julienne
1 onion, cut into ¼-inch (0.7-cm) julienne
2 pounds (910 g) Sauerkraut (page 320), drained
2 cups (475 ml) Riesling
2 legs Classic Duck Confit (page 23)
4 links Apple & Black Rice Morcilla (page 81)
1 loop Polska Kielbasa (page 86)
4 slabs (each 3 ounces/90 g) Maple Smoked Bacon (page 13)
2 x Corned Beef Tongue (4 tongues; page 66)
4 slices (each 3 ounces/90 g) Cotechino (page 78)
kosher salt

potato purée
5 pounds (2.3 kg) Yukon gold potatoes, peeled and quartered
2 pounds (910 g) unsalted butter, cut into ½-inch (1.3-cm) dice
2 cups (475ml) heavy (double) cream, warmed
kosher salt

gravy
1 x Ham Hock Stock (page 336)
2 tablespoons lard or bacon fat
¼ cup (60 g) all-purpose (plain) flour
freshly cracked black pepper
kosher salt (optional)

to serve
2 cups (475 ml) Two-Ingredient Applesauce (page 306)
2 cups (475 ml) Apple Cider Mustard (page 318)
2 cups (475 ml) Pickled Cornichons (page 314)

make the vol-au-vent shell

Classic vol-au-vent shells are circular, either in one large shell or individual rounds. We're going rectangular.

On a lightly floured work surface, roll out 2 sheets of puff pastry, each measuring 9 × 11 inches (23 × 28 cm) and about ¼ inch (0.5 cm) thick. Freeze the dough on a sheet tray for 10 minutes before moving on. Don't let it freeze solid, just allow it to get a little hard. This will help prevent the layers from pinching together, and it'll help it rise more evenly. More puff!

On a baking sheet with a Silpat, carefully place the first pastry sheet upside down.

For the second pastry sheet, with a utility or paring knife, score a 1½-inch (3.8-cm) border into the dough, creating a second rectangle inside the first. Only press halfway down into the dough, making sure not to cut through to the bottom. Hold your knife at a 90-degree angle, cutting a straight line. Do not remove the second rectangle.

In a small bowl, whisk to combine the egg yolk, milk, and salt for an egg wash. With a pastry brush, brush the egg wash onto the first sheet of puff pastry on your Silpat. Be careful not to get the egg wash onto the sides of the dough, which will seal the side and prevent a good puff. Once it's brushed with the egg wash, place the second sheet of puff pastry, upside down, on top. Make sure it lines up perfectly. Brush the top sheet all over with the egg wash, again avoiding the sides of the dough. With the dull edge of your knife, make shallow, angled cuts along the outside edge of the rectangle every few centimeters, to help aerate the dough.

Chill the dough for 20 minutes.

Meanwhile, preheat your oven to 400°F (200°C), with a rack set in the middle.

Bake the puff pastry for 10 to 15 minutes, or until golden brown. Allow the shell to cool on the tray before using a knife to cut away the center rectangle. Slice through the shell at an angle and then carefully pull out the middle. Keep the top to finish the dish. While the puff pastry is cooling, reduce your oven to 300°F (150°C).

make the braised meats and kraut

In a wide braising pan on medium-high heat, cook the guanciale, stirring. It should start to look as translucent as gummy bears. Continue to cook until it's a little bit crispy, then add the onion and cook them until translucent. Add the drained sauerkraut, Riesling, duck legs, morcilla, kielbasa, and bacon.

Cover and cook in the oven for 20 to 25 minutes, then add the tongue and cotechino, cover, and cook for 5 more minutes. Adjust the seasoning with salt.

make the potato purée

In a large pot, cover the potatoes with cold water, adding 1 tablespoon of salt per 1 quart (0.9 liter) of water. Bring to a boil, then reduce to a simmer and cook for 30 to 40 minutes. The potatoes should be very soft and easily mashable but not falling apart.

Drain the potatoes in a colander or strainer. Press the potatoes through a ricer into a wide pot and return them to the stove. On medium heat, gently stir the potatoes with a wooden spoon or firm silicone spatula. This will cook off the excess moisture. Add ¼ cup (60 g) diced butter, then whip with your wooden spoon to combine. Add about 1 ounce (30 ml) of cream, then whip. Repeat until all the butter and cream are used, whipping as you go. Adjust the seasoning with salt. The potatoes should resemble vanilla pudding from the container that you may have enjoyed as a child, or perhaps late last night as an adult.

make the gravy

Remove the meat from the sauerkraut to a bowl. In a fine-mesh sieve set over another bowl, strain the sauerkraut from the braising liquid. There shouldn't be too much left, most should have cooked away. Combine the strained liquid with enough of the ham hock stock to equal 2 cups (475 ml).

In a medium saucepan over medium heat, melt the lard until hot. Carefully sprinkle in the flour and whisk it with the hot lard. Allow it to combine and bubble. Now, while whisking with one hand, slowly add the ham hock stock mixture with the other. Keep whisking. It will start to bubble and thicken as it warms. Check the seasoning. Add black pepper and salt if necessary. Transfer to a warmed gravy boat.

to serve

Place the prepared pastry shell (case) on a large platter. To it, add the drained sauerkraut, spreading it in an even layer. Next, top the sauerkraut with the potato purée, spreading it with an offset spatula. Arrange the meats on top of the potatoes. Break or cut the pastry top into shards and arrange those on there, too. Fill in any holes with your cornichons.

Carry the monstrosity to the table and serve immediately with the gravy boat and side dishes of applesauce, cider mustard, and pickled cornichons.

STARTERS	170 → 183
SOUPS & STEWS	184 → 194
FRIED	195 → 205
HOT PLATES	206 → 223
ENTRÉES & LARGE FORMAT	224 → 235

Poultry & Rabbit

Rabbit Mortadella, Fava Beans, Pistachio & Mint

Harold McGee, a titan in the food world, is also just a really nice man. I got to cook for him often at Manresa when I was the sous chef there. He got me a reservation at The Fat Duck while I was in London, as well as opportunities to stage at Restaurant Gordon Ramsay and St. John. It was improbable that a young cook like me would have gotten in on my own. That Fat Duck meal was transformative for me. McGee's book, *On Food and Cooking,* is on every serious chef's bookshelf. Like I said, he's a titan.

Beyond the street cred that knowing Harold McGee gives, I'm dropping his name because I'm using McGee's tip here to blanch the fava (broad) beans. Adding the baking soda (bicarbonate of soda) helps the inner bean slip out of its shell; the ones that don't slip out on their own come out with very little resistance when pinched between your fingers. Shocking the beans in ice water removes any residual taste from the baking soda.

This is a springy little dish and an excellent starter. If you can't find favas, try English peas instead.

Serves 4

1¼ cups (325 g) fava (broad) beans, shucked (see Note)
kosher salt
baking soda (bicarbonate of soda), for blanching
3 tablespoons shelled pistachios
¼ cup plus 2 tablespoons (90 ml) Nasturtium Salsa (page 304)
20 to 25 fresh mint leaves, torn (I like spearmint)
2 tablespoons fresh lemon juice
12 ounces (340 g) Rabbit & Myrtle Berry Mortadella (page 57), sliced 1/16-inch (2 mm) thick
freshly ground black pepper

Note: 2 pounds (900 g) of fava (broad) bean pods usually yields about 1 cup (170 g) of beans before they're shucked. It's not an exact science, more like a rule of thumb, and a good stat to know when you head to the market.

Preheat your oven to 350°F (180°C).

Blanch the fava (broad) beans in heavily salted water with 1 tablespoon of baking soda (bicarbonate of soda) per quart (liter) of water. Per Harold McGee: if you start to see the bright green favas coming out of their shells, scoop those out so they don't absorb the baking soda taste. Any that don't immediately pop can be boiled for 2 to 3 minutes, shocked, and then popped out of their hard outer skins.

Dry the shocked beans on paper or kitchen towels, discarding the outer skins.

Toast the pistachios in the preheated oven for 6 minutes, then allow to cool slightly. You can leave the pistachios whole or give them a very rough chop. Personally, I always like my chopped nuts to contain about 15 percent powder.

In a mixing bowl, add the favas, nasturtium salsa, toasted pistachios, and torn mint leaves. Give the mix a gentle stir. Season with salt and black pepper, then add the lemon juice a little at a time until the flavor is where you want it (you may not end up using it all).

To serve, arrange the mortadella on 4 plates and top with the fava mixture.

Buffalo Deviled Eggs

In 2011, I moved to Los Angeles to consult on the menu of a soon-to-open gastropub named Freddy Smalls on Pico and Robertson. Like most things with me at the time, I burnt that bridge to the ground (you can read the intro of *On Vegetables* if you want to know more), but this recipe remains. There have been a few versions, but this is my favorite… until I change my mind again.

This recipe makes thirty-six deviled eggs, which is a point of contention in my house. My wife would say make only fourteen: twelve to fit in her pretty chicken-themed deviled egg dish and two extra to eat before guests arrive. I say that's nonsense. If you're going to go to the trouble of making deviled eggs, you should MAKE deviled eggs.

Makes 36

hard-boiled eggs
18 large eggs (not super fresh; fresh from the chicken are much harder to peel)

filling
8 ounces (225 g) cream cheese, room temperature
5 ounces (140 g) blue cheese, room temperature
3 tablespoons hot sauce (I like Frank's RedHot)
¼ cup (60 ml) Aioli (page 321)

to serve
Chicken Crackling (page 340), chopped
celery leaves (the inner, smaller, pale green leaves)
flaky sea salt
freshly ground black pepper
sweet paprika, for dusting

make the hard-boiled eggs

Remove your eggs from the refrigerator 1 hour before you're ready to boil them.

Then, fill a large saucepan with water and bring it to a gentle simmer. Fill a wide wire basket (sometimes called a pasta basket or a steamer basket) with your tempered eggs and gently submerge them into the simmering water. Once the water begins to simmer again, set your kitchen timer for 10 minutes.

After 10 minutes, remove the basket from the simmering water and immediately transfer your cooked eggs to a bowl of cold water set in your kitchen sink. Let the water run over the eggs and into the bowl until the temperature drops and the water in the bowl is the same as what's coming out of your tap. I like to peel them under a gentle stream of water. Place them on a parchment-lined sheet tray as you peel, so they don't roll away from you.

With a clean, wet knife, cut each egg in half lengthwise. The knife should be clean and wet each time, you don't want to get streaks of yellow yolk on your bright whites. You're not a monster. Pop the yolks into the bowl of your food processor, this should yield you 11 ounces (310 g) of yolks. Spread the whites, cut side down, on your tray lined with fresh parchment paper.

make the filling

To the food processor with the yolks, add the cream cheese, blue cheese, and hot sauce. Process the mixture until ultra creamy, scraping down the sides. Remove the blade from your food processor and fold in the aioli. Transfer the yolk mixture to a pastry (piping) bag. I don't use a star tip here; I like to dome the yolk mixture into the whites so later, when we dip it in the chopped chicken crackling, we have a lot of surface area. But I'm getting ahead of myself. First, the mixture must chill in the pastry bag for 4 hours or, ideally, overnight. Tightly cover your tray of whites with plastic wrap (clingfilm), so they don't dry out, and chill those too.

Once the yolk filling and the whites have chilled, remove everything from the refrigerator and let's fill 'em. You want to pipe the filling into each half, so it makes a generous dome. It can't be too crazy, you still have to be able to bite it, but let's be generous. Once they're all filled, line them up on your tray and refrigerate until you're ready to serve; they will hold overnight, if needed.

to serve

Sprinkle each filled egg half with the chopped chicken crackling, coating it generously. Once complete, they're nestled in your version of a chicken-deviled egg serving plate situation, garnished with the pretty celery leaves, flaky sea salt, black pepper, and a dusting of sweet paprika.

Chicken Liver & Allium Toast

I don't usually force cooks to abide by specific plating parameters, but for this toast from Birdie G's, I made an exception. Once covered in chicken liver, the toast is decorated with onion jam, chives, and crispy shallots—all lining up to look like a flag. A flag from Nowhere, the capital of my mind.

Serves 4

onion jam
¼ cup (60 ml) Schmaltz (page 338)
4 cups (1.7 kg) white onions, sliced into ⅛-inch (0.3-cm) thick julienne
2 teaspoons kosher salt, plus extra to taste
3 cloves
3 allspice berries
1 star anise
1 cup (237 ml) concord grape red wine (I use Manischewitz)

crispy shallots
neutral-tasting oil, for frying
½ cup (80 g) shallots, sliced into ¹⁄₁₆-inch (2-mm) rings
½ cup (60 g) all-purpose (plain) flour
kosher salt

to serve
4 slices (1½ inches/3.8 cm thick) Pain de Mie (page 328)
2 ounces (60 g) unsalted butter, melted
pinch of kosher salt
2 cups (500 g) Chicken Liver Parfait (page 44)
¼ cup (60 g) thinly sliced chives

make the onion jam

In a 3- to 4-quart heavy-bottom pan on medium heat, add the schmaltz, onions, and salt. As the onions break down, turn the heat to low and gently caramelize the onions. For this application, I like to actually "crowd the pan," as the water from the onions is released and combines with the fat to create a "bath" in which to cook. Too large a pan will likely lead the edges of the onions to burn. You may need to add 1 tablespoon of water intermittently to replace the liquid as it evaporates.

Make a mini sachet out of the cloves, allspice berries, and star anise. It'll make it easier to fish the spices out of the onions later. Sachets are easy to make with a bit of cheesecloth (muslin) and butcher's twine. Cut a double-layer-square of cheesecloth and arrange all the spices in the center. Gather up the corners of the cheesecloth around them, twist, and tie it together at the top with the butcher's twine, leaving long ends of twine.

Once the onions are nice and golden brown, add the wine. Suspend the sachet in the pot, loosely tying the long ends of twine to the handle. Continue to cook until the wine has reduced to a syrup.

Remove from the heat and let the mixture cool to room temperature. Untie and discard the sachet. Once cooled, finely chop the jam or pass it through a food mill. This can never be foolproof, so if the jam needs more moisture, add 1 teaspoon of water at a time; if it's too loose, drain through a fine-mesh sieve or cheesecloth. Adjust the final seasoning with salt as needed. The onion jam will keep, tightly covered and refrigerated, for several weeks.

make the crispy shallots

In a medium saucepan, heat the oil to 250°F (120°C).

In a bowl, use a fork or kitchen tweezers to make sure the shallots loosen into their rings and don't clump, but don't murder them, be nice. Coat the shallots with the flour, then place in a metal steamer or pasta basket or coarse-mesh strainer to remove excess flour.

Add the shallots to the hot oil and stir/agitate them with a spider as they cook so they brown evenly. With the same spider, remove them from the oil and spread them evenly on a sheet tray lined with paper towels. While they're still hot, sprinkle them lightly with salt. Fight the urge to eat them all before you assemble your dish.

to serve

Brush the bread slices on both sides with the melted butter and sprinkle with the salt. Cook the slices in a cast-iron skillet on medium heat until golden on both sides and warmed all the way through.

Spread the liver parfait to cover the entire surface of the bread. Now, imagine the surface of the bread has 5 even sections; devote 2 for the onion jam, 2 for the crispy shallots, and 1 for the chives… or go rogue if you prefer. Serve with a fork and steak knife and have at it.

Soft-Boiled Eggs, Lovage Gribiche & Allumette Potatoes

My dear friend Eric Korsh is one of my favorite chefs of all time. To me, everything he makes is perfect. His food is the unattainable goal that lives in the back of my head, and I wish I could emulate it if only I could get out of my own way. He feels similarly about my food. I'm pretty sure my wife likes his cooking better than mine. She'll deny it, but it's not as enthusiastic a denial as one would hope. While dining at his sadly-now-closed New York City restaurant Calliope in 2013, Rachael and I had the most amazing lunch. His *oeufs mayonnaise* stood out among giants, and I've been thinking about them since. His version consists of perfectly cooked eggs with the silkiest mayonnaise and celery salt. I'm pairing my version with shoestring potatoes and gribiche. I might be trying too hard.

Serves 4

lovage oil
3 ounces (90 g) lovage leaves
1½ teaspoons kosher salt
½ cup (120 ml) grapeseed oil, refrigerated for 30 minutes

gribiche
¾ cup (180 g) Aioli (page 321)
1 tablespoon finely diced Pickled Cornichons (page 314)
1 tablespoon chopped capers
1 tablespoon chopped lovage
1½ teaspoons chopped fresh parsley
1½ teaspoons chopped fresh tarragon
2 teaspoons Dijon mustard
1 teaspoon freshly ground black pepper
kosher salt

soft-boiled eggs
6 large eggs

fried potatoes and capers
4 large Russet potatoes
neutral-tasting oil, for frying
2 tablespoons capers, drained
kosher salt
freshly ground black pepper

make the lovage oil

Mix the lovage with the salt and add to a blender cup, then refrigerate for 20 minutes. Yes, in the blender cup. Chilling down the cup helps with the color later. Remove from the refrigerator, and blend with the chilled grapeseed oil until very smooth, paying attention to the temperature of the blender container. If it gets too hot, it will cause your oil to take on a drabber green hue instead of bright green.

Strain the blended oil through cheesecloth (muslin) or a coffee filter into a lidded container, discarding solids, and freeze overnight. As it freezes, any natural water from the lovage will sink to the bottom and freeze solid, while the oil will remain pourable.

You're going to essentially decant the oil by slowly tilting the container and pouring off the oil into a fresh lidded container. Lovage oil will hold in the freezer for several months. Save the leftover liquid from the bottom of the first container for your next pot of vegetable soup.

make the gribiche

In a small mixing bowl, mix together the aioli, cornichons, chopped capers, lovage, parsley, tarragon, mustard, and black pepper. Add salt to taste. Store refrigerated in an airtight container until you're ready to serve the dish.

make the soft-boiled eggs

Remove your eggs from the refrigerator 1 hour before you're ready to boil them.

Then, fill a large saucepan with water and bring it to a gentle simmer. Fill a wide wire basket (sometimes called a pasta basket or a steamer basket) with your tempered eggs and gently submerge them into the simmering water. Once the water begins to simmer again, set your kitchen timer for 6 minutes.

Set up an ice bath while the eggs cook. After 6 minutes, plunge the hot eggs into the ice bath and let them sit for 30 minutes. Peel the eggs under cool running water. Dry them with paper towels and cut each egg in half lengthwise, wiping the knife clean and wetting it before slicing each new egg. Place 3 egg halves, yolk side down, on individual plates, or arrange them all on a large serving plate, leaving room in the middle for the potatoes.

make the fried potatoes and capers

Set up 3 containers of cold water. Peel the potatoes, adding the peels to one container and potatoes to another. Save those peels for Tallow-Fried Potato Peels (page 238).

Cut the potatoes (crosswise) into $\frac{1}{8}$-inch-thick (0.3-cm-thick) sticks with a sharp mandolin, ideally one that stands, using the julienne setting. Add the cut potatoes to the third container of water, then flush them under cold running water, agitating with your hands, until the water runs clear. This washes off extra starch, which makes your potatoes darker sooner when frying. Drain the potatoes and dry on paper or kitchen towels, with towels set on top as well.

In a large saucepan, heat the oil to 300°F (150°C).

First, let's fry the capers. Fried capers are one of life's greatest joys in my opinion. Drain and dry the capers well. Fry the capers until bloomed and crispy, 30 to 60 seconds. Drain on paper towels.

Return the temperature of your oil back up to 300°F (150°C).

Fry the dried potatoes in batches, stirring continuously, until crispy. I prefer little to no color. Scoop the finished fried potatoes into a mixing bowl lined with paper towels, give a little shake, pull out the towels, and season the shoestrings with salt and pepper.

To serve, top each egg half with gribiche and fried capers. Settle the hot, fried potatoes around the eggs. Sprinkle everything with a bit more salt and enjoy.

Chicken Liver Cannoli with Hoshigaki & Red Walnut

We started making these cannoli at Rustic Canyon for a special wine dinner, and now I want to pipe them full of all sorts of savory options. I hope this recipe inspires you to do the same. You could fill them with the deviled egg mixture (page 172) and tap the ends in chopped capers, or even the Smoked Tomato 'Nduja (page 54). Of course, you can buy the pastry shells (cases); they'll work fine. But I'll go to my grave insisting that cooking something from scratch makes it better, even if it's not as good. Does that make sense? Give it a try and let me know how you do.

Makes 12

cannoli shells (cases)
2 cups (240 g) all-purpose (plain) flour, plus extra for dusting
1 tablespoon plus 1½ teaspoons granulated sugar
½ teaspoon kosher salt
1 large whole egg plus 1 large egg white
1 tablespoon Leaf Lard (page 339), melted and cooled
¼ cup (60 ml) madeira
3 tablespoons whole (full-fat) milk
oil, for frying (I like rice bran here)

to finish
2 cups (500 g) Chicken Liver Parfait (page 44)
½ cup (60 g) chopped toasted red walnuts
2 persimmon hoshigaki (see Sources, page 350, and Note)

Notes: When slicing the hoshigaki (described on page 137), gently flatten them with your palm so they're uniform and easier to manage. Don't murder them, just gently flatten. Slice with a sharp knife into ¼-inch (0.5-cm) pieces.

You'll need 12 cannoli molds for shaping the dough (see Sources, page 350).

make the cannoli shells (cases)

Into a large bowl, sift the flour, sugar, and salt and make a well in the center. Add to the well the whole egg, lard, madeira, and milk. With a fork, begin whisking everything in the well, incorporating bits of the flour mixture as you go. Keep mixing until the dough looks like pancake batter and then switch from the fork to a wooden spoon to finish mixing up the dough. Knead until smooth, cover with plastic wrap (clingfilm), and let rest for 1 hour at room temperature.

On a floured work surface, cut the dough into 2 equal pieces, and roll out each piece to a thickness of 1/16 inch (2 mm) and about 5½ inches (14 cm) long. Using a 5-inch (13-cm) round cutter, punch out as many disks as possible, then let them rest for 20 minutes. Lightly beat the egg white.

Wrap the dough disks around cannoli molds and seal the overlapped edges with the beaten egg white.

In a wide pot, heat your oil to 350°F (180°C). Using a spider, gently lower the cannoli shells (on their molds) into the hot oil and fry until golden brown. With a spider, remove them from the oil and let cool slightly before slipping the shells off the mold. Cool the shells completely on a sheet tray lined with paper towels. If stored properly in an airtight container, the shells will last for several weeks at room temperature.

to finish

When you're ready to assemble the cannoli, remove your chicken liver parfait from the refrigerator so it can sit at room temperature for a short period. You don't want it super cold or warm, you want to just take the chill off.

Using a flexible silicone spatula, aerate the liver a few times, giving it a couple of good stirs at an angle to incorporate a little air. We're not whipping cream, just giving the parfait some life.

Load the parfait into your pastry (piping) bag and cut the opening wide enough to fit into the cannoli shell. You don't need a pastry tip; the bag is fine. To fill, load one side of the cannoli, turn the shell, and load the other side. Dip the loaded ends into the toasted red walnuts and arrange with slices of hoshigaki.

Matzo Ball Soup

Matzo ball soup is, in my opinion, the holy grail of Jewish cuisine. I had long been trying to incorporate matzo balls into my menus, but nothing was coming out how I envisioned it in my mind. Nothing was scratching that itch. So, instead of running from it, I went back to the classic.

I wanted the broth to be the best it could be, with lots of dill, a custardy-light matzo ball. Something that came out perfect every time. Taking on something like matzo ball soup is taking on beloved memories, not just my own but for others as well. I didn't want to disappoint. I set out to make my ancestors proud here, to make the best bowl of matzo ball soup in the city, and thank Yahweh, I think we nailed it.

My grandmother Gladys made matzo ball soup for all my cousins and me. In the silverware drawer, mixed with the mismatched soup spoons, was one gold soup spoon that we all fought over. It felt like a prize to be won. So now, at Birdie G's, where the G represents Glad herself, we serve our matzo ball soup with a gold soup spoon. But only one. If you split the bowl, you'll need to grab for the prize. We accommodate pretty much every special request, but we do not budge on the gold spoon rule.

There are so many ways to say, "I love you. I miss you. I still think of you." This is one of mine.

Serves 8

matzo balls

7 ounces (190 g) Matzo Ball Soup mix; I use The Matzo Project's (see Sources, page 350)
½ cup plus 1 tablespoon (130 ml) Schmaltz (page 338), melted
6 large eggs, lightly beaten
¼ cup plus 2 tablespoons (3 g) fresh dill, coarsely chopped (save the stems)
1½ teaspoons kosher salt, plus extra to taste

soup

3 quarts (2.75 liters) Rachael's Chicken Stock (page 334)
8 ounces (227 g) carrots, cut into ¼-inch (0.6-cm) slices
8 ounces (227 g) celery stalks, cut into ¼-inch (0.6-cm) slices
1 cup (60 g) Gribenes (page 338)
4 teaspoons white miso
2 teaspoons dill pollen (see Sources, page 350)

make the matzo balls

In a large mixing bowl, combine the matzo soup mix, schmaltz, eggs, 2 tablespoons of chopped dill, and the salt. Gently mix together and roll into 8 balls. Don't overwork, use light hands. If you compact the mixture, you'll end up with a hard, dense matzo ball. We want light, custardy floaters.

make the soup

In a large pot, bring the chicken stock up to a gentle boil, add the carrots and celery, and give it a good stir. Now gently add the matzo balls and cover the pot. Cook at a low simmer for 45 minutes. Do not stir. Do not remove the lid. Set a timer and practice your issues with trust.

After 45 minutes, remove the pot from the heat and let sit for 1 hour. With a small spider, carefully transfer the matzo balls to a container and wrap tightly with plastic wrap (clingfilm) so they don't dry out. Strain the stock into another large pot, reserving the carrots and celery.

Add the gribenes and reserved dill stems to the stock, cover, and steep on low heat for 20 minutes. Strain again, discarding the solids.

Now put the steeped and strained stock back in a pot with the matzo balls and reserved carrots and celery. Bring to a gentle boil and adjust the seasoning with salt.

At Birdie G's, we serve the matzo ball in warm bowls with the carrots and celery. Then we put a small dollop of miso on top of each matzo ball, cover that with the remaining chopped dill and the dill pollen, and pour the hot stock over it to melt the miso and dill into the soup. If that feels like too much fuss, feel free to just combine it all at the last minute. Make sure to serve with a gold soup spoon.

Chicken Pot Pie Profiteroles

My wife doesn't know how to cook in small quantities. In theory, she does, and I think she sets out to do so, but she always ends up cooking for a hoard. Because of this, I end up taking in leftover bits and bobs to the restaurants a lot. "For family meal!" she'll say. Cookies, vats of marmalade, an entire brisket, and after one Thanksgiving, containers and containers of leftovers. It was the first year of COVID, the world was upside down, and she had cooked a feast for twenty, though for two adults and a four-year-old.

When I got to work, I combined everything she sent me into a pot: turkey, gravy, mashed potatoes, peas, and stuffing, making a thick pot pie-like filling. I made gougères, slicing off the tops and filling them profiterole-style with the filling. They were delicious. We later recreated the dish with classic chicken pot pie flavors.

A little note about Gribenes (page 338). At Birdie G's, we produce schmaltz in 50-pound (23-kilogram) batches and, in turn, produce a lot of delicious fried pieces of chicken skin and onions left behind. If you want to substitute them with onions fried until melting in chicken fat, that's great, that'll work. If you want to go to the store and buy those crispy fried onions in a can that typically top a certain green bean casserole, that'll work, too.

Serves 4 to 6

gougères
1 cup (120 g) all-purpose (plain) flour
½ cup (120 ml) whole (full-fat) milk, plus 1 tablespoon for the egg wash
4 teaspoons kosher salt
3 ounces (80 g) unsalted butter, cut into 1-inch (2.5-cm) cubes
5 large eggs
3 ounces (80 g) grated Gruyère cheese, plus extra for sprinkling

chicken pot pie filling
8 tablespoons (110 g) salted butter
3 ounces (90 g) carrots, cut into ⅓-inch (0.8-cm) dice
3 ounces (90 g) celery stalks, cut into ⅓-inch (0.8-cm) dice
½ cup (60 g) all-purpose (plain) flour
5 cups (1.2 liters) Rachael's Chicken Stock (page 334)
½ cup (120 g) Gribenes (page 338), chopped
2 skinless, boneless chicken breasts, cut into 1-inch (2.5-cm) pieces
kosher salt
freshly ground black pepper

to serve
Chicken Crackling (page 340; optional)
3 tablespoons finely chopped fresh Italian parsley

Notes: If your chicken pot pie filling doesn't thicken as you'd like it to, you can always make a beurre manié by mixing together equal parts softened butter and all-purpose (plain) flour. Try starting with 2 tablespoons each. Whisk the mixture into your bubbling stew. If you still want it thicker, repeat the process. This is a great little trick to remember when you're making any stew or quick gravy.

Also, I wouldn't hate it if you added some frozen peas to the filling, microwave-dinner style.

make the gougères

Making gougères means making choux pastry. First, line a baking sheet with parchment paper and set aside. Sift the flour into a bowl and set aside.

In a large, heavy-bottom saucepan, add the ½ cup (120 ml) milk, ½ cup (120 ml) water, salt, and unsalted butter and set it over low heat. We want the butter to melt before the mixture boils. Once it comes to a boil, immediately remove the pan from the heat. Add the flour all at once to shock it, and, with a wooden spoon, begin mixing the flour into the hot butter mixture. Keep mixing until a smooth dough forms. Return the pan to medium heat for 3 to 4 minutes, stirring constantly, to dry out the dough. You'll know it's ready when your wooden spoon can be pushed into the center of the dough and stand up straight without falling over.

Remove from the heat and transfer the dough to a bowl. With your wooden spoon, smooth the dough evenly around the edges of the bowl, essentially spreading it out to help it cool slightly. Give it 5 minutes to cool, then add 4 of the eggs, one at a time, beating with the wooden spoon. When you add your first egg, you'll think you've ruined it. Keep stirring; it'll come together. I like to stir with a wooden spoon and scrape the sides of the bowl with a flexible spatula. Once the last egg has been incorporated, and the mixture is smooth, add the grated Gruyère. Don't overwork the dough! Immediately transfer your dough to a pastry (piping) bag; you don't need to fit it with a tip.

Preheat your oven to 400°F (200°C).

Make an egg wash by mixing together the remaining egg and 1 tablespoon of milk, then set aside.

To pipe the choux onto the parchment-lined sheet, cut the end of your pastry bag to a ¾-inch (2-cm) opening. We're going to stagger them in rows, so they have room to puff up. Holding the pastry bag straight and hovering about ½ inch (1.3 cm) above the sheet, pipe a mound that builds on itself until it's 2 inches (5 cm) in diameter and 2½ inches (6.4 cm) tall. When the mound is the correct size, sweep the tip to the right, cutting off the flow.

Brush each mound with some egg wash, gently smoothing the top as you go, and sprinkle with a bit of grated Gruyère.

Bake the pastries for 15 to 20 minutes, or until they are dry, crisp, and golden brown. Cool on a wire rack.

make the chicken pot pie filling

In a large, heavy-bottom pot, melt the butter over medium heat. When the butter stops foaming, add the carrots and celery, then sauté for 3 minutes. Sprinkle in the flour, mixing it into the vegetables well. Cook the flour and vegetables for 2 minutes, scraping the bottom and sides of the pot. In a slow stream, add the chicken stock, a little at a time, stirring to combine. Now add the gribenes and chicken breast pieces. Cook the stew at a low simmer for about 20 minutes. The sauce will thicken, and the chicken will cook through. Season to taste with salt and black pepper.

to serve

With a serrated knife, cut the tops off the gougères, exposing the hollow center and creating a lid. Plate the shells (cases), then fill them with the chicken pot pie filling. Top with the chicken crackling and chopped parsley. Return the pastry lid to the top, a little askew. Enjoy!

Chicken Paprikash with Board-Cut Spaetzle

Serves 4 to 8

chicken paprikash
8 chicken leg quarters (about 4 pounds/1.8 kg)
3 tablespoons sweet paprika
1 tablespoon kosher salt, plus extra to taste
2 to 3 tablespoons Schmaltz (page 338)
1 pound (455 g) red bell peppers, seeded and cut into ½-inch (1.3-cm) dice
8 ounces (225 g) white onion, cut into ½-inch (1.3-cm) dice
1½ cups (355 ml) white wine
2½ cups (590 ml) Rachael's Chicken Stock (page 334)
3 tablespoons sweet paprika
2 tablespoons fresh dill leaves, chopped, plus stems tied together tightly with twine
1 cup (240 ml) heavy (double) cream

spaetzle
3 cups (360 g) all-purpose (plain) flour
1 tablespoon kosher salt
6 large eggs
1 cup plus 2 tablespoons (270 ml) whole (full-fat) milk
5 tablespoons (70 g) unsalted butter

to serve
1 cup (or more) Crème Fraîche (page 322)
1 cup (160 g) Ohio Peppers (page 317)

I've been making spaetzle forever, but not like this. We had a cook at Rustic Canyon named Cal Egan, who came to us from Roberta's in New York City. Just a great natural cook. There was an Elizabeth David quality to his cooking. Cal became known for making great family meals, and for one such meal, he made spaetzle. Up until that point, I had only made spaetzle by pushing the dough through a perforated hotel pan. But watching Cal slice noodles off a board was new for me. It creates a more rustic spaetzle, more misshapen. It feels like a method someone's grandma uses, not a chef hack. I love learning new things from the cooks in my kitchens. I only know what I know, so it's nice to feel that old curiosity bubble up.

This spaetzle method takes some practice, but keep at it. You'll get faster and faster, though anything that forces you to slow down a bit and focus on one task is a good thing.

Served with paprikash, this dish is a big bowl of comfort.

make the chicken paprikash

On a cutting (chopping) board, separate the thighs from the drumsticks. Of course, you can buy thighs and legs separately, but I find that leg quarters are cheaper, and your pieces will be more uniform. Rinse the pieces in cold water and dry on paper towels.

In a mixing bowl or large container, evenly season the chicken with the paprika and salt. Refrigerate the chicken, covered, for at least 6 hours, or overnight. Once marinated, transfer the chicken to dry on paper towels.

Add 2 tablespoons schmaltz to your sauté pan over medium-high heat. Once the schmaltz begins to smoke, sear the chicken, making sure not to crowd the pan or else you'll end up with very sad chicken. Cook it in batches if necessary, and turn the chicken so it caramelizes on all sides. After the chicken is seared, transfer to a plate while you start the sauce in the same pan.

Scrape up any fond, the little caramelized bits that stick to the pan, as this is flavor gold. You may need to add another tablespoon of schmaltz to the pan if none is left. Add the bell peppers and onions, sautéing until you get just a bit of color.

Add the white wine and reduce by half, scraping up any fond that's still stuck to the pan. Add the chicken stock, paprika, and dill stems while also returning the chicken to the pan.

Bring the stock to a boil, then lower the heat to a simmer and braise the chicken in the sauce for about 30 minutes. Add the cream and return to a boil one last time, making sure the chicken reaches an internal temperature of 175°F (79°C). Typically, chicken is cooked to 165°F (74°C), but I prefer the texture of dark meat that's cooked a little longer.

make the spaetzle

First, let's mix up the dough. Stir to combine the flour and salt in a mixing bowl. Separately, lightly beat the eggs and whisk in the milk to incorporate nicely. Next, pour the egg mixture into the dry ingredients while whisking to combine.

Bring a large pot of salted water to a boil. Once the water is boiling, cut in the spaetzle. To do this, you'll need a small cutting (chopping) board, something at least as wide as your bench scraper. Dip the board into the boiling water to wet it. Now top the wet board with one-third of the spaetzle dough. Using your bench scraper, flatten the dough, "wiping" it toward the end of the board. Next, cut a ¼-inch (0.6-cm) ribbon off the end of the board. Scrape it toward the cliff and let it fall into the boiling water. Keep repeating this process until all the spaetzle are in the water. Remove from the boiling water with a spider strainer to a bowl. Toss the spaetzle with the butter so they don't stick to themselves.

to serve

Transfer the chicken and spaetzle to a large platter or bowl or individual bowls. Pulse the sauce with an immersion blender, just enough to break up the large pieces of bell peppers and onions. Adjust the seasoning with salt to taste and add the chopped dill. Smother the chicken and spaetzle with the sauce, then top with a dollop of crème fraîche and pickled Ohio peppers.

And be sure to say, "Waiter, there is too much pepper on my paprikash. But I would be proud to partake of your pecan piiiiiiie," as you serve it.

Braised Rabbit Legs Provençal

The first time I ever had rabbit was at a French restaurant called Mistral in Charleston, South Carolina, where I ordered *lapin a la moutarde* (rabbit with mustard). I was maybe 19 or 20 and in culinary school. The dish cost $15, a real splurge for such a poor student like me. Because of this initial experience, rabbit always feels French in my mind; it's an association that stuck. This recipe would pair nicely with polenta, Potato Purée (page 166), or some roasted eggplant (aubergine) dripping with olive oil and covered in parsley. Oh, and don't go to cooking school. Just don't. I didn't even graduate. Save your money and stage everywhere and anywhere you can. Learn on the fly. I just saved you a lot of money.

Serves 6

braised rabbit legs
6 rabbit hind legs (about 2½ pounds/1 kg)
1 tablespoon kosher salt
¼ cup plus 2 tablespoons (90 ml) Schmaltz (page 338) or a neutral oil such as grapeseed
1 pound (455 g) white onion, cut into 2-inch (5-cm) pieces
8 ounces (225 g) celery stalks, cut into 2-inch (5-cm) pieces
½ bunch thyme
1 bay leaf
2 tablespoons tomato paste (purée)
2 cups (475 ml) white wine
6 cups (1.4 liters) Rachael's Chicken Stock (page 334)

tomato chips (crisps)
6 medium tomatoes, cored (I like Early Girl tomatoes)
olive oil, for brushing
fresh thyme leaves, for sprinkling
flaky sea salt
freshly ground black pepper

sauce
½ cup (120 ml) olive oil
1 pound (455 g) fennel bulb, cut into ¾-inch (2-cm) pieces, plus 3 tablespoons chopped fronds
2 tablespoons grated garlic
1 tablespoon fresh rosemary leaves, coarsely chopped
½ teaspoon chili flakes
kosher salt
1 pound (455 g) assorted cherry tomatoes
4 tablespoons (56 g) unsalted butter
¼ cup plus 2 tablespoons (65 g) nice olives, cracked and pitted

make the braised rabbit legs

Preheat your oven to 300°F (150°C).

Season the rabbit legs with the kosher salt and let them sit for 1 hour. In a Dutch oven on high heat, add the schmaltz. Once the schmaltz shimmers, sear the legs on both sides, then transfer to a plate while you sauté the vegetables.

To the same Dutch oven, add the onion, celery, thyme, and bay leaf and caramelize lightly over medium heat, 5 to 7 minutes. Add the tomato paste (purée) and stir to coat the vegetables. Deglaze with the white wine, scraping up any brown bits, and reduce by two-thirds. Add the chicken stock, bring it to a boil, and return the rabbit legs to the pot; they should almost be submerged in liquid. Add a cartouche (see page 35). Cover the pot with the lid or aluminum foil and put it into the oven for 2 hours.

Remove the pot from the oven, let it cool down to just warm, and gently remove the legs. Strain and reserve the braising liquid, discarding the solids.

make the tomato chips (crisps)

Slice the medium tomatoes as thinly as possible. Arrange them on the trays of a dehydrator, without overlapping. Brush them lightly with some of the olive oil and top with a few thyme leaves. Then sprinkle each slice with a few grains of flaky sea salt and a twist of a black pepper mill. Dehydrate at 140°F (60°C) for 12 to 18 hours, or until crisp. You can pull one out and let it cool to gauge crispness. Ideally, keep them in the dehydrator until you're ready to serve, or stash in a warm area.

make the sauce

In the same Dutch oven, add the olive oil on medium heat and sweat the fennel, garlic, rosemary, chili flakes, and a pinch of kosher salt. Add the strained braising liquid and one-quarter of the cherry tomatoes. Simmer until the liquid is reduced by half, then check the seasoning and add more salt to taste. You can always dilute the sauce with water if it becomes over-reduced.

Add the rest of the cherry tomatoes and return the rabbit legs to the pot with the butter and continually baste the legs until glossy, about 5 minutes. Add the olives and fennel fronds, gently folding them into the sauce.

To serve, spoon the sauce over the rabbit legs and top with the tomato chips.

Rabbit Foreleg Confit, Kriek BBQ & Pistachio Dukkha

I've been cooking with lambic, called kriek when it's infused with sour cherries, ever since I staged at the now-closed De Snippe restaurant in Bruges, Belgium. This kriek-infused barbecue sauce utilizes dried cherries (order them online from Andy's Orchard if you can; see Sources, page 350) as well as cherry lambic. The sauce recipe will work with pretty much any dried fruit, although due to the natural pectin in some fruits, you may need to dilute it with a touch of water if it gets too thick.

This recipe has all the things: tender meat, crispy exterior, sticky sauce, and a crunchy, salty, nutty topping. If you're new to rabbit, this is a great place to start.

Serves 4

kriek barbecue sauce
1 cup (160 g) dried sour cherries
1½ cups (350 ml) cherry lambic (aka kriek)
½ cup (120 ml) ketchup
½ cup (120 ml) apple cider vinegar
1 tablespoon brown mustard seed
½ teaspoon cayenne powder
1½ teaspoons Worcestershire sauce
1 tablespoon kosher salt
2 teaspoons freshly ground black pepper

pistachio dukkha
3 tablespoons pistachios
1 tablespoons benne or white sesame seeds (untoasted)
1 teaspoon coriander seed
1 teaspoon cumin seed

rabbit confit
8 rabbit forelegs (about 2½ pounds/1 kg)
1 ounce (30 g) Poultry Cure (page 341; see Note)
4 to 6 cups (950 ml to 1.4 liters) Schmaltz (page 338) or duck fat
oil, for frying (I like rice bran oil)

to serve
flaky sea salt

Note: For the poultry cure, use 2.5 percent of the rabbit's total weight.

make the kriek barbecue sauce

In a medium-size nonreactive saucepan, combine the dried cherries and lambic and simmer on medium heat for 5 minutes.

Add the ketchup, cider vinegar, mustard seed, cayenne, Worcestershire, kosher salt, and black pepper to the pan and simmer for an additional 10 to 15 minutes. Cool the mixture to room temp, then blend until smooth and cool completely. Store in an airtight container in the refrigerator, up to 1 month.

make the pistachio dukkha

Preheat the oven to 350°F (180°C). On oven-safe pans or rimmed baking sheets, separately toast the pistachios, benne or sesame seeds, and combined coriander and cumin seed: 8 minutes for the pistachios, 4 to 5 minutes for the benne seeds and spices.

Once they cool slightly, grind or mortar the spices. Chop the pistachios. I like to chop them so there is a nice mixture of sizes and textures, including some that's basically dust. Slice the benne seeds into thin strips. I'm kidding. Combine all ingredients, cool completely, and store in a sealed container at room temperature until ready to use, up to 1 week.

make the rabbit confit

Preheat your oven to 275°F (135°C).

In a large bowl or container, toss the rabbit in the poultry cure and let it sit at room temperature for 30 minutes. This will help to flavor the meat. Drain off any liquid that leaches out and pat the rabbit legs dry with paper towels.

Melt the schmaltz in a small casserole dish that can hold all the rabbit (or a "third pan" for the pros out there, although you probably wouldn't be cooking only 8 rabbit forelegs unless you're writing a book, of course). Add the cured legs and make sure they are submerged in the melted fat. Cover with parchment paper, pressing it directly on the surface of the fat. Now, cover with a lid or aluminum foil (the parchment paper will stop the legs from sticking to the foil as they cook) and place in the oven. Cook until the rabbit is tender, around 1 hour 45 minutes. Remove from the oven and allow the legs to cool at room temperature in the fat. If you're not serving them right away, cover and refrigerate.

There are two ways you can warm and sauce the legs: My favorite way is to deep-fry them at 350°F (180°C) for 3 to 4 minutes, or until crispy and golden. Then brush generously or toss in a bowl with the barbecue sauce (like chicken wings).

Alternatively, you can bake them in a 450°F (230°C) oven, brushing with barbecue sauce every few minutes, until just crispy, around 10 minutes. Remove from the oven, and brush with more of the sauce.

But honestly, just fry them.

Transfer the crispy, sticky legs to plates and sprinkle with the chopped pistachio dukkha, as well as some flaky sea salt.

Kasha Cakes

I've really been trying to make kasha happen. Kasha is the porridge form of roasted buckwheat groats, which was a staple for me growing up. My grandmother made it all the time. For years now, I've been trying to introduce it to the masses. These cakes are one such attempt, a sort of Jewish falafel. By pairing these with the tangy and creamy yogurt sauce and a topping of chicken bouillon and crispy chicken skin, they exhibit all the characteristics of a must-order dish. As the kids say, "10 out of 10 would smash." They say that, right?

Makes 8 cakes

kasha cakes
7 ounces (205 g) kasha (see Note)
1 pound (455 g) Sauerkraut (page 320), drained and chopped
5 ounces (150 g) Gribenes (page 338)
¼ cup plus 2 tablespoons (90 ml) Schmaltz (page 338)
2 tablespoons plus 1½ teaspoons Apple Cider Mustard (page 318)
⅓ cup (70 g) potato starch
kosher salt
freshly ground black pepper

yogurt dipping sauce
1 cup (240 g) plain Greek-style yogurt
¼ cup (60 g) thinly sliced chives

to finish
oil, for frying (I like rice bran oil)
2 teaspoons chicken bouillon powder
¼ cup (60 g) chopped Chicken Crackling (page 340)
2 tablespoons chopped fresh Italian parsley
½ cup (120 g) Aioli (page 321)

Note: The kasha must be rinsed/washed just like rice. Agitate the groats in cool water and drain. Repeat three to four times until the water becomes clear.

make the kasha cakes

In a wide saucepan, combine the kasha and 2 cups plus 2 tablespoons (500 ml) cold water and bring to a simmer over medium-high heat, then reduce to a slight simmer and cook while stirring occasionally until the kasha is tender, around 16 to 20 minutes. Turn off the heat and fold in the sauerkraut, gribenes, schmaltz, and mustard. Season with salt and black pepper, add the potato starch, and spread on a sheet tray to cool.

make the yogurt dipping sauce

Meanwhile, in a small bowl or container, combine the yogurt and chives and refrigerate, covered, until ready to serve.

to finish

Bring a pot of frying oil to 325°F (165°C).

Form the kasha mix into 4-ounce (120-g) balls and shape each into an oval. Fry the cakes until completely golden brown. Once the cake is golden brown, test the internal temperature with a cake tester; if it comes out warm to hot to the touch, the cake is done.

If the cakes are golden brown but still cold inside, finish them in a 350°F (180°C) oven.

Dust the cakes with the chicken bouillon and top with the chicken crackling and parsley. Serve with the chive-yogurt sauce and aioli.

Pickle Chick

When opening Birdie G's, I really wanted our kids' menu to be super solid. It had to be things parents would approve of but also things that kids would actually eat. At the time, my daughter Birdie was only three and a pretty picky eater. She still is. All in good time. She wouldn't even eat chicken tenders, but I hoped if I made a great one, she would. I also wanted the tenders to be gluten free, so they were more available to everyone. I worked on this gluten-free breading a lot, really tinkering with it to get it right. Our chicken tenders at Birdie G's are top notch. But if you're wondering, no, my kid won't eat them.

When COVID hit and Birdie G's, like most restaurants, had to switch to takeout only, the Pickle Chick was born. We use the same gluten-free breading from the chicken tenders that Birdie won't eat, and we sprinkle the fried chicken pieces in dill pollen. Serve them with Dill Pickles (page 312) and Dill Pickle Sauce (page 313) on the side. Fourteen orders (a Birdie's Dozen) are available nightly.

Serves 4

chicken
2 whole chickens (each about 3 pounds/1.4 kg)
2 quarts (1.9 liters) All-Purpose Meat Brine (page 337)
1 pound (455 g) potato flakes
1 cup (120 g) cornstarch (cornflour)
¼ cup (30 g) Birdie Bay Spice (page 311)
2 tablespoons plus 1½ teaspoons kosher salt
1 cup (120 g) rice flour
8 large eggs, lightly beaten with ¼ cup (60 ml) water
2 quarts (1.9 liters) neutral oil, such as rice bran, peanut (groundnut), or canola (rapeseed)
1 tablespoon dill pollen

to serve
Dill Pickles (page 312)
Dill Pickle Sauce (page 313)

make the chicken

Separate the 2 whole chickens into 20 pieces as follows: 4 breasts, each cut in half; 4 thighs; 4 drumsticks; 4 wings, with flat and drumette connected. Submerge the chicken in the cold brine, either in a large plastic resealable bag or an airtight container. Let brine in the refrigerator for 24 hours.

Remove the chicken from the brine and dispose of the brine. Transfer the chicken to a sheet pan fitted with a rack. Refrigerate, uncovered, for 24 hours.

In a food processor, combine the potato flakes, cornstarch (cornflour), bay spice blend, and salt and process until you achieve a fine powder. Store in an airtight container at room temperature.

To bread the chicken, in 3 wide, shallow bowls, set out your flour, whisked eggs, and potato mixture. Toss the pieces with the flour to coat evenly. Transfer the chicken to the eggs, one piece at a time, making sure each piece is evenly coated and letting any drips fall back into the egg container before adding the pieces to the potato mixture, again coating each piece completely. Transfer the fully breaded pieces to a sheet pan with a rack.

To fry the chicken, in a large, heavy-bottom pot, bring the oil to a temperature of 325°F (165°C). Carefully add each piece of chicken, cooking in batches if necessary to avoid crowding the pot. Fry until each registers an internal temperature of 165°F (74°C). Remove the chicken, dust with the dill pollen, and quickly let dry on paper towels to absorb any extra oil.

to serve

Arrange the chicken on a plate with a pile of dill pickles and a side of dill pickle sauce.

Chicken Kyiv with Escargot Butter

Serves 4

12 ounces (340 g) Escargot Butter (page 323), room temperature
4 skinless, boneless chicken breasts (about 1½ pounds/700 g)
2 cups (240 g) all-purpose (plain) flour
6 large eggs, lightly beaten with 2 tablespoons water
2 cups (160 g) panko breadcrumbs
oil, for frying (I like rice bran oil)
kosher salt
freshly ground black pepper

This is a particularly nostalgic recipe for me. Microwaveable chicken Kyiv (and cordon bleu) was one of my favorite childhood dinners. Serve with anything you think will help absorb the butter: Potato Purée (page 166), rice, or mashed peas could all be nice.

On a piece of plastic wrap (clingfilm), use an offset spatula to spread the softened escargot butter into a 4 × 5-inch (10 × 12-cm) sheet, ¾ inch (2 cm) thick. This is where your kitchen ruler comes in handy. Cover with another piece of plastic wrap, then freeze the butter until solid.

Place the chicken breasts between 2 layers of plastic wrap and gently pound to a thickness of ¼ inch (0.6 cm). Place each pounded chicken breast on a large piece of plastic wrap.

To stuff the chicken, cut the chilled escargot butter into quarters, so each piece is 4 × 1¼ × ¾ inch (10 × 3 × 2 cm). Place a butter piece on each breast, 2 inches (5 cm) from the edge nearest you. Roll the nearest edge over the butter and form a seal, rolling it forward by ½ inch (1.3 cm), then fold the left and right edges inward by 1 inch (2.5 cm) and continue rolling forward into a log.

Torque (see page 34) each rolled and stuffed chicken breast to form a tight log and seal the edges. Place your "chicken logs" in the freezer for about 30 minutes, or refrigerate for 2 hours.

To bread the chicken, in 3 wide, shallow bowls, set out your flour, whisked eggs, and panko. First, roll each log in the flour, shaking off any extra. Now, roll in the eggs, letting excess drip back into the bowl, then coat each log with the panko.

Transfer the fully breaded pieces to a sheet pan with a rack and refrigerate, uncovered, for 2 hours.

To fry the chicken, preheat your oven to 325°F (160°C) and heat the oil in a heavy-bottom pot to 325°F (160°C). Carefully add each log to the hot oil and cook until golden, 5 to 6 minutes.

Transfer the fried chicken to a sheet pan fitted with a rack and slide it into your preheated oven until the meat has reached an internal temperature of 165°F (74°C). Sprinkle the hot chicken all over with salt and pepper and serve.

Pressed Chicken Confit Parmesan

This is one of my favorite recipes, left over from a consulting gig I once did at the now closed gastropub, Freddy Smalls. Well, this and Buffalo Deviled Eggs (page 172).

Serves 4 to 6

3 pounds (1.4 kg) bone-in, skin-on chicken thighs
¾ ounce (20 g) Poultry Cure (page 341)
4 cups (480 g) Schmaltz (page 338) or duck fat (¾ cups strained & decanted reserved)
1¼ pounds (570 g) provolone cheese, in ½-inch (1.25 cm) dice
¾ cups finely grated Parmesan cheese, plus extra
½ cups fresh basil leaves, chiffonade, plus extra
2½ tablespoons dried Sicilian oregano
2 cups (240 g) all-purpose (plain) flour
6 eggs + 2 tablespoons cold water, whisked
2 cups (160 g) panko bread crumbs
Clarified Butter, for pan-frying (page 323)
3 cups (700 ml) Easy Tomato Sauce (page 306)
1 bunch dried Sicilian oregano
kosher salt
freshly ground black pepper

Pat the chicken thighs dry and evenly distribute the cure among them, coating all sides. Transfer the thighs to a rack on a rimmed baking sheet and refrigerate, uncovered, for at least 2 hours, or overnight.

Preheat the oven to 275°F (135°C). Dry the thighs with paper towels and load them into a cooking vessel large enough to hold them without touching.

In a large saucepan, melt the duck fat or schmaltz. Once the fat has reached 200°F (93°C), gently pour the warmed fat over the chicken thighs until they're submerged by 1 inch (2.5 cm). Cover the fat with a cartouche (see page 35), then heavy foil, and place in the preheated oven. No convection please. Gently confit the legs for 2½ to 3 hours. Remove from the oven and allow the thighs to cool to room temperature in the hot fat.

Remove the skin and set aside. Pull the meat off the bone in large chunks, discarding the bone. Give the chicken skin a rough chop and add to the pulled meat. In a mixing bowl, combine the meat chunks, chopped skin, diced provolone, grated Parmesan, oregano, and basil. Now pour over the reserved and cooled fat. Mix gently to combine.

Line your terrine mold with plastic wrap (cling film; see page 33). Spoon the chicken mixture into a terrine mold, close off the plastic wrap at the top and place a weight on the surface of the plastic wrap to weigh down slightly. Refrigerate overnight.

Remove the terrine by lifting the plastic wrap and pulling up. On a cutting board, cut the terrine into 1-inch (2.5 cm) thick slices.

Set up your breading station: one shallow bowl of flour, one shallow bowl of the egg and water mixture, and one shallow bowl of the panko. Have a rimmed baking sheet with a rack set at the end for the finished slices. Dip a slice in flour, then egg, then panko; make sure that all sides are covered. Once all your slices are breaded and ready, warm the clarified butter in a shallow frying pan until it reaches 325°F (163°C). The butter should come halfway up the slice so that, once we flip it, all sides will be equally cooked. Add your first slice—it should sizzle and bubble—followed by more slices, working in batches, without crowding the pan. Cook until the bottom is golden brown and then gently flip and continue to cook the other side. Remove your crispy, golden slices back to the tray with the rack to drain.

Warm the tomato sauce over medium heat. Each plate should get a generous spoonful of sauce on the bottom, followed by the crispy chicken slice. Top each slice with basil leaves, oregano, freshly grated Parmesan, and salt and pepper. Serve warm.

Dressed Chicken Bones "Isadore"

Serves 2 to 4, or 1 great-grandfather

4 tablespoons (56 g) unsalted butter
1 teaspoon kosher salt
1 teaspoon grated garlic
½ cup (120 ml) Rachael's Chicken Stock (page 334)
1 pound (455 g) chicken bones (feet, wings, necks) after making the stock, warmed
2 tablespoons capers
2 tablespoons finely chopped fresh Italian parsley
zest and juice of 1 lemon
flaky salt

I used to tag along with my grandmother Gladys to my great-grandparents' apartment. We would take spent chicken bones from the chicken stock she had just made, and my great-grandfather would sit and gnaw on them. He might have been on to something, as he lived to 94. His name was Isadore Katz, though I knew him as Pup-Pup, and my great-grandmother was Esther. Here I've made a nice little sauce to toss the chicken bones in. If you don't have spent bones, you could always poach chicken feet until they're soft and gelatinous.

In a saucepan on medium-high heat, brown 3 tablespoons of butter with the kosher salt. Stir in the garlic and cook quickly, just to make it fragrant, or toast it lightly if you prefer that flavor. Dealer's choice. Add the chicken stock and reduce to ¼ cup (60 ml). Remove from the heat, and mount with the remaining 1 tablespoon butter.

In a mixing bowl, toss the chicken bones with the reduced chicken stock, then add the capers, parsley, and lemon zest and juice. Sprinkle with flaky sea salt and servo.

Chicken Scrapple

Scrapple, or pannhaas, is a Pennsylvania Dutch recipe traditionally made from pork. Famously, it usually includes "everything but the oink" and is a delicious way to use up bits and leftovers. My version makes use of chicken gribenes, the oniony-chicken by-product of making schmaltz. When I opened a restaurant called Rotisserie & Wine with Tyler Florence in 2010, this was one of my favorite dishes on the menu.

Serves 8

sautéed livers and hearts
1 pound (455 g) chicken livers
8 ounces (230 g) chicken hearts
whole (full-fat) milk, to cover
1 tablespoon Schmaltz (page 338), more if needed

broth and meat paste
2 cups (475 ml) Rachael's Chicken Stock (page 334)
1 cup (240 ml) Ham Hock Stock (page 336)
2 cups (475 ml) whey (see Note)
6 garlic cloves, smashed
2 red bell peppers, seeded and cut into 1-inch (2.5-cm) pieces
1 white onion, cut into 1-inch (2.5-cm) pieces
24 fresh sage leaves
3 rosemary sprigs, leaves picked
1 bay leaf
½ bunch thyme, leaves picked
1 teaspoon Fox Spice (page 311)
1 tablespoon freshly ground black pepper
½ teaspoon freshly ground white pepper
8 ounces (225 g) chicken gizzards, tied in a sachet
1 pound (455 g) Gribenes (page 338)

scrapple
2 cups (240 g) coarse polenta (see Sources, page 350)
nonstick cooking spray, for loaf pan
Clarified Butter (page 323), for frying
fine semolina, for frying
Smoky Honey Mustard (page 302), for serving

Note: You can substitute the whey with 1 cup plain yogurt (240 ml) mixed with 1 cup (240 ml) water.

make the sautéed livers and hearts

Inspect the livers one at a time, removing any sinew, fat, or green bits (when a little of the gallbladder is still attached). Now, remove the veins: Each liver is composed of 2 halves connected with a strand of sinew. Get a firm grip on the vein with one hand (index finger and thumb) and cradle one end of the liver with the other hand; pull gently to slide the liver loose from the vein. Repeat. All you want is bright red liver. Each liver should be uniform in color.

Add the cleaned livers to a container and run under cold water until the water runs clear. Drain the livers on paper or kitchen towels.

In separate containers, cover the livers and hearts with milk and let soak for 2 hours.

Pour off the milk and flush the chicken pieces with cold running water until it runs clear. Drain the pieces and pat them dry with paper towels.

Season the livers and hearts lightly with salt. In a large cast-iron skillet on high heat, add the schmaltz. Once it just begins to smoke, add the hearts, not crowding the pan, and cook while rolling them around to caramelize for 3 to 4 minutes. Fish the hearts from the pan and reserve.

[...]

[...]

Next, get the pan hot again, adding another 1 tablespoon schmaltz if needed, and add the livers, again not crowding the pan; cook for 2 minutes on each side until caramelized. Remove them from the heat, combine with the cooked hearts, and cool to room temperature.

make the broth and meat paste

In a large pot on medium heat, combine both stocks, whey, garlic, bell peppers, onion, herbs, fox spice, black and white pepper, and sachet of chicken gizzards, tying it to the side of the pot so it's easier to fish out later.

Bring the mixture to a simmer and keep it at a steady temperature, ideally 180°F (82°C), to slowly extract the flavors. Once the gizzards are tender, 1½ to 2 hours, stir in the gribenes and then remove from the heat and strain through a fine-mesh sieve. Save the solids and broth separately.

Once they're cool enough to handle, roughly chop the gizzards. Add the gizzards and other solids to a food processor and pulse to a coarse paste.

make the scrapple

Return the reserved broth to the pot, bring to a boil, and stir in the polenta. Reduce the heat so it barely bubbles and cook, stirring occasionally, for 1½ to 2 hours. Once the raw crunch of the polenta is gone, fold in the gizzard paste, bring to a bare simmer, and remove from the heat. Adjust the seasoning.

First, line the loaf pan: coat the interior with nonstick cooking spray, and set the pan horizontally about 6 inches (15 cm) in front of your roll of plastic wrap (clingfilm); pull the plastic wrap over the pan, then take a rolled kitchen towel and push it into the well of the pan, flattening down the wrap. You want at least 4 inches (10 cm) of overhang on each side.

Pour the polenta and meat mixture into the lined pan. Tap it on the counter a few times to help compress the mixture and release any air bubbles. Use the overhang of plastic wrap to wrap the top. Refrigerate overnight.

When ready to fry off the scrapple, invert the pan onto a cutting (chopping) board and remove the plastic wrap. Slice the loaf ½ inch (1.3 cm) thick. Rewrap and refrigerate any scrapple you won't be frying up immediately.

We're going to shallow-fry the scrapple. Heat a large, high-sided cast-iron skillet over medium heat; after a few minutes, add enough clarified butter so the melted depth is ½ inch (1.3 cm).

Once the clarified butter is hot enough to sizzle immediately when a tiny bit of semolina flour is added to it, coat the scrapple lightly with semolina. Fry on each side until golden and crispy, 2 to 3 minutes. Serve it up hot, with the honey mustard alongside.

Chef's note: There are no standing laws (I think) prohibiting you from serving this as a "soft" scrapple with poached or fried eggs.

Egg Salad Croque Madame on Texas Toast

My career has been a struggle of two sides: I either strip everything away, bare bones, nothing on the plate except what absolutely needs to be there, or I go decadent, big, whole hog. I'm not sure I know how to be in the middle or what that would even look like. This recipe is a perfect example. I love egg salad. My grandmother made it for me as a kid. Hell, I'll even buy it from a gas station, I love it that much. When I knew I wanted to put it on the menu at Birdie G's as part of our Texas Toast section, the decadent side took over and I married it with a *croque madame*. Clearly, this is not Gladys's egg salad.

Serves 4

egg salad
9 large eggs, room temperature (take them out of the refrigerator 1 hour before cooking)
¾ cup (180 g) Aioli (page 321)
¼ cup (20 g) thinly sliced scallions (spring onions)
1 tablespoon sherry vinegar
kosher salt

to serve
4 slices Pain de Mie (page 328), sliced 1½ inches (3.8 cm) thick
12 ounces (340 g) Rosemary Pork Loin (page 70), sliced ⅛ inch (0.3 cm) thick
2 cups (475 ml) Béchamel (page 322), cold
truffle pecorino cheese, for shaving (see Note)
1 ounce (30 g) fresh black truffle (optional)
flaky sea salt

Notes: I like to use the microplane "large cheese shaver" for the pecorino and the fine microplane for the truffles.

At the restaurant, we bake the truffle pecorino and béchamel over the egg salad under the salamander. In a home kitchen, you will need a really good broiler (grill) to melt the cheese quickly without heating up the egg salad too much. I like that little bit of chill against the piping hot topping. So, if you don't have a proper broiler, but you have a toaster oven, bust out that bad boy. Some air fryers also have a broil function. I'm sure you can make it work, get creative.

make the egg salad

Fill a medium saucepan three-quarters of the way with water. Bring it to a full boil over high heat and, using a slotted spoon, place the eggs gently into the boiling water. Return the water to a boil and then lower the heat to a bare, consistent simmer. Cook the eggs for 9 minutes. Drain the eggs and transfer to a large ice bath.

Let the eggs remain in the ice bath for at least 10 minutes, then peel them under running water, or in that same ice bath, and transfer them to a cutting (chopping) board. The yolks should be fully set with just the slightest bit of jamminess.

For this egg salad, you want large chunks of egg rather than a mash. I like to slice the egg into sixteenths: Cut the eggs in half lengthwise, placing each egg cut side down on the cutting board. Slice in half again, this time lengthwise. Then cut each quarter crosswise into 4 pieces. Alternately, if you have a gridded cooling rack, the kind for cookies and cakes, you can set it over a bowl and push the eggs through the grid. Boom, instant dice.

Place the eggs, aioli, scallions (spring onions), and vinegar in a mixing bowl and fold gently until combined. Season with salt.

If not using immediately, the egg salad can be covered and refrigerated for up to 24 hours.

to serve

Heat your broiler (grill) or use a toaster oven to lightly toast the bread. The slices are probably too thick for a pop-up toaster.

Working on a rimmed baking sheet (broiler method) or your toaster oven tray, top each piece of bread with the sliced ham, then evenly divide the egg salad among the toasts, piling it on and spreading it all the way to the edge (you should not see the top of the bread) so the bread doesn't burn.

Spoon the béchamel over the egg salad as evenly as possible, or spread it gently with an offset spatula. Using a large cheese shaver, grate the truffle pecorino over the egg toast, evenly coating with a thin layer. Broil until nicely caramelized or pop the tray in the toaster oven.

Transfer to plates, sprinkle with flaky salt, and finely grate black truffle over the top if you like.

Duck Neck Sausage, Green Walnuts & Apples

At the restaurants, we process a lot of whole ducks and are left with all of the bits. Not everything can be used to make confit or stock. At first, I stuffed the necks with mortadella (which works great if you want to go rogue here), but then I settled on this stuffing made from our leg trim and Birdie G's house-made candied green walnuts. This is one of those projects that's going to give you a lot of confidence and, I hope, get your creative juices flowing. Once you nail the method, you'll realize you can do all sorts of things within these parameters. If the accompanying apples and walnuts evoke Passover charoset vibes, that is by design.

Serves 4

sausage
4 duck necks
1 tablespoon kosher salt, plus extra for soaking solution
1 pound (455 g) duck leg meat
6 ounces (170 g) pork fatback
1 teaspoon freshly ground white pepper
¼ teaspoon curing salt #1
3 ounces (90 ml) madeira
¼ cup (20 g) minced shallots
2 ounces (60 g) candied green walnuts, diced (see Sources, page 350)
2 tablespoons Schmaltz (page 338) or duck fat

to serve
3 apples of your choosing (I love Honeycrisp, Fuji, and Pink Lady), cored and cut into 1-inch (2.5-cm) pieces
1 lemon, halved
1 ounce (30 g) toasted walnuts, chopped
kosher salt
flaky sea salt (optional)

make the sausage

First, remove the skin in one piece from one of the duck necks. To do this, turn the skin inside-out at one end and roll it down the neck, removing it. You'll want a firm grip, but not so firm that you tear the skin. You should be left with a hollow-sock-without-the-foot situation. A leg warmer if you will. Save the inside of the neck for your next stock. Repeat with the remaining 3 necks.

Soak the neck skins overnight in a solution made with 6 percent kosher salt and water. The next morning, remove the necks from the brine and discard the brine. Dry the neck skins well on paper or kitchen towels.

Set up your meat grinder (see page 30) and grind (mince) together the duck leg meat and the pork fatback using a ³⁄₁₆-inch (4-mm) plate.

In a large mixing bowl, combine the ground mixture with the 1 tablespoon kosher salt, white pepper, curing salt, madeira, shallots, and candied green walnuts. With a wooden spoon, mix well to combine. Divide the sausage mixture into 4 equal portions, one for each neck skin.

To fill, tie off one end of the skin with butcher's twine. With a spoon or your hands, stuff one portion of the meat mixture into the skin. Really pack it in, we don't want air holes. Tie off the other end. Repeat with the remaining skins and filling. Now, roll each neck tightly in plastic wrap (clingfilm).

Still wrapped in plastic, poach the sausages in a pot of 180°F (82°C) water to an internal temperature of 165°F (74°C). Once the sausages reach this temp, remove them immediately and shock them in ice water for 30 minutes.

Remove the plastic wrap from each neck and any gelled stock or rendered fat from the skin. You can usually pop it off like melted candle wax. If not, try pouring a little warm water to loosen. Dry by rolling in paper or kitchen towels.

In a cast-iron skillet on medium-high heat, heat the schmaltz. Add the poached sausages and cook, rolling them in the pan to achieve even browning, until each link once again reaches an internal temperature of 165°F (74°C) and is nicely browned and crispy on all sides. Remove from the heat and allow the sausages to rest as you prepare the apples.

to serve

In a large mixing bowl, combine the apples with 1 tablespoon of fat from the skillet, tossing to coat. Adjust the seasoning with kosher salt and a squeeze of lemon.

Slice the sausages ¼ inch (0.6 cm) thick, and finish with flaky sea salt if needed. Arrange the slices haphazardly on plates with the dressed apples and a sprinkle of the toasted walnuts.

Duck Ham & Heart Skewers with Grapes

I like to come up with funny restaurant names and then build really serious menus around them. It's how I unwind, we all have our thing. The Brothel is my idea for a soup spot. Our tagline would be: "I dipped my ladle at The Brothel." Perfection. Then there's Sammy Spiedini's: Home of the Wood-Fired Weenie. All sorts of grilled meats on skewers with dipping sauces. I have the menu if you want to see it. The web domain as well.

This is a spiedini from the menu of that mythical restaurant come to life. Duck hearts are so nice; the flavor is mild and the texture is perfect. Grilling them as here highlights the hearts instead of them disappearing into something else.

I'd love for you to cook these on a Japanese hibachi if you have one, but a regular charcoal or gas grill (barbecue) is great, too. You can also use a cast-iron grill pan on the range.

Serves 4

20 duck hearts
kosher salt
freshly ground black pepper
2 Duck Hams (page 65), sliced ⅛ inch (0.3 cm) thick
½ white onion, cut into 2 × 1½-inch (5 × 4-cm) petals
24 seedless red grapes
olive oil, for drizzling
¼ cup (60 ml) Nasturtium Salsa (page 305)
flaky sea salt
nasturtium leaves and flowers, to garnish

Note: For the skewers, you can strip rosemary stems, leaving about 1 inch (1.5 cm) of leaves on one end and save the leaves for another use. Wooden skewers, soaked in water so they don't burn, also work great. As do metal skewers, no soaking required.

Set up your hibachi or grill (barbecue) according to the manufacturer's directions. Otherwise, wait to heat a griddle pan over high heat until the skewers are ready to go.

Lightly season the duck hearts with kosher salt and black pepper. Thread the skewers by alternating a few folded slices of duck ham with horizontally-pierced duck heart and onion petals, then a few more slices of duck ham, and finally a grape. Repeat until everything is skewered.

Drizzle the skewers lightly with olive oil. Grill, turning, until the duck hearts are nicely charred and just warm in the center, about 3–5 minutes.

Serve on a platter with the nasturtium salsa spooned over. Finish with flaky sea salt and nasturtium leaves and flowers.

Duck Tongue Fried Farro

I love 99 Ranch Market. If you're looking for hard-to-find cuts of meat or just inspiration, it will be the place for you as well. If you're unfamiliar, it's the largest Asian supermarket chain in the United States. H Mart is also a favorite. This recipe came from one such trip to 99 Ranch. I was on a mission to buy my daughter a Korean soda, frozen udon noodles, and cute plush toys, and I came across these duck tongues. Farro, the toasty ancient grain, gives this dish a great bite and chew, but you can, of course, use rice. Leftover rice usually works best.

Serves 4

1 ½ cups (300 g) farro (see Sources, page 350)
1 tablespoon kosher salt, plus extra to taste
1 pound (455 g) duck tongues
2 tablespoons sesame oil
1 cup (120 g) diced white onion
¾ cup (90 g) diced carrot
¾ cup (75 g) diced celery stalk
½ cup (60 g) thinly sliced scallion (spring onion)
3 garlic cloves, grated
½ teaspoon freshly ground white pepper
1 tablespoon (14 g) unsalted butter
4 large eggs, lightly beaten with a pinch of kosher salt
2 tablespoons Tiki Sauce (page 303)
¼ cup (10 g) cilantro (coriander) leaves and stems, coarsely chopped (optional)

Combine the farro and 1 quart (0.9 liter) water in a small saucepan with the salt. Bring to a boil, then reduce the heat and simmer for 15 to 20 minutes until the grains are tender. Drain the farro and reserve the cooking liquid. Spread the drained farro on kitchen towels to dry.

In the same pan, combine the duck tongues and reserved farro cooking water and bring to a boil, skimming foam from the surface. Reduce the heat to a slow simmer and cook for 15 to 20 minutes until tender.

Let the tongues cool to a workable temperature, then remove the bone by holding the tongue in one hand and use kitchen tweezers to pull the bone out with the other. Dry the tongues on kitchen towels and discard the bones.

In a large wok or cast-iron skillet, heat the sesame oil on medium-high heat. Sauté the onion, carrot, and celery for 3 to 4 minutes until slightly caramelized and beginning to soften. Add the farro, duck tongues, scallion (spring onion), garlic, and white pepper, and cook for another 2 minutes.

Push the contents of the pan to one side, melt the butter on the other, and scramble the eggs in the butter. Then break the eggs up as you introduce them to the farro mixture.

Mix in the tiki sauce and cilantro (coriander), adjust the seasoning with more salt to taste, and serve.

Joel's Chicken Riggies

I "inherited" Joel Spadafore when I took over the kitchen at Rustic Canyon in 2013. Joel was one of the cooks that mercifully didn't quit on me. It's hard to take over an established kitchen; turnover is inevitable, and you only hope you can staunch the bleeding. At the time, Joel worked the burger station until I, much to the angst of the regulars, removed the burger from the menu. This was actually my marching order when I got the job. The burger station was in the corner of the hotline, utilizing an old griddle that constantly caught on fire underneath. But Joel handled it like a champ. He is fiercely opinionated, dedicated, and passionate about using up kitchen scraps—sometimes to a fault. We ended up working together for many years, from Rustic Canyon to the opening of Birdie G's.

In the very early days of Birdie G's, Joel, by then a sous chef, made chicken riggies for me. It's a regional dish from his hometown of Syracuse, New York. I had never heard of it, but I instantly fell in love. We put it on the menu at Birdie G's as a weekly Blue Plate Special. Chef Dave Beran of Pasjoli would come in to eat it because he's also from Syracuse, and he'd never seen it on a menu outside of that city. America is full of these kinds of dishes and it's so fun to learn about them, to get a peek inside these pockets you didn't know existed.

Joel is back in Syracuse now. But this dish remains imprinted on my memory. I remain grateful to Joel for sticking around, especially in those early days.

Serves 4

4 boneless, skinless chicken breasts
¼ cup (30 g) all-purpose (plain) flour
1 tablespoon extra-virgin olive oil
1 tablespoon grated garlic
½ cup (120 ml) dry sherry
3 cups (710 ml) Easy Tomato Sauce (page 306)
¼ cup (60 ml) red hot sauce
1 tablespoon plus 1½ teaspoons brine from Ohio Peppers (page 317)
½ cup (120 ml) heavy (double) cream
1 pound (455 g) dried rigatoni
1 tablespoon chopped fresh Italian parsley
kosher salt
freshly ground black pepper

To make the sauce, slice the chicken breasts into strips that are 2 × 1 inch (5 × 2.5 cm) long and season them lightly with salt and black pepper. Dredge the chicken lightly with the flour and shake off any excess.

In a heavy-bottom rondeau or a Dutch oven, heat the olive oil on medium-high heat until a tiny bit of flour added to it sizzles immediately. Add the floured chicken, reduce the heat to medium, and cook until ever so lightly browned, about 5 minutes each side.

Add the garlic and cook quickly, just until fragrant. Deglaze the pot with the sherry and cook until mostly evaporated. Add the tomato sauce, hot sauce, and Ohio pepper brine, and bring to a simmer. Add the cream and simmer for about 5 minutes as the sauce thickens.

To cook the pasta, bring about 4 quarts (3.75 liters) salted water to a boil and cook the rigatoni until al dente. Drain the pasta, reserving a little pasta water.

To finish the dish, adjust the seasoning of the sauce with more salt to taste, then toss it in a large bowl with the drained pasta and the parsley. If it needs thinning, add a tablespoon or so of the reserved pasta water. Then plate it up in wide bowls and dig in.

BTW: I wholeheartedly endorse finishing with crumbled blue cheese, but I don't dare officially add it to this recipe.

Jeremiah's Chicken

There was a stretch at Rustic Canyon when we were down a cook and just couldn't find that special someone. Then, right before Christmas, Jeremiah Lacsamana walked in. He had staged at a few other places, but he ultimately took the job with us. It's how he became known as "our Christmas present." You know that super cheerful guy, that hardworking, stand-up guy that everyone loves? That's Jeremiah. He worked the meat station at Rustic, and he got hammered every weekend.

    He became famous for his family meals: huge trays of nachos that other chefs in town would give him props for when they toured the kitchen. He once made the timpano from the movie *Big Night*. Pretty soon he was grilling jerk chicken from the back of his pickup truck on a makeshift grill (barbecue) with wood chips and hotel pans, in the alley behind the restaurant… I have photos. The first time I tried his jerk chicken, I told him, "You should work on this. This should be the chicken on the opening menu at Birdie G's." He did work on it, and we tweaked it over time. It stayed on the menu for three years. Once Jeremiah left Birdie G's, it didn't feel right to make it without him, in case he wanted to open a restaurant built around his chicken.

    As a chef, you learn to spot "the good ones," and Jeremiah remains on my short list. People like him will always have a job with me, no questions, even if I'm fully staffed. I still root for Jeremiah and want the world for him. And this chicken is really, really good.

Serves 4 to 6

marinade
⅔ cup (150 ml) extra-virgin olive oil
3 tablespoons tamari
2 ounces (60 g) lime, coarsely chopped (rind and all)
2 ounces (60 g) scallions (spring onions), thinly sliced
2 fresh habañero peppers, stemmed and finely minced
2 tablespoons dark brown sugar
2 tablespoons fresh thyme leaves and chopped stems
1 tablespoon minced peeled fresh ginger
1 tablespoon allspice berries
1½ teaspoons grated garlic
1 teaspoon smoked cinnamon (see Sources, page 350)
1 teaspoon cumin seed
½ teaspoon grated nutmeg
¼ teaspoon whole cloves

grilled chicken
2 fresh whole chickens (about 3 pounds/1.4 kg)
kosher salt
oil, for the grill (barbecue)

tropical sauce
3 ounces (85 g) carrot, cut into ½-inch (⅓-cm) dice
3 ounces (85 g) white onion, cut into 1-inch (2.5-cm) pieces
2 tablespoons extra-virgin olive oil
pinch of kosher salt
1 tablespoon grated garlic
5 ounces (150 g) fresh pineapple, peeled and cored
¼ cup plus 2 tablespoons (90 ml) honey
½ cup (120 g) Dijon mustard
¼ cup (60 g) Pickled Mustard Seeds (page 318)
¼ cup (60 g) cape gooseberries, plus extra, halved, for serving
2 tablespoons apple cider vinegar
1 teaspoon (2 g) xanthan gum (optional)

make the marinade

Preheat your oven to 225°F (105°C).

In a large pot or Dutch oven, combine all the marinade ingredients. Cover with a lid or aluminum foil and cook slowly in the oven for 24 hours.

The next day, after removing from the oven, let the marinade cool down a little; while still warm, transfer to a blender and purée until smooth, adding ⅔ cup (150 ml) lukewarm water in a slow, steady stream with the motor running to emulsify.

Let the marinade cool to room temperature, then refrigerate in an airtight container until ready to use, up to 1 week.

make the grilled chicken

Muster all your chutzpah, we're going to spatchcock. Meaning we are going to remove the backbone and flatten the chicken so it cooks evenly.

On a cutting (chopping) board, place the bird, breast side down, with the legs facing you. The fatty, fleshy bit that sticks out at the end of the bird is where the tail, sometimes referred to as the pope's nose, once was, and that's where we'll be cutting: straight up along the backbone using the pope's nose as a guide. With good kitchen shears, cut along the backbone on either side of the bird. You'll be cutting through the little rib bones. There might be crunching; it's okay, you're doing it right.

Once you cut up both sides of the backbone, it will lift right out of the chicken. Pop it in the freezer and save for a batch of stock later on.

Now, flip the bird over, breast side up, legs still pointing toward you; with the heel of your hand, push down on the breastbone to flatten the bird. *Et voila*!

Next, repeat the whole process with the other chicken.

Dry the birds with paper or kitchen towels and then lightly salt them. On a sheet pan, generously coat them with the marinade, reserving ½ cup (120 ml) for cooking. Refrigerate the chicken overnight, uncovered. Also return the reserved marinade to the refrigerator. (Now is a good time to make the tropical sauce, below.)

Set up your charcoal or gas grill (barbecue) for direct heat cooking. We want to reach a temperature of 450 to 500°F (230 to 260°C). Remove the chickens from the refrigerator and let sit at room temperature for 30 to 45 minutes before grilling.

Once they are hot, oil the grates of your grill. Cook the chickens, breast side down, for 5 to 7 minutes until nicely caramelized, then flip them. If the chicken won't flip cleanly by now, wait; it'll loosen with time, don't force it.

Once you can flip the chickens, you'll want to cook them slowly through. If using a charcoal grill, elevate the birds to a higher rack. For a gas grill, reduce the temperature to low. Either way, brush with the reserved marinade as the chicken cooks, about 40 minutes, or until the thickest part of the leg near the bone reaches 165°F (74°C).

Remove the chicken from the grill and let rest for 5 to 10 minutes before carving.

make the tropical sauce

Do this while the chicken is marinating.

Preheat your oven to 350°F (180°C).

On a flat baking sheet, toss the carrot and onion with the olive oil and a pinch of salt. Spread the mixture evenly, and cook until very soft, 20 to 25 minutes.

Remove from the oven and toss the hot vegetables with the grated garlic. Let cool slightly; while still warm, transfer to a blender along with the pineapple, honey, Dijon mustard, pickled mustard seeds, cape gooseberries, and vinegar. Purée until smooth.

With the motor running, sprinkle in the xanthan gum, if using, and purée for an additional 2 minutes.

Check the seasonings for salt. Push the mixture through a fine-mesh sieve and then let it cool to room temperature. Refrigerate the sauce in an airtight container until you're ready to use it, up to 3 days; reheat before serving.

To serve, arrange the chicken pieces onto warmed plates or a warmed platter along with the tropical sauce and some halved cape gooseberries.

You could even do Jeremiah's signature cuts before presenting: Simply make an incision at the joint between the drumsticks and thighs, but don't cut all the way through. Then make 3 incisions, evenly spaced apart along the length of the breasts. By doing so, you're making life a little easier for other people. Just like Jeremiah.

Lemon Pepper Roast Chicken

Last year, while feeling particularly nostalgic, I asked Birdie G's then-executive chef, Matt Schaler, to work on a lemon pepper chicken dish for the menu as the sequel to Jeremiah's Chicken (page 224). I had been missing my late mother Trudy, and lemon pepper was something she put on everything. For me, feeling nostalgic can sometimes mean diving deep into a food memory, and sometimes it's handing it off to someone else with capable hands. Matt did not disappoint; in truth, he never did. He and sous chef CJ Sullivan worked on this iteration, and I think it's perfect. It hits all my favorite notes: It's delicious, it invokes a memory, it utilizes overlooked ingredients in our pantry, and it can be served with mashed potatoes.

Serves 4

roast chicken
2 fresh whole chickens (each about 3 pounds/1.4 kg)
¼ cup (30 g) Lemon Pepper Rub (page 310)
kosher salt
1 lemon, halved
2 bay leaves

beurre poulet
3 cups (710 ml) Rachael's Chicken Stock (page 334)
2 tablespoons olive brine (we use the brine from Castelvetrano olives)
5 ounces (150 g) unsalted butter, cut into ¼-inch (0.6 cm) dice
kosher salt
lemon juice, to taste

fried lemons
oil, for frying
8 ounces (225 g) thinly sliced lemons (as thin as possible), seeded
¼ cup (30 g) cornstarch (cornflour)
kosher salt

to serve
picked fresh Italian parsley and dill leaves
snipped fresh chives

make the roast chicken

A day ahead of time, season the exterior of each chicken with the lemon pepper rub, saving a little to sprinkle into each cavity. After the rub is on, sprinkle the chickens with salt and place a halved lemon and bay leaf into each cavity.

Now, to truss or not to truss? That's really up to you. Trussing can help the bird cook more evenly, but it's about personal preference. If you don't want to truss completely, maybe at least tie the legs loosely together so that the lemon half and bay leaf stay secure. Sometimes, I tuck the wings under, but more often than not, I find myself leaving them untucked so they get crispy. I'm a man of whims.

Refrigerate the chickens overnight on a rack-lined sheet pan, uncovered.

The next day, before cooking, let the chickens sit at room temperature for 30 to 45 minutes while preheating your oven to 500°F (260°C).

Roast the chickens on the same rack-lined pan for 10 minutes. Rotate the pan and cook for another 5 minutes. Remove from the oven and lower the heat to 250°F (120°C), leaving the oven door open a bit to expedite cooling. There's nothing worse than a dry bird overcooked at too high a temperature.

Return the chicken to the oven and cook until the thickest part of the leg near the bone reaches 165°F (74°C), about 40 minutes. Let the chickens rest for 10 minutes before carving.

make the beurre poulet

Do this while the chicken roasts. In a wide saucepan on medium-high heat, reduce the chicken stock by half, then add the olive brine. Remove the pan from the heat and slowly add the butter pieces while whisking by hand or using an immersion blender; add a hunk, whisk, whisk, whisk, add another hunk. Once all the butter is emulsified, set the sauce aside, leaving it on the warm stovetop so it doesn't break. Before serving, whisk any pan sauces that have accumulated into the sauce and check the seasoning, adding salt and lemon juice to taste.

make the fried lemons

Do this while your chickens rest. In a medium saucepan, heat the oil to 300°F (150°C). Double-check your lemon slices for seeds, pick out any that escaped your notice, and dredge the slices in the cornstarch (cornflour), tapping off any excess. Lower the dredged slices gently into the oil and fry until crispy, about 2 minutes. Remove to a plate topped with a paper towel and sprinkle with salt.

to serve

Carve the chicken into pieces, reserving the backbone to make a lemony stock later.

Arrange the pieces onto warmed plates or a warmed platter and spoon the beurre poulet over the chicken, then top with the fried lemons and herbs.

Chicken Cutlets with Date, Almond & Yogurt

This dish can be thrown together relatively quickly, at least within the context of many of this book's recipes, especially if you prep the dates in advance. I love it served with a simple cucumber, melon, and feta salad, or just some lightly dressed arugula (rocket). Keep it loose and you can't go wrong. For the dates, seek out barhi, empress, medjool, or a mix of all three.

Serves 4

date chutney
½ cup (100 g) granulated sugar
4 ounces (120 g) fresh ginger, peeled and thinly sliced
8 ounces (225 g) pitted fresh dates
1 ounce (30 g) preserved lemon rind, finely diced

fried chicken
4 boneless, skin-on chicken breasts
oil, for greasing
2 cups (240 g) all-purpose (plain) flour
2 teaspoons kosher salt, plus extra for seasoning
2 teaspoons freshly ground black pepper
6 large eggs, lightly beaten with 2 tablespoons cold water
2 cups (260 g) panko breadcrumbs, finely ground (see Note)
Clarified Butter (page 323), for shallow-frying

to serve
½ cup (120 ml) plain Greek yogurt
2 ounces (60 g) roasted almonds, toasted
picked fresh mint leaves

Note: You can buy fine-ground panko, or just zip, zip, zip the regular version in your food processor.

make the date chutney

In a medium saucepan, bring 1½ cups (350 ml) water and the sugar to a boil. Add the sliced ginger, then lower the heat and simmer until its spiciness is dulled, about 30 minutes.

Using the fine disk of your food mill, purée the dates. It's a sticky business, so if any mashed dates won't go through the grate, scoop them out of the food mill and add to the processed dates; just no pits, please. That would be, ahem, the pits.

Remove the ginger from the syrup and chop finely. Combine the dates, preserved lemon, ginger, and ¼ cup plus 1 tablespoon (75 ml) of the ginger syrup (reserve the remainder for another use). The chutney will keep for up to 6 months in an airtight container in the refrigerator.

make the fried chicken

Using the flat side of a meat mallet, pound the chicken, shiny side up, between layers of greased parchment paper or plastic wrap (clingfilm) to a thickness of ⅓ inch (1 cm). I recommend starting from the center and working out.

In a wide, shallow bowl, whisk together the flour, salt, and black pepper. In two more separate bowls, put the beaten eggs and panko.

To shallow-fry the cutlets, heat a large, high-sided cast-iron skillet over medium heat; and after a few minutes, add enough clarified butter to your skillet so the melted depth is ½ inch (1.3 cm).

Meanwhile, dip each piece of chicken into the seasoned flour, tapping off any excess. Next, dip the chicken into the eggs, letting any excess drip back into the bowl, then dredge in the breadcrumbs, coating completely. Place the chicken on a rack set in a sheet tray until it's time to fry.

The clarified butter is hot enough when a tiny bit of flour added to it sizzles immediately. Add the chicken to the hot butter one piece at a time. If you have enough room for 2 pieces in your skillet, great, but don't overcrowd them. Fry until golden, about 3 minutes, then flip and fry the other side. Remove the fried chicken to paper towels and sprinkle with salt. Repeat the frying method with the other pieces.

to serve

The plating of this dish is really up to you. You could serve the chicken with a quenelle of date chutney and yogurt and then sprinkle it all over with the roasted almonds and mint. Or, you can serve little dishes of everything on the side and let folks choose their own adventure. There are no rules.

page 233

Lonnie's Quail

In the penultimate scene of *Flirting with Disaster*, David O. Russell's brilliant, second full-length movie, Ben Stiller's character meets his birth parents, played by Lily Tomlin and Alan Alda. Their other son, Lonnie, feels threatened by his new brother, but he prepares the special quail that he "bagged that morning" for the occasion. The quail doesn't look that good, and also, it is laced with LSD, but I've always dreamed of helping Lonnie cook something that really impresses. Maybe it would give him confidence.

Serves 4

chicken mousse
1 pound (455 g) boneless, skinless chicken breast, cut into ½-inch (1.3-cm) pieces
1 cup (240 ml) heavy (double) cream
3 large egg whites
¼ teaspoon kosher salt

choux pastry
¼ cup (60 g) whole (full-fat) milk
4 tablespoons (56 g) unsalted butter
¼ teaspoon kosher salt
2 tablespoons all-purpose (plain) flour
1 large whole egg

morel and truffle stuffing
1 tablespoon (14 g) unsalted butter
8 ounces (225 g) morel mushrooms, cleaned and thinly sliced
4 ounces (120 g) black truffles, chopped
2 ounces (60 g) shallots, minced
1 tablespoon grated garlic
¼ cup (60 ml) port

poached stuffed quail
4 quail (see Note)
kosher salt
freshly ground black pepper
2 tablespoons olive oil
2 tablespoons (28 g) unsalted butter

truffle sauce
6 tablespoons (84 g) unsalted butter
3 ounces (85 g) shallots, thinly sliced
2 cups (475 ml) dry vermouth
2 cups (475 ml) Rachael's Chicken Stock (page 334)
2 cups (475 ml) heavy (double) cream
1 tablespoon grated garlic
2 ounces (60 g) black truffles, finely chopped
kosher salt
2 tablespoons thinly sliced chives

sautéed spinach
2 tablespoons (28 g) unsalted butter
1 pound (455 g) Bloomsdale spinach, washed, excess stems removed
kosher salt

Note: Each quail should be entirely deboned as you would a chicken; your butcher may be able to do this for you.

make the chicken mousse

In the bowl of your food processor, add the chicken pieces, cream, egg whites, and salt. Process until smooth. Remove from the food processor, cover, and set aside.

make the choux pastry

In a heavy-bottom saucepan, add the milk, butter, and salt. Cook over low heat so the butter melts before the mixture comes to a boil. Once boiling, immediately remove the pan from the heat. Add the flour all at once to shock it, then, with a wooden spoon, begin mixing the flour into the hot butter mixture. Keep mixing until a smooth dough forms. Return the pan to medium heat for 3 to 4 minutes, stirring constantly, to dry out the dough. You'll know it's ready when your wooden spoon can be pushed into the center of the dough and stand up straight without falling over.

Remove from the heat and transfer the dough to a mixing bowl. With your wooden spoon, smooth the dough evenly around the edges of the bowl to help it cool slightly. Give it 5 minutes to cool and then add the egg, beating it in with the spoon. When you add the egg, you'll think you've ruined it. Keep stirring, it'll come together. I like to stir with a wooden spoon and scrape the sides of the bowl with a flexible spatula. Cool the dough to room temperature.

make the morel and truffle stuffing

While the choux pastry is cooling, in a medium saucepan over medium heat, melt the butter; once it stops foaming, add the morels, black truffles, shallots, and garlic. Cook until the shallots are soft but have no color, about 6 to 8 minutes. Add the port and reduce by half. Remove from the heat and cool to room temperature.

Fold the cooled choux pastry into the chicken mousse, followed by the cooled morel mixture. Cover and set aside.

make the poached stuffed quail

Weigh out your stuffing, dividing it into 4 equal portions.

Now, it's time to torque (see page 34). With a roll of plastic wrap (clingfilm) about 2 feet (60 cm) in front of you, pull out a piece of plastic wrap but do not remove it from the roll. Flatten the pulled wrap and set one of the deboned quail, skin side down, in the center, about 4 inches (10 cm) in front of you. The quail should be positioned sideways on the wrap, with the leg meat facing the right-hand side. Grab a portion of the stuffing and, with your hands, roll it into a large ball and then form into an oblong cylinder. Place the stuffing onto the quail, about 1 inch (2.5 cm) in, running horizontally from neck to leg.

Next, lift the edge of the plastic wrap closest to you and start rolling it over the meat, tightening it as you go. Twist one end, creating tension, and tie it off with butcher's twine. Twist and tie the other end and secure with twine.

Repeat the entire process with the remaining quail and stuffing.

Set your immersion circulator to 135°F (57°C). Sous-vide (aka poach) the wrapped quail for 1 hour.

When the quail is done poaching, move it to an ice bath and chill for 30 minutes. At this point, the quail can be refrigerated until you're ready to serve it, up to 2 days. If serving right away, leave it to come to room temperature.

make the truffle sauce

While the quail poaches, in a sauté pan over medium heat, melt half of the butter and cook the shallots until soft but do not take on any color, about 2 minutes. Add the vermouth and reduce by half. Add the chicken stock and reduce by half. Next, add the cream and, you guessed it, reduce by half.

Remove from the heat and cool for a few minutes, then transfer to a blender and purée until smooth. Strain through a fine-mesh sieve, discarding the solids.

In a clean pan, melt the remaining butter with the garlic and truffles over low heat, cooking just enough to make fragrant. The combo of butter/garlic/truffles is perfect; really take in that smell, waft it on yourself like cologne.

Add the strained sauce to the pan and adjust the seasoning with salt. Wait to add the chives until right before serving... like right before. I'll remind you. Don't do it yet, we have to crisp up the quail.

Unroll the plastic wrap from the poached quail. If it has been refrigerated, allow it to sit at room temperature for at least 30 minutes. Dry each one with a kitchen towel and season with salt and black pepper.

In a large, high-sided skillet on medium-high heat, heat the olive oil and butter. Once the butter has stopped foaming, add all the stuffed quail and cook until browned on each side, rolling it through the fat to get the skin nice and crispy. Once the internal temperature reaches 165°F (74°C), remove the quail from the pan to a cutting (chopping) board to rest for 5 minutes.

make the sautéed spinach

In the same skillet, melt the remaining 2 tablespoons butter over medium heat, scraping up any fond from the pan as it melts. Once the butter has stopped foaming, add the spinach and sauté until wilted. Season with salt.

to serve

Carve each quail into rounds, about ¾ inch (2 cm) thick. Plate the spinach, followed by the quail rounds. Stir the chives into the truffle sauce and serve it on the side or pour it around the quail on each plate. Make sure you eat the dish while watching *Flirting with Disaster*.

STARTERS & SNACKS	238 → 249
HOT PLATES	250 → 261
OFFAL	262 → 278
ENTRÉES & LARGE FORMAT	279 → 296

Beef & Lamb

Tallow-Fried Potato Peels

Serves as many as you like

potato peels
Beef Tallow (page 339)
Birdie Bay Spice (page 311)

This is not a fixed recipe, but a guide for using potato peels as you produce them. Start with 1 quart (about 1 liter) of beef tallow and add more from there, depending on the quantity of peels. There should be enough oil so that the peels are completely submerged and have room to cook evenly. After frying, strain the tallow through a coffee filter set in a fine-mesh sieve that's resting over a bowl. Reserve the tallow at room temperature, covered, and reuse it several times in this way.

    I added these peels to the menu at Rustic Canyon years ago, joking far too frequently that they paid for our annual holiday party.

As you're peeling potatoes, add the peels to a bowl of cold water, flush, and agitate with more cold water until the water runs clear. This will wash off all the starch. Dry the peels on paper or kitchen towels.

In a heavy-bottom pot, heat the tallow to 325°F (165°C) and fry the peels until golden and crispy. Drain the fried peels on paper towels and then toss them in a little spice mix.

Steak Tartare "Birdie G's" with Mushroom Carpaccio

Elevating button mushrooms is one of my favorite things to do. Look, heirloom produce is wonderful. Obviously. We're super privileged here in California, we get outstanding produce. But there's something so nice about elevating something most folks think of as ordinary or pedestrian.

Making this mushroom carpaccio is an excellent lesson for any cook. Here's why: it can't be seasoned beforehand. It's not a salad where you can take a leaf out to test for salt and acid. You have to use your "brain palate." You have to work on developing your muscle memory for seasoning. It's instinctual. What do the grains of salt feel like? How many drops of lemon juice are needed? How much olive oil? You're tasting it in your mind. If it's not perfectly seasoned, it's not very good. If done right, it's a beautiful dish. It's a surprise.

The carpaccio can be served as is but gets further elevated when paired with the tartare. Try it both ways. If you're a young cook—if you bought this book hoping to glean some knowledge—master the mushroom carpaccio. Work that part of your culinary journey and learn to trust your instincts. Button mushrooms are cheap, it won't be a wasted exercise. Any surplus from your training can easily be added to scrambled eggs or sautéed to serve alongside a steak, among other applications.

Serves 4

steak tartare
1 pound (455 g) lean beef (sirloin, tenderloin, or flatiron)
3 ounces (90 g) Beef Tendon Terrine (page 47), cut into fine brunoise
2 tablespoons extra-virgin olive oil
3 tablespoons Sungold Tomato Ketchup (page 300)
2 tablespoons Aioli (page 321)
2 tablespoons Dijon mustard
1 tablespoon Mushroom Worcestershire, made with porcini (page 319)
1 teaspoon hot sauce
3 tablespoons minced shallot
3 tablespoons finely sliced chives
3 tablespoons finely diced Pickled Cornichons (page 314)
3 tablespoons chopped capers
2 large egg yolks
kosher salt
freshly ground black pepper

mushroom carpaccio
8 ounces (225 g) white button mushrooms
3 to 4 tablespoons olive oil
lemon juice, for seasoning
kosher salt
2 tablespoons finely sliced chives

to serve
flaky sea salt

make the steak tartare	Before I start cutting the beef, I fold a paper towel into a 1-inch (2.5-cm) strip, wet it, and then fold it in half lengthwise. I use this to clean my knife after each slice, helping the blade glide through the beef.
	Slice the beef against the grain into strips, about ⅛ inch (0.3 cm) thick. Slice, wipe the knife clean, slice, and repeat. Next, cut the slices into ⅛-inch (0.3-cm) batons (a fancy word for matchsticks). Then, dice the batons into ⅛-inch (0.3-cm) cubes.
	In a large mixing bowl, combine the beef, tendon terrine, and olive oil and mix with a fork. Add the ketchup, aioli, mustard, Worcestershire, and hot sauce, and mix well. Add the shallot, chives, cornichons, and capers, then mix well. Lastly, add the egg yolks and mix to combine. Season with kosher salt and black pepper.
make the mushroom carpaccio	First, peel the mushrooms. Holding a mushroom stem side up, use a bird's beak knife to reach under the cap and peel back the thin outer layer, working all the way around the mushroom. Repeat with the remaining mushrooms, then slice them all paper thin on a mandoline.
	Arrange the mushroom slices on the bottom of each of 4 plates, dividing evenly. Season with the olive oil, some drips of lemon juice, kosher salt, and the chives, again dividing evenly.
to serve	Center a portion of tartare in the middle of each plate and sprinkle with flaky sea salt.

Beef Carpaccio ZZ's Style

In 2013, my wife and I were in New York City, and stumbled into ZZ's Clam Bar, a just-then-opened spot from the folks at Carbone. It was a tiny place that maybe sat fifteen people. I ordered a cocktail that came in a coconut. The coconut was smoking a cigarette. Everything on the menu seemed a little over the top and irreverent. I loved it.

One dish's $150 price tag jumped off the page: a beef carpaccio covered in all the most expensive things. We were so curious. And also, young. And drunk on and in New York City. When it came and we dug in, we were instantly furious, mad that it was as delicious as it was. Mad that we got our money's worth?

We still talk about that dish. "Remember that carpaccio from ZZ's?"

This is my take, covered in all the things. Ready for you to be furious about.

Serves 6

beef carpaccio
1 tablespoon black peppercorns, coarsely ground
1 tablespoon coriander seed, coarsely ground
1 tablespoon kosher salt
18 ounces (510 g) prime beef tenderloin
¼ cup (60 ml) Dijon mustard
3 tablespoons grapeseed oil
nonstick cooking spray, for plastic wrap (clingfilm)

shrimp
12 shrimp (prawns), shell on, cleaned
2 lemons

geoduck clam
1 geoduck clam, cleaned
kosher salt

to top
3 tablespoons Yuzu Kosho Sauce (page 302)
18 oysters, shucked
12 uni tongues
3 ounces (85 g) caviar
flaky sea salt

make the beef carpaccio

Mix together the black pepper, coriander, and kosher salt. Coat the tenderloin in the mustard and then the spice mixture.

Heat the grapeseed oil in a heavy-bottom skillet and sear the tenderloin, about 2 minutes per side, until browned all over. Remove the meat from the skillet and let cool to room temperature. Tightly wrap the cooled tenderloin in plastic wrap (clingfilm) and freeze for 1 hour to help the meat firm up for easier slicing.

Remove the tenderloin from the freezer and unwrap it. On your cutting (chopping) board, slice the tenderloin against the grain into ½ inch (1 cm) slices. Next, place each slice between pieces of plastic wrap sprayed with nonstick cooking spray. With the flat side of your meat mallet, pound to roughly the thinness of 2 sheets of paper; start in the center of the slice and pound out to the edges. Work in even strokes, taking care not to rip or mash the meat. Keep each freshly pounded slice between the plastic until you're ready to plate the dish, and chill the slices while you prepare the other components.

make the shrimp

To poach the shrimp (prawns), combine 2 quarts (1.9 liters) of water, 2 tablespoons of kosher salt, and the 2 lemons (halved and squeezed) in a large pot. Bring the mixture to a boil, then remove from the heat and add the shrimp. Wait 1 minute, then add enough ice to cool it down, 3–4 minutes. Remove the shrimp from the pot with a large spider and spread them out on kitchen towel to drain. Peel and devein the shrimp.

make the geoduck clam

Purge the geoduck clam in cold water heavily salted with kosher salt for 1 hour. This will help remove any silt or sand. Lift from the water and cut it off with a knife just above where the shell starts. Blanch the clam in boiling water for 10 seconds, then shock it in ice water. To peel, start at the end where you cut it away from the shell; you'll see a loose membrane that almost looks like sausage skin. Pull it all the way down the length of the clam and discard the membrane. Slice the peeled clam into ⅛-inch (0.3-cm) pieces. Refrigerate in an airtight container until you're ready to serve.

to top

On a chilled platter, arrange the slices of tenderloin, slightly overlapping at times to close up any gaps. Brush the meat with a thin layer of the yuzu kosho sauce. Arrange the shrimp on top of the beef, followed by (in this order): the clam slices, oysters, uni tongues, and small dollops of the caviar. Sprinkle all over with flaky sea salt, and serve.

Beef Tendon, Tofu, Sweet Chili & Almond

I usually crave this kind of snack: soft, creamy, crunchy, sweet, nutty, spicy, and salty.

    Healthy, even.

Serves 4

16 ounces (450 g) extra-soft kumidashi cup tofu (see Sources, page 350)
¼ cup (60 ml) Sweet Chili Sauce (page 303)
2 tablespoons toasted almonds, chopped
zest and juice of 1 lime
8 ounces (225 g) Beef Tendon Terrine (page 47), cut into 1½ × ⅛-inch (3.8 × 0.3-cm) strips
8 ounces (225 g) yuba (tofu skin), cut into 1½-inch (3.8-cm) strips
extra-virgin olive oil, for drizzling
flaky sea salt
fresh basil leaves, to garnish
flowering cilantro (coriander), to garnish

Gently spoon the tofu into the center of a plate or bowl, disturbing its structure as minimally as possible. Smother with the chili sauce, then top with the almonds and lime zest and juice. Arrange the tendon and yuba strips on top, obscuring the tofu completely. Finish with a drizzle of olive oil, some grains of flaky sea salt, and a sprinkling of basil leaves and flowering cilantro (coriander).

Spanish Tortilla but Like a Reuben

If you're doing a good job as a chef in a restaurant, you're constantly trying to come up with ways to use up the scraps and leftovers. The trick is creating something that feels authentic and tastes delicious. Not just a hodge-podge of trimmings with no rhyme or reason. This is one such dish. I've been making Spanish tortilla since my Ubuntu days, but this version is very much Birdie G's.

Serves 8

Russian dressing
2 cups (475 ml) Aioli (page 321)
1 tablespoon brine from Dill Pickles (page 312) or Pickled Cornichons (page 314)
1 tablespoon ketchup (see Note)
1 tablespoon hot sauce
2 teaspoons prepared horseradish
1 teaspoon honey

tortilla
14 large eggs
1 cup (240 ml) heavy (double) cream
2 teaspoons kosher salt
2 pounds (910 g) Russet potatoes, peeled
1 pound (455 g) Sauerkraut (page 320), drained
1 pound (455 g) Corned Beef Brisket (page 73), coarsely chopped (great use of scraps)
8 tablespoons (110 g) unsalted butter

Note: You can use the Sungold Tomato Ketchup (page 300) for the dressing, but you may prefer to buy the standard red ketchup for the color.

make the Russian dressing

Mix together all the ingredients and refrigerate, covered, until you're ready to serve, up to 1 week.

make the tortilla

Preheat your oven to 350°F (180°C).

Crack the eggs into a large mixing bowl and whisk to combine. Add the cream and salt and stir to combine. Using either a box grater or food processor, shred the potatoes, hash browns-style, adding them to the egg bowl as you go to avoid oxidation. Next, add the sauerkraut and corned beef brisket and mix well.

In a 12- or 14-inch (30- or 36-cm) cast-iron skillet or nonstick pan, melt the butter on medium-high heat. When the butter starts to brown, pour in the egg mixture, but do not shake the pan. Don't even let the thought of shaking the pan enter your mind. I feel like you just thought about it.

When a little bit of color appears on the edges, gently put the pan into the oven. Be careful not to tilt the pan as you put it in. You only narrowly avoided shaking.

Cook for 15 minutes, turn the oven down to 275°F (135°C), and continue cooking for an additional 30 minutes, or until golden brown and a cake tester inserted in the middle comes out clean. Remove the pan from the oven.

Use an offset spatula to loosen the sides of the tortilla from the pan, then carefully slide it onto a sheet pan fitted with a rack and let it rest for about 15 minutes.

Cut into triangles, the size of which is up to you. Serve with the Russian dressing.

Waffled Corned Beef Hash

This is another great way to use up leftover Corned Beef Brisket (page 73). You could, of course, serve these with Crème Fraîche (page 322), Aioli (page 321), or the Russian dressing from the Spanish Tortilla but like a Reuben (page 247). Or get really fancy and top them with caviar and sea urchin.

I recommend steaming and peeling the potatoes ahead of time, so you can throw the dish together quickly when you're ready.

Serves 4 to 6

1½ pounds (680 g) Russet potatoes
1 pound (455 g) Corned Beef Brisket (page 73), coarsely chopped
6 tablespoons Clarified Butter (page 323), warmed
4 ounces (120 g) white onion, thinly sliced into half-moons
1 teaspoon kosher salt, plus extra to taste
1½ teaspoons potato starch
2 tablespoons chopped fresh dill
2 tablespoons chopped fresh Italian parsley
nonstick cooking spray, for waffle iron

Fill a saucepan with water and bring to a simmer, then place the potatoes in a steamer basket set over the pan. Cover and cook the potatoes for 25 to 30 minutes. They shouldn't be super soft, more par-cooked, so check them often to rate their progress.

Remove the potatoes to a rack set over a sheet pan and cool them to room temperature. Remove the skins; they should peel right off, but if there are stubborn spots, use a paring knife to help them along. Once the skins are removed, chill the potatoes in the refrigerator. (Save the potato skins to make Tallow-Fried Potato Peels on page 238).

Once chilled, shred the potatoes with the largest holes of a box grater, not the slicer side, into a mixing bowl and gently mix in the corned beef brisket, clarified butter, onion, salt, potato starch, dill, and parsley with a fork.

Heat your waffle iron, and grease with nonstick cooking spray. Test a bit of the mix by frying 1 tablespoon. Taste it for seasoning and adjust with more salt if necessary. Once you're pleased as punch with the seasoning, cook the remaining mix in the waffle iron according to the manufacturer's directions. Serve hot and crispy.

Sloppy Jeremy

My version of a Sloppy Joe, the Sloppy Jeremy, is a grown-up, cheffed-up ode to a childhood favorite I ate from the can.

Serves 4

sloppy
1¾ pounds (800 g) ground (minced) beef, 80/20 blend
1 tablespoon kosher salt, plus extra to taste
1 tablespoon minced shallot
2 teaspoons grated garlic
2 teaspoons porcini powder
2 teaspoons fennel seed, coarsely crushed
2 teaspoons freshly cracked black pepper
½ cup (120 ml) Rachael's Chicken Stock (page 334)
¼ cup (60 g) Strawberry Sofrito (page 307)
¼ cup plus 2 tablespoons (90 ml) balsamic vinegar
6 tablespoons (84 g) unsalted butter, cold, cut into pieces

horseradish cream
8 ounces (225 g) cream cheese, room temperature
¼ cup (60 g) prepared horseradish plus 2 tablespoons brine from the jar

to serve
8 tablespoons (110 g) unsalted butter, room temperature
4 slices Pain de Mie (page 328), sliced 1½ inches (3.5 cm) thick
spicy greens, such as nasturtium, arugula (rocket), or watercress, for finishing

make the sloppy

In a large, high-sided skillet over medium heat, cook the ground (minced) beef while adding the salt until the meat is brown with no signs of pink, then drain off the fat. Stir in the shallot, garlic, porcini powder, fennel seed, and black pepper and cook just until fragrant. Add the chicken stock, strawberry sofrito, and balsamic vinegar. Cook at a slight simmer until it reaches the familiar sauciness, 10 to 15 minutes. Remove from the heat, mount with the butter, and check the seasoning for more salt.

make the horseradish cream

Combine the cream cheese, prepared horseradish, and horseradish brine and mix well to combine. Refrigerate in an airtight container until ready to serve.

to serve

Butter the bread slices on both sides and toast in a hot skillet until golden brown, flipping them halfway through.

Put a piece of toast on each plate, cover it with the sloppy, and top with a dollop of horseradish cream and a sprinkling of greens.

Mongolian Flanken Ribs

Mongolian beef became one of my favorite things as an early teenager, after my mom started taking me to a place near our house in Atlanta called Golden Empress. By this time, she had begun to make enough money in the cemetery business for the weekly dinner out, and Golden Empress was the first place where I became a regular. To this day, I use their Mongolian beef as the blueprint in combining flavors and textures.

The lovely woman who owned Golden Empress, Phong Lee, also owned a salon and cut my hair. Between my time in her salon chair and a booth at the restaurant, Phong Lee was probably the person I conversed with the most during those years. I've never been much of a talker. It's not that I don't want to, I do, but it's just not something I ever figured out how to do. It feels like attempting to join in on a game of Double Dutch and not being able to make the jump. I still think of her, and Golden Empress, every once in a while. Her kindness lingers.

Serves 4 to 6

4 pounds (1.8 kg) bone-in beef flanken ribs, thinly sliced
2 cups (475 ml) Tiki Sauce (page 303)
1 cup (90 g) each thinly sliced white and green parts of scallions (spring onions)
1 cup (240 ml) grapeseed oil
kosher salt
freshly ground black pepper
flaky sea salt
¼ cup (35 g) benne or white sesame seeds (untoasted)

In a large container, combine the ribs with half of the tiki sauce, turning to coat, then cover and marinate overnight in the refrigerator.

The next day, to a mixing bowl, add the sliced white scallion (spring onion) parts. In a small saucepan, heat the grapeseed oil until smoking, then slowly pour the hot oil over the scallion whites (it will sizzle) and mix with a fork. Season with kosher salt.

Remove the ribs from the marinade and allow them to come to room temperature, about 1 hour.

Set up your grill (barbecue) for direct heat cooking. Season the tempered ribs with salt and black pepper and grill them briefly, brushing with the remaining tiki sauce, until just cooked through, 3 to 5 minutes per side. Remove from the grill and brush with more sauce. Sprinkle with flaky sea salt.

Plate with a scattering of sliced scallion tops, and benne or sesame seeds.

Merguez Sausage with Loaded Eggplant

I like serving whole vegetables that haven't been fussed with a lot—what I call "on the bone," as if they're rustic cuts of meat. Here, instead of scooping out the flesh, we're serving the eggplants (aubergines) baked potato-style in their charred skins. Allowing them to steam after grilling helps infuse the flesh with even more flavor and lets the excess liquid seep out. Merguez with eggplant is a classic pairing, and I think this method turns it on its head a little, while still being rustic and not fussy.

Serves 4

4 Italian eggplants (aubergines; each about 6 inches/15 cm)
2 pounds (910 g) Merguez Sausage (page 77)
1 cup (240 ml) plain full-fat Greek yogurt
¼ cup (60 g) Ohio Peppers (page 317)
¼ cup (60 g) thinly sliced scallions (spring onions)
2 tablespoons thinly sliced chives
1 tablespoon preserved lemon rind, pith removed, cut into ½-inch (1.3-cm) strips
2 lemons, halved
extra-virgin olive oil, for drizzling
kosher salt
flaky sea salt
fresh spearmint leaves, to garnish

How you prepare your grill (barbecue) depends on whether it uses charcoal or gas.

If you're using a charcoal grill, you'll need to prepare it for both direct and indirect heat cooking from the start. Build your coals in 2 piles on opposite sides of the grill for direct heat; the middle zone is your indirect heat. Place the rack 6 inches (15 cm) above the embers once they're glowing.

If you're using a gas grill, heat one side to medium-high direct heat (you can adjust the settings once you are ready to grill the sausages).

First, grill the eggplants (aubergines) over direct heat, turning as they cook, until the skin is blackened and crisp all over, about 8 to 10 minutes.

Transfer the charred eggplant to a heat-safe container, spread them out, and cover tightly with plastic wrap (clingfilm). Let them steam in the residual heat until softened all the way through, 20 to 30 minutes. Discard the released liquid or save it for another application; it'll be smoky and slightly viscous.

Meanwhile, grill the sausages. You don't want them to char and split before they're cooked through, so I cook them on indirect heat until they're almost done, then finish them over direct heat.

On your prepared charcoal grill, start them in the middle zone until they reach an internal temperature of 165°F (74°C), then move over the hot coals to get nice and browned.

For a gas grill, raise the heat to high on either side of the grill and turn the middle to very low. The same cooking principle applies.

Remove the sausages from the grill and let rest on a plate for 5 minutes.

To serve, cut a slit across the top of each eggplant and squeeze so the flesh protrudes from the skin, baked potato-style. Season with kosher salt, then top with the yogurt, Ohio peppers, scallions (spring onions), chives, and preserved lemon, dividing evenly.

Plate an eggplant next to the sausage, with lemons for squeezing. Drizzle the eggplant with olive oil, sprinkle with flaky sea salt, and finish with spearmint leaves.

Lamb Shawarma Platter

Here, chef Adam Lambert's Lamb Shawarma (page 62) is served in a way that best translates how the gyros were presented at Gyro Wrap Cafe, a small place I worked at during high school in Atlanta—with pita, cucumbers, yogurt, herbs, and spreads. In no way do I claim that this is an authentic presentation, but it is 100 percent nostalgic.

Serves 4 to 6

garlic-mint yogurt
1 cup (240 ml) plain Greek yogurt
1 garlic clove, grated
20 fresh mint leaves, chopped
kosher salt

smashed cucumbers
12 ounces (340 g) Persian cucumbers
1 tablespoon olive oil
juice of ½ lemon
20 fresh Italian parsley leaves, chopped
1 teaspoon kosher salt

gyro lamb slices
1½ pounds (700 g) Ohio City Provision's Lamb Shawarma (page 62)

to serve
8 spearmint sprigs
8 Italian parsley sprigs
1 tablespoon Aleppo chili powder
olive oil, for drizzling
4 pita breads, halved to form 8 pockets
kosher salt

make the garlic-mint yogurt — In a mixing bowl, stir to combine the yogurt, garlic, and mint leaves. Season with salt and chill the yogurt until you're ready to assemble the platter.

make the smashed cucumbers — With the back of your chef's knife, smash the cucumbers, cut off the ends, then cut them roughly into manageable chunks along the bash lines. Toss them with the olive oil, lemon juice, chopped parsley, and salt. Set aside.

make the gyro lamb slices — After being chilled, the sous-vide loaves of the gyro meat will be covered in a layer of lamb fat. Not only does this layer help preserve the product, but it keeps the interior moist and will be handy for warming the meat or adding to other dishes.

Take one of the loaves from the sealed bag and remove this outside layer of fat. It should pop off much like candle wax. Save the fat. While still cold, cut the loaves into slices the width of thick-cut bacon. Weigh as you go; we're looking for 1½ pounds (700 g) of sliced meat for 4 to 6 people.

In a large cast-iron skillet, warm 1 tablespoon of the reserved lamb fat over medium heat. Working in batches to avoid crowding the pan, cook the slices until warmed through but not crisp, 1 to 2 minutes per side. Add another tablespoon of fat between batches to keep the meat coated and juicy.

to serve — Get together all your bits, leaving the sprigs of spearmint and parsley whole for guests to pick the leaves. Have the Aleppo chili powder and some kosher salt and olive oil in separate dishes.

For the assembly, you have options. You can fill the pitas with the lamb and place them on one large platter, plate 4 to 6 individual servings, or set out the lamb, pita, and accompaniments in multiple dishes that folks can grab from to serve themselves.

Beef Pelmeni Stroganoff

Pelmeni are like cute little Russian ravioli. My introduction to pelmeni was made by chef Christopher Kostow when he was the final guest chef of Birdie G's first annual "8 Nights" dinner series in 2022. He left the molds behind, and we began using them soon after. I am a sucker for stroganoff, as I am with pretty much anything that reminds me of the frozen meals from Stouffer's during my childhood.

Serves 8 to 12

filling
1 pound (455 g) ground (minced) beef, 80/20 blend
1 cup (125 g) white onion, cut into fine dice
2 large eggs
4 teaspoons Mushroom Worcestershire, made with porcini (page 319)
3 tablespoons fresh dill leaves, finely chopped
2 tablespoons finely sliced chives, plus extra to serve
1 tablespoon grated garlic
1 tablespoon kosher salt
1 teaspoon freshly ground white pepper

dough
4 cups (480 g) all-purpose (plain) flour, plus more for dusting
1 tablespoon kosher salt
4 large eggs
3 tablespoons white wine

sauce
1 pound (455 g) beef chuck, cut into 1-inch (2.5-cm) pieces
1 teaspoon kosher salt, plus extra to taste
1 teaspoon black peppercorns
2 teaspoons fresh rosemary leaves, chopped
1 teaspoon fresh thyme leaves, chopped
1 bay leaf
3 tablespoons Beef Tallow (page 339)
8 ounces (225 g) mushrooms of choice (porcini, cremini, button, or king trumpet), cut into randomly shaped pieces no larger than bite-size
1 large white onion, cut into ½-inch (1.3-cm) pieces
1½ cups (375 ml) white wine
1 quart (0.9 liter) Rachael's Chicken Stock (page 334)
2 teaspoons porcini powder
2 tablespoons Dijon mustard
1 tablespoon Mushroom Worcestershire, made with porcini (page 319)
1 cup (225 g) Crème Fraîche (page 322), plus extra to serve

Note: For this recipe, you'll need a traditional pelmeni mold, which looks like a honeycomb-shaped stencil and makes multiple ravioli at once.

make the filling

Using your stand mixer and the paddle attachment, beat together all the ingredients until combined. Cook a piece in a small skillet to test for seasoning, adjusting with more salt and black pepper to taste. Cool to room temperature and refrigerate, covered, until ready to use.

make the dough

In the clean bowl of your stand mixer, this time fitted with the dough hook, mix the flour and salt for 30 seconds.

In a separate bowl, stir together the eggs and wine.

With the mixer on low speed, slowly pour the egg mixture into the flour mixture. Beat on low until the dough is smooth and slightly shiny. If it is too dry, add a little water, 1 teaspoon at a time. Turn the dough out of the bowl and knead it briefly by hand to incorporate any crumbs. Wrap in plastic wrap (clingfilm) and allow it to rest at room temperature for 1 hour before rolling out.

make the sauce

While the dough is resting, in a mixing bowl, season the beef chuck with the salt and mix well.

Line an additional mixing bowl with cheesecloth (muslin), then add the black peppercorns, rosemary, thyme, and bay leaf. Set aside.

In a large Dutch oven on medium-high heat, heat the tallow until it reaches the smoking point. This may seem like a lot of fat but it helps the ingredients caramelize more evenly, and you'll drain it off later.

Working carefully to avoid splashing the tallow, add the beef chuck to the pot; kitchen tongs help with this task. Spread the pieces evenly… this is not a "crowd-the-pan" situation. You may need to work in batches. Let the meat chunks sit undisturbed until they have a nicely caramelized sear underneath, then gently stir (or flip them) to allow the other sides to caramelize, about 8 to 10 minutes. Reduce the heat to medium if it seems too aggressive. Remove the meat from the pan with a slotted spoon to a strainer set in a heatproof container, leaving the tallow behind.

To the tallow, add the mushrooms and cook until deeply caramelized, stirring often to brown evenly, about 8 to 10 minutes. Remove them from the pan with a slotted spoon to the cheesecloth-lined bowl containing the peppercorns and herbs.

Now, add the onion to the same pot and caramelize these nicely as well, stirring frequently; this will take 4 to 5 minutes. Transfer to the cheesecloth-lined bowl. With butcher's twine, tie off the cheesecloth into a sachet.

Increase the heat to fairly high again and deglaze it with the wine, scraping the beautiful golden-brown bits (aka fond) from the pot. Bring the wine to a boil, reduce the heat to a gentle simmer, and reduce the wine by 75 percent.

Return the beef to the pot along with the chicken stock, herb sachet, porcini powder, mustard, and mushroom Worcestershire. Bring to a boil, reduce to a simmer, and reduce the liquid by half, about 30 minutes, at which time the sauce should be silky but not at all sticky.

Turn off the heat, transfer the sachet to a bowl, and whisk the crème fraîche into the stock mixture in the pot.

Strain this mixture through a fine-mesh sieve into a large heatproof container, pushing on the meat with a wooden spoon to remove as much liquid as possible. At this point, the sauce should resemble melted coffee ice cream.

[…]

[...]

Re-introduce the contents of the sachet to the sauce, adjust the seasoning with more salt to taste, and cool to room temperature. Refrigerate, covered, until ready to use.

The strained-off meat, while no longer leading-lady status, can still be enjoyed in cameo roles, such as added to scrambled eggs or gravy, or at the very least as a meal for canine royalty. Even when you're extracting a lot of flavor, as you did here, try not to waste anything.

To form the pelmeni, on a large, floured work surface, cut the dough into 4 equal sections with your bench knife. Keep the pieces wrapped in plastic wrap when you're not using them.

Dust your pelmeni mold with flour.

Roll out one piece of the dough to a round large enough to drape over the mold and a thickness of about 2 mm. Place the dough round over the pelmeni mold, pressing lightly to see the honeycomb pattern and individual circles. Scoop out 1 tablespoon of filling, rolling it between your palms into a little meatball, and place it in the middle of one of the little dough circles. Repeat the process until all the circles are filled.

Roll out another piece of the dough to the same shape and thickness. Drape it over the mold, covering up the meatball filling. Using a rolling pin, roll over the top of the mold, flattening the 2 pieces of dough together and causing the pattern of the mold to cut through entirely (the individual rounds will remain in the mold). Trim away the dough overhang around the edge of the mold. Now, invert the mold onto a floured work surface to release the pelmeni, giving any stuck ones a gentle nudge.

Repeat the process with the remaining 2 dough pieces and filling.

Fill a large pot with salted water, which should be salty like the sea, and bring to a boil. Gently add the pelmeni in batches and cook them for 3 to 4 minutes, or until they float to the top. Scoop the cooked pelmeni out of the water with a spider and transfer them to a bowl. Toss them with the sauce and serve in wide, shallow bowls, topped with a spoonful of crème fraîche and a sprinkling of chopped chives.

Corned Beef Tongue, Cornichon & Lovage

The combination of corned beef, pickles, and mustard is not my most creative work, but it's still a classic for a reason. I was surprised, though, by just how much the lovage elevated something so simple into a whole new idea. This combo instantly joined the ranks of my favorites.

Serves 4

lovage oil
2 teaspoons kosher salt
4 ounces (120 g) lovage leaves
½ cup (237 ml) grapeseed oil, cold

to serve
12 ounces (340 g) Corned Beef Tongue (page 66), thinly sliced
48 Pickled Cornichons (page 314)
2 tablespoons Pickled Mustard Seeds (page 318)
parsley leaves

make the lovage oil

In a mixing bowl, add the salt to the lovage leaves and let them sit for 30 minutes in the refrigerator. This next part may seem weird, but also put the base and container of your blender in the refrigerator as well. You want the oil to be as vibrantly green as possible, and that means using cold ingredients and equipment.

In the now-cold blender, combine the lovage leaves and oil and purée until very smooth. Strain the mix through 2 layers of cheesecloth (muslin) into an airtight container and freeze overnight.

The next day, decant the oil that is on top, leaving any frozen water that has leached from the mixture behind (and discarding).

At this point, the lovage oil can be frozen, tightly covered, for a few months, or kept in the refrigerator where the color may start to dull after a week or so.

to serve

On each of 4 plates, arrange the thinly sliced beef tongue, cornichons, and pickled mustard seeds, dividing evenly. Drizzle with the lovage oil and add a scattering of parsley leaves.

Creamed Chipped Beef Tongue

I used to love the boxed creamed chipped beef from Stouffer's as a kid. I knew how to use a microwave and could also handle dropping some bread in the toaster. I've heard the recipe has changed, and I'm devastated if that's true. If I see creamed chipped beef at a diner, I order it. My mother-in-law makes a dried beef dip around the holidays that hits all the creamed chipped beef notes, and I loathe sharing it.

This recipe is a cross between the classic version with béchamel and a rarebit sauce, one of my other favorite things. It's the best of each of my worlds. And it serves four to six folks or one hungry me.

Serves 4 to 6

4 tablespoons (56 g) unsalted butter
kosher salt
¼ cup (60 g) all-purpose (plain) flour
2 cups (475 ml) whole (full-fat) milk
12 ounces (355 ml) beer (see Note)
2 tablespoons Worcestershire sauce
1 tablespoon Dijon mustard
1 teaspoon hot sauce
1 cup (130 g) shredded white Cheddar cheese
9 slices Pain de Mie (page 328), sliced ½ inch (1.3 cm) thick
1 pound (455 g) Corned Beef Tongue (page 66), cut into 1/16-inch (2-mm) slices
freshly cracked black pepper

Note: You can use any beer in this recipe. Chances are if you like to drink it, you'll like it in the sauce.

Preheat your oven to 350°F (180°C).

Start by making the zinged-up béchamel sauce. In a large saucepan over medium heat, melt the butter with a pinch of salt. When it has stopped foaming, sprinkle in the flour and quickly whisk until a bubbling paste forms. Do not let the mixture take on any color. Whisking, add the milk in a slow, steady stream and continue whisking until well incorporated. Allow the mixture to bubble and thicken, whisking every few moments to prevent lumps.

In a small saucepan—sorry, you'll have to wash 2 pans—bring the beer to a boil and simmer until it's reduced by 75 percent. We're making a hoppy beer syrup. Remove from the heat and fold the syrup into the béchamel along with the Worcestershire, mustard, and hot sauce. Now, sprinkle in the cheese as you continue to whisk. You're looking for a pancake-batter consistency, not gloop. Adjust the seasoning with more salt to taste and remove the sauce from the heat. This can sit for a bit if you're moving on to other tasks; just rewarm it over medium heat and thin as needed with a little hot water.

Toast the slices of bread in a toaster or the preheated oven, then halve them diagonally.

Spread the thin slices of tongue on a baking sheet and heat in the oven for 30 to 45 seconds, just enough to warm through.

Divide the warm tongue among the toast triangles, smother with the sauce, and finish with cracked black pepper.

Grilled Lamb Heart, Spigarello & Bagna Cauda

I started cooking lamb hearts during my first year at Rustic Canyon and fell hard for this dish. It felt like a huge step forward into an exploration of simple and rustic cuisine, a far cry from the esoteric nature of my previous style. The meat of the hearts is very lean, and when grilled to a rested medium, they're quite steak-like.

Serves 4

bagna cauda
3 ounces (90 g) anchovy filets, crushed in a mortar and pestle
3 tablespoons grated garlic
½ teaspoon chili flakes
½ cup (120 ml) extra-virgin olive oil
¼ cup (60 g) unsalted butter, room temperature

lamb hearts
4 fresh lamb hearts, 8 ounces (225 g) each
kosher salt
freshly ground black pepper

to finish
10 ounces (300 g) young spigarello, washed and dried
1 shallot, minced
juice and zest of 1 lemon
2 tablespoons chiffonade parsley
2 cups (70 g) Garlic Bread Croutons (page 326)
4 tablespoons Crispy Kasha (page 329)
Parmesan, for grating

make the bagna cauda

In a nonreactive pan, sweat the anchovy, garlic, and chili flakes in the olive oil. We're not looking for any color here, just to activate the fragrancy of the garlic and anchovy. Cook gently on low heat until the rawness of the garlic is cooked out, around 20 to 25 minutes. Remove from the heat, let sit for 5 minutes, then whisk in the butter. Keep warm until ready to serve.

make the lamb hearts

Begin by trimming off any exterior fat from a heart. Inspect the heart and find the slanted line running on the outside; we'll use this as a guide on where to cut. With your knife, carve into the heart along this slanted line to create a loose piece of meat. It will look like a piece of meat that's "hugging" the rest of the heart. Work around and cut it off the main muscle. Trim off any fat or sinew and set aside. Insert the tip of your knife into the cavity of the remaining heart and open it out into one flat piece. Trim away any tubes and web-like vessels, and remove any interior veins with kitchen tweezers. Slice this piece into 2 even pieces. You'll now have 3 pieces in total. Repeat this process with the remaining lamb hearts.

Season all sides of each heart piece with salt and pepper. Set up your grill for direct heat cooking. Grill on each side for about 2 minutes, until they reach an internal temperature of 135°F (57°C)—remember, that first outer piece is a bit thinner, so it may need less cooking time. Rest for 5 minutes, then slice against the grain into ¼-inch (0.6 cm) slices.

to finish

Fill a mixing bowl with water and submerge the spigarello for 5 minutes. Drain from the water and dry with paper towels.

To a large mixing bowl, add the spigarello, torn if the leaves are larger than one bite, the shallots, lemon juice and zest, parsley, and the warm sliced lamb heart. Add half of the warm bagna cauda, croutons, and crispy kasha, then toss. If you desire more bagna cauda, add it now. Adjust the seasoning.

Transfer to plates or wide bowls. It should appear as though the salad fell from the sky and landed precisely where it wanted. Finish by ribbon-grating Parmesan over the top.

Tripe & Chickpea Gratinata

The first time I had tripe, other than in menudo, was in San Francisco. It was my first Valentine's Day in the city and I was a cook at Rubicon. I didn't have to work that night, so I walked to The Mission neighborhood and sat at the bar at Delfina, one of the restaurants that inspired me to come to California. They had tripe alla Fiorentina on the menu, so I ordered it. I could see everyone in the kitchen kind of looking at me. Craig Stoll, the chef-owner, walked over to me and said, "Tripe? You're either a food writer or a cook and you don't look like a food writer." I said, "Yes, Chef, I'm a cook." Every time I order tripe, it's good. I guess that if you put tripe on your menu, chances are high that you love it and know how to prepare it.

This is an ode to that dish, with the addition of chickpeas and the elements of a gratin. Texturally, I love the long pieces of tripe, with the small chickpeas and crunch of the breadcrumbs.

Serves 4 to 6

tripe
¾ cup (180 ml) white wine vinegar
¼ cup (40 g) kosher salt
1½ teaspoons vanilla extract
2 bay leaves
2 pounds (910 g) beef honeycomb tripe

chickpeas
¼ cup (60 ml) olive oil
2 white onions, cut into ½-inch (1.3-cm) dice
4 celery stalks, cut into ½-inch (1.3-cm) dice
2 carrots, cut into ½-inch (1.3-cm) dice
3 tablespoons chopped garlic
2 tablespoons chopped fresh rosemary leaves
1 teaspoon chili flakes
1½ cups (355 ml) Rachael's Chicken Stock (page 334)
1 teaspoon baking soda (bicarbonate of soda)
1 quart (0.9 liter) good-quality canned tomatoes, whole ones broken by hand or pulsed with an immersion blender
8 ounces (225 g) dried chickpeas, soaked in water overnight, drained, and rinsed
2 tablespoons (28 g) unsalted butter, cold
3 tablespoons chopped fresh Italian parsley
kosher salt

to finish
2 teaspoons freshly ground black pepper
1 cup (120 g) coarsely crushed Garlic Bread Croutons (page 326)

make the tripe

In a large pot, mix 4 quarts (3.8 liters) water with the vinegar, salt, vanilla, and bay leaves. Add the tripe and bring to a boil on high heat, skimming foam from the surface. Reduce the heat to a low simmer, add a cartouche (see page 35), and cook until the tripe is fork-tender, 1½ to 2 hours.

Remove the pot from the heat and cool the tripe in the cooking liquid. Once cool, remove the tripe and discard the cooking liquid. Cut the tripe into 2 x ¼-inch (5 × 0.6-cm) strips.

make the chickpeas

Preheat your oven to 300°F (150°C).

In a large Dutch oven, heat the olive oil on medium heat. Then add the onions, celery, and carrots with a pinch of salt and cook 5 to 7 minutes until the vegetables soften. Add the garlic, rosemary, and chili flakes, then cook, stirring so the garlic doesn't burn, for another 3 minutes.

Next, add the stock, baking soda (bicarbonate of soda), tomatoes, and soaked chickpeas. Cover, move to the oven, and cook until the beans are tender and creamy, checking every 10 minutes or so after 1 hour. Strain the mixture, reserving the solids.

to finish

Return the liquid to the pot and reduce by 40 percent on the stovetop. Then return the chickpeas and vegetables to the pot along with the tripe. Gently simmer to reduce by another 10 percent of liquid. Remove the pot from the heat, mount with the butter, and add the parsley. Adjust the seasoning with the pepper and more salt.

Raise the oven heat to 450°F (230°C). Transfer the tripe mixture to a gratin or casserole dish, top with the breadcrumbs, and bake for 5 to 7 minutes until golden brown on top. Let cool slightly before serving.

Sweetbreads a la Jocko's

Jocko's is a 100-year-old steakhouse in central California wine country. While I was a sous chef at Manresa, the kitchen team took a little "meat road trip" down the coast, trying tri-tip barbecue from roadside stands and eventually ending up at Jocko's.

Jocko's is my kind of place. You can see the large fire pit where they grill everything over red oak. Their menu descriptions are short and sweet, so I didn't know anything other than we had ordered grilled sweetbreads. When they arrived at the table, they had been grilled and charred to perfection, roughly chopped, and served with Texas toast cubes, toothpicks, and drawn butter. It blew my mind. I didn't know you could grill sweetbreads from raw; I thought they had to be poached first. We started cooking them this way at Manresa after that experience. I knew if I ever had my own place, I'd want a dish to honor Jocko's on the menu, as it had made such an impact on me.

I put this dish on the opening menu at Birdie G's. In place of the drawn butter, we serve a meat jus broken with brown butter to mimic the juices of a large cut of roasted meat. Shortly after opening, a family came in and was shocked to see the sweetbreads on the menu; it turned out they owned Jocko's.

Serves 6 to 8

sweetbreads
2 pounds (910 g) veal sweetbreads, ideally from the heart area (see Note)
3 tablespoons kosher salt
1 lemon, quartered

brown butter sauce
9 tablespoons (250 g) unsalted butter
½ bunch thyme
2 bay leaves
6 garlic cloves, smashed, skin on
1½ cups (355 ml) All-Purpose Meat Jus (page 336)
1 tablespoon Banyuls vinegar

to finish
2 tablespoons Montreal Steak Rub (page 308)
8 slices Pain de Mie (page 328), cut 1-inch (2.5-cm) thick
flaky sea salt

Note: I find that sweetbreads from around the heart of the animal, versus the neck, are squatter, meatier, cleaner, better.

make the sweetbreads

Start by cleaning the sweetbreads: In a large container, combine 3 quarts (2.8 liters) of cold water with the kosher salt and lemon. Add the sweetbreads and let them sit in the refrigerator for at least 3 hours, or overnight. As with bone marrow, soaking will help purge any residual blood or toxins; it will also brine the veal.

Remove the sweetbreads, pour out the brine, return the sweetbreads to the container, and flush under a steady stream of cold running water for 15 to 20 minutes. Give the sweetbreads a test squeeze to see if any blood seeps out. If it does, repeat the soaking and flushing steps. Once free of blood, dry the sweetbreads well on paper or kitchen towels and move to a cutting (chopping) board.

With a utility knife, trim off the membrane enrobing the sweetbreads, as well as any extraneous fat. This step isn't semantics; the membrane would make chewing difficult. Transfer them to a rack set over a sheet pan and refrigerate, uncovered, for 4 hours. By doing this, we make sure the soaking and flushing process hasn't waterlogged the sweetbreads, so they don't weep on the grill and decimate your caramelization.

make the brown butter sauce

In a medium saucepan on medium-high heat, add the butter and allow it to brown. Remove the pan from the heat and add the thyme, bay leaves, and garlic. Let the mixture steep for 20 minutes, then remove the herbs and garlic, and reserve them for later. Add the meat jus and Banyuls vinegar to the pan with the brown butter, stirring to combine, then strain through a fine-mesh sieve, discarding the solids, and set aside.

to finish

Remove the sweetbreads from the refrigerator and allow them to sit at room temperature for 45 minutes.

Meanwhile, set up your grill (barbecue) for direct cooking over medium-high heat.

Pat the sweetbreads dry and coat them in the Montreal steak rub. Grill, turning to hit all surfaces, until the pieces are nicely charred as far as the eyes can see. Don't worry about grill marks. Ever. Cook them to an internal temperature of 165 °F (74 °C). Remove from the grill, cover with the reserved thyme, bay leaves, and garlic, and let rest.

Grill your toast until nicely browned on both sides, then cut into bite-size squares.

Also cut the sweetbreads into bite-size pieces and sprinkle with flaky sea salt. Arrange the pieces on a warm platter with the warm butter sauce in dipping bowls.

Serve with toothpicks, the frilly kind; use one to poke a piece of the sweetbread and then a piece of toast. Dip the tasty bite into the butter sauce and enjoy!

"Popcorn" Sweetbreads with Fermented Peppercorn Sauce

I go crazy for an *au poivre* sauce, which is essentially what this recipe includes. When we received some samples of salted pepper berries from The Reluctant Trading Experiment, I was excited to try them. The pepper berries are so delicious, dried but packed in salt; they're not dense or hard like a classic black peppercorn. I highly recommend them. The sauce pairs so well with, of course, a great steak, but here it's a nice accompaniment with the crispy fried sweetbreads. It's in the doing that cooking with sweetbreads stops feeling overwhelming. Don't overthink it or psych yourself out. Buy the best you can afford, follow the steps below, reap the benefits.

Serves 6 to 8

sweetbreads
2 pounds (910 g) veal sweetbreads, ideally from the heart area of the animal (see Note, page 270)
6 tablespoons kosher salt
1 lemon, quartered, seeds removed
2 cups (475 ml) white wine
3 celery stalks, cut into 4-inch (10-cm) lengths
3 garlic cloves, smashed
1 white onion, quartered
10 thyme sprigs
2 bay leaves

fermented peppercorn sauce
¼ cup (60 g) sliced shallots
½ teaspoon kosher salt, plus extra to taste
4 tablespoons (56 g) unsalted butter
½ cup (120 ml) cognac
3 tablespoons salted pepper berries, crushed (see Sources, page 350)
2 tablespoons brined green peppercorns
1 tablespoon pink peppercorns, crushed
2 cups (475 ml) All-Purpose Meat Jus (page 336)
¼ cup (60 g) Dijon mustard
1 cup (240 ml) heavy (double) cream

to finish
2 cups (240 g) all-purpose (plain) flour
2 teaspoons kosher salt, plus more for sprinkling
1 teaspoon freshly ground black pepper
8 large eggs, beaten
2 cups (90 g) panko breadcrumbs
oil, for frying

make the sweetbreads

Start by cleaning the sweetbreads: In a large container, combine 2 quarts (1.9 liters) cold water with 3 tablespoons of the kosher salt and lemon. Add the sweetbreads and let them sit in the refrigerator for at least 3 hours, or overnight. As with bone marrow, soaking will help purge any residual blood or toxins; it also brines the veal.

Remove the sweetbreads, pour out the brine, return the sweetbreads to the container, and flush under a steady stream of cold running water for 15 to 20 minutes. Give the sweetbreads a test squeeze to see if any blood seeps out. If it does, repeat the soaking and flushing steps. Once free of blood, dry the sweetbreads well on paper or kitchen towels.

Next, poach the sweetbreads: In a pot, bring the white wine to a boil and cook off the alcohol. Add 2 quarts (1.9 liters) water, the celery, garlic, onion, thyme, bay leaves, and the remaining 3 tablespoons of kosher salt. Bring to a boil. Add the sweetbreads and turn off the heat. Top with a cartouche (see page 35) and cover with a lid. Check the doneness of the thickest piece after 30 minutes; we're looking for an internal temperature of 145°F (63°C). Continue cooking if needed, checking again after another 5 minutes.

Remove the sweetbreads from the poaching liquid and wrap each in plastic wrap (clingfilm). Poke each plastic-wrapped piece with a fork, knife, skewer, or whatever you have, making several holes in each piece. Press each wrapped sweetbread between 2 sheet pans and place in the refrigerator, weighing them down with a pot or a jug of milk, or whatever you have that's heavy, until completely chilled, about 2 to 3 hours. This step will help flatten them and remove any excess poaching liquid.

After pressing, remove the plastic wrap from the sweetbreads and pop the meat nodules from the outer membrane. Discard the membrane.

make the fermented peppercorn sauce

In a small bowl, combine the shallots and salt and let the mixture sit for 15 to 30 minutes. In a small saucepan, melt the butter over medium heat and sweat the shallots until translucent. Add the cognac and reduce it by 90 percent. Strain the mixture through a fine-mesh sieve into a pot, add the pepper berries and both peppercorns, meat jus, and mustard, and reduce by half. Now, add the cream and reduce by 25 percent. Adjust the seasoning with more salt to taste.

to finish

Set up a little frying station for the sweetbreads. In one wide, shallow bowl, whisk together the flour, the 2 teaspoons salt, and 1 teaspoon black pepper. In 2 separate bowls, add the well-beaten eggs and the panko. Coat the sweetbread pieces in the flour, tapping off excess, then dip in the eggs, allowing excess to drip back into the bowl, and dredge in the breadcrumbs.

In a heavy-bottom pot, heat the oil to 350°F (180°C). Using a small spider or large slotted spoon, lower the breaded sweetbreads into the oil. Fry them until golden, 3 to 4 minutes. Remove to a paper towel-lined plate or a rack set over a sheet pan and sprinkle them with salt.

Serve the crispy "popcorn" sweetbreads with the warm peppercorn sauce.

Bone Marrow, Miso-Creamed Spinach & Artichoke Flower

I will eat spinach-artichoke dip anytime and from anywhere—even from a certain warehouse store. Driving across the country and stopping at a Cracker Barrel? Sign me up. Your mom's recipe you make in a crock-pot? Yes, please, and thank you. It's an unfair power dynamic. This version has all the traditional dip vibes, with the fun of an actual artichoke to peel and eat, plus whole bone marrow to scoop from to top the leaves. It's still a dip, but interactive.

Serves 4

roasted bone marrow
4 beef marrow bones (each about 4 inches/10 cm)
kosher salt, for brine solution
flaky sea salt
freshly ground black pepper

miso-creamed spinach
1 tablespoon (14 g) unsalted butter
2 tablespoons minced shallot
kosher salt
1 ½ pounds (680 g) Bloomsdale or baby spinach
2 cups (475 g) Béchamel (page 322)
2 ounces (60 g) cream cheese, room temperature
3 tablespoons miso
1 teaspoon grated nutmeg

artichoke flowers
1 quart (0.9 liter) white wine
2 lemons, quartered
2 tablespoons kosher salt
1 teaspoon black peppercorns
1 bay leaf
4 globe artichokes
olive oil, for drizzling
flaky sea salt

to serve
2 cups (80 g) Garlic Bread Croutons crushed into coarse crumbs (page 326)
2 tablespoons finely chopped fresh Italian parsley

make the roasted bone marrow

A day ahead, in a brining bag or container depending on the size of your refrigerator, soak the bones in a 2 percent saltwater brine for 12 to 24 hours in the refrigerator. (No judgment, my home refrigerator is pretty tiny.) This step will help extract the blood and give your marrow a clean white hue.

Remove the bones, discard the brine, and drain on paper or kitchen towels.

Preheat your oven to 350°F (180°C).

On a rimmed baking sheet, spread the marrow bones evenly and roast until the marrow inside is jiggly, 5 to 8 minutes. Remove from the oven and sprinkle with a few grains of flaky sea salt and some black pepper.

make the miso-creamed spinach

In a large sauté pan, melt the butter and sweat the shallot with a tiny pinch of kosher salt until translucent, with no color. Add the spinach and quickly sauté just until wilted. Spread the spinach onto a sheet pan to cool, then coarsely chop.

In a medium saucepan, heat the béchamel, fold in the cream cheese and miso, and cook until heated through and bubbling. Stir in the chopped spinach and adjust the seasoning with the nutmeg and more salt to taste. Remove from the heat and set aside, covering the pan to keep warm.

make the artichoke flowers

In a large, heavy-bottom pot, combine 3 quarts (2.8 liters) water, white wine, lemons, kosher salt, peppercorns, and bay leaf.

To trim each artichoke, use a serrated knife to cut off the top 1 inch (2.5 cm). Then cut off the bottom stem so the artichoke sits flat. You'll need to cut pretty close to the base, but not the base itself. Remove the small leaves around the base by pulling them back and snapping them off. Add the artichokes to the pot as you go to keep from discoloring.

Top the pot with a cartouche (see page 35), pressing it directly on the surface of the liquid. Cover with a lid and cook at the slightest simmer until the artichokes are tender, 15 to 20 minutes. You can test this by using kitchen tongs to pry off a leaf. If you need to tug hard, they need more cooking. If the leaf comes right off, they're ready.

Unless you're eating them right away, let the artichokes cool to room temperature in the pot. If you are eating them right away, remove them from the pot to a rack set over a sheet pan to cool more quickly. Once cool enough to handle, carefully open up the outer leaves while gently pressing down to form a flower shape. Using a spoon, scoop out the hard leaves and fuzz from the center, revealing the artichoke heart. Drizzle with a little olive oil and sprinkle with flaky sea salt.

to serve

Spoon enough hot creamed spinach to cover the base of each plate. Combine the breadcrumbs and parsley, and sprinkle generously over the spinach. Place a warm artichoke flower in the center and rest a marrow bone right on top of the flower.

Banana Shank & Banana Stew with Sweet Potato

This recipe came about after a shopping trip to Ranch 99, my go-to market in Los Angeles for Asian ingredients. Banana shank... bananas... so obvious. What could just be "good on paper" actually worked, like really well. The sugar from the bananas balances out the savory aspects of the stew, especially when paired with the coconut milk. If you can't find banana vinegar, I suggest apple cider vinegar in its place.

Serves 6

lime leaf sachet
4 makrut lime leaves
4 star anise
1 lemongrass stalk, cut crosswise into thirds, then halved lengthwise
1 cinnamon stick
1 tablespoon madras curry powder

stew
2½ pounds (1 kg) boneless beef banana shank, cut into 2-inch (5-cm) pieces
¼ cup (30 g) all-purpose (plain) flour
¼ cup (60 ml) Schmaltz (page 338) or duck fat
4 to 5 ripe bananas, peels reserved
1 tablespoon fresh rosemary leaves, coarsely chopped
1 tablespoon madras curry powder
2 cups (475 ml) white wine
3 cups (710 ml) Rachael's Chicken Stock (page 334)
3 tablespoons banana vinegar (see Sources, page 350)
2 tablespoons coconut aminos
1 white onion, cut into 1½-inch (3.8-cm) pieces
1 pound (455 g) Japanese sweet potatoes, cut into 1½-inch (3.8-cm) pieces
1½ cups (355 ml) unsweetened coconut milk
kosher salt
freshly ground black pepper

to serve
cilantro (coriander) leaves and flowers, to garnish
zest of makrut limes (optional, but I have a tree in my front yard... humble brag)
2 regular limes, quartered

make the lime leaf sachet

To a square of double-thick cheesecloth (muslin), add the lime leaves, star anise, lemongrass, cinnamon stick, and curry powder. Gather the corners of the cheesecloth, twist them, and tie with butcher's twine. Leave a long tail that can be tied to the handle of your pot.

make the stew

Preheat your oven to 300°F (150°C).

Season the banana shank with salt and black pepper and let sit for 30 minutes. Coat the meat with the flour and shake off any that doesn't adhere.

In a large braising pan or Dutch oven on high heat, sear the shanks on all sides, about 3 minutes per side, then transfer to a plate and reserve.

Into the same pan on medium-high heat, break up the peeled bananas along with the rosemary and curry powder, mashing with a wooden spoon as they start to caramelize, as you would with tomato paste (purée). Deglaze the pan with the white wine, scraping up any fond, and add the lime leaf sachet. Bring to a boil, then lower the heat to a simmer and reduce the liquid by 75 percent.

Return the shanks to the pan, along with any accumulated juices, then the chicken stock, banana vinegar, coconut aminos, onion, and sweet potatoes. Bring to a boil, then lower the heat to the slightest simmer.

Top with the reserved banana peels (instead of a cartouche), cover with a lid, and place in the oven. Cook for 3 to 3½ hours, or until the meat is fall-from-the-bone tender. Remove from the oven, squeeze the sachet to remove any liquid and flavor, and discard the sachet.

Return the pan to a burner on medium heat and skim any fat that has risen to the top. Add the coconut milk and heat until just before simmering. Remove from the heat and adjust the seasoning with more salt and black pepper.

to serve

Serve in wide, shallow bowls topped with cilantro (coriander) flowers and leaves and, if using, makrut lime zest, with regular lime quarters on the side.

Oxtails with Noodles

You can consider this your blueprint for red wine-enriched beef stew. Oxtails are delicious, and eating them off the bone has a primal quality I really enjoy. You could add bacon lardons, as this recipe leans more toward beef Bourguignon. Here, I pair the stew with egg noodles, but Potato Purée (page 166) or polenta are also viable options.

Serves 6

oxtail stew
3 pounds (1.4 kg) oxtails, cut 1½ to 2 inches (3.8 to 5 cm) thick
¼ cup (30 g) all-purpose (plain) flour
3 tablespoons Beef Tallow (page 339) or fat of your choosing
4 carrots, halved lengthwise and cut into 2-inch (5-cm) lengths
2 tablespoons tomato paste (purée)
3 cups (710 ml) red wine
2 medium onions, cut into eighths, root intact
4 celery stalks, cut into 2-inch (5-cm) lengths
1 tablespoon fresh thyme leaves
2 bay leaves
2 teaspoons porcini powder
8 ounces (225 g) cremini (chestnut) mushrooms, stems trimmed, cleaned and halved
3 cups (710 ml) All-Purpose Meat Jus (page 336)
3 tablespoons Mushroom Worcestershire (page 319)
2 tablespoons red wine vinegar
1 tablespoon (14 g) unsalted butter, cold
kosher salt
freshly ground black pepper

gremolata
4 garlic cloves, finely grated
2 tablespoons chopped fresh Italian parsley
zest of 1 lemon

to serve
1 pound (455 g) dried egg noodles
1 tablespoon unsalted (14 g) butter
kosher salt

make the oxtail stew

Preheat the oven to 300°F (150°C).

Season the oxtails with salt and black pepper, and coat with the flour, shaking off any excess.

In a large braising pan or Dutch oven on high heat, add the tallow or other fat. Sear the oxtails until nicely caramelized on all sides, 8 to 10 minutes, then use kitchen tongs to transfer them to a plate.

Add the carrots to the pan and brown slightly. Stir in the tomato paste (purée) to coat the carrots and toast for 1 to 2 minutes. Deglaze the pan with the red wine, scraping up any fond, and add the onions, celery, thyme, bay leaves, and porcini powder. Bring to a boil, then reduce the heat and simmer until reduced by 80 percent.

Return the oxtails to the pan along with the mushrooms, meat jus, Worcestershire, and vinegar.

Top with a cartouche (see page 35), cover with a lid, and place in the preheated oven. Cook for 3 to 4 hours, or until the meat is fall-from-the-bone tender, skimming off any fat that rises to the top.

Transfer the pan to the stovetop and place on medium heat to do a final skim of the surface. Turn off the heat, mount with the butter, and adjust the seasoning with more salt and pepper.

make the gremolata

In a small mixing bowl, mix together the garlic, parsley, and lemon zest.

to serve

In a pot of heavily salted water, cook the noodles until al dente, then drain and toss with the butter and a good pinch of kosher salt. Divide the noodles among wide, shallow bowls, spoon the stew over each dish, and sprinkle with the gremolata.

Corned Beef Steak Frites

When we were firmly in the throes of all things corned beef upon opening Birdie G's, we felt compelled to prepare it as many ways as we could. For all the testing of this and that, it turned out that simply cooking a thick slice over the wood-fired grill was the most satisfying. Before this, I had only eaten corned beef thinly sliced in a sandwich, or unrecognizably in hash. How could something so basic be so eye-opening? Within a few months, *The New York Times* declared it one of the best dishes of 2019.

Serves 4

frites
6 Russet potatoes
oil, for frying (I like rice bran)
2 tablespoons chopped fresh Italian parsley
kosher salt

brisket
2 pounds (900 g) Corned Beef Brisket (page 73), cut into four 8-ounce (225 g) "steaks" (see Note)
2 tablespoons Dijon mustard
1 tablespoon Montreal Steak Rub (page 308)

to serve
spicy greens, such as arugula (rocket) or watercress
½ cup (120 g) Aioli (page 321)

Note: I prefer slices that are about ½ inch (1.3 cm) thick and include both the point and flat of the brisket, with fat in between.

make the frites

Have a bowl of cold water ready. Working with one at a time, peel the potatoes and cut them into ⅓-inch (0.8-cm) slices the length of the potato, then cut these slices into ⅓-inch (0.8-cm) batons (matchsticks). As you finish slicing the batons, drop them into the bowl of cold water.

To get these nice and crispy, we have to wash off the potato starch, much like washing rice. To do it, agitate them gently in the cold water. Tip out all the water, add more, and continue the process until the water is no longer cloudy.

In a large pot, cover the potatoes with 8 quarts (7.5 liters) of cold water and add ¼ cup plus 2 tablespoons (90 g) of kosher salt. Bring to a boil on medium-high heat, then immediately shut off the heat. Let the potatoes sit until they are just starting to fray at the edges, about 12 to 15 minutes.

Once they are done, gently transfer them to a rack set over a sheet pan. Refrigerate for 2 hours.

In a heavy-bottom pot, heat your frying oil to 250°F (120°C). Lower the potatoes into the hot oil and blanch for about 10 minutes, making sure that they keep a blonde color. Remove the frites from the oil and return them to the cooling rack. Return to the refrigerator and chill for another 2 hours.

Bring your frying oil back to 350°F (180°C), add the cold potatoes, and this time fry them until they have turned golden brown and crispy.

Remove the potatoes with a spider or strainer to drain briefly on paper towels; while still warm, toss them in a mixing bowl with the parsley and salt to taste.

make the brisket

Brush one side of each brisket "steak" with the mustard and sprinkle with the Montreal steak rub.

Next, you have a choice. You can either grill the steaks, mustard side down, over direct heat, then flip and elevate to warm through. OR you can bake them at 300°F (150°C), mustard side up, for 5 to 8 minutes, depending on how tempered they are.

to serve

Arrange the steak slices on each plate, with a pile of frites, greens, and a small dish of aioli (for dipping the frites) alongside.

Beef Borscht, Horseradish, Crème Fraîche & Caviar

I imagine you might make this in the fall when only a few leaves are hanging onto the trees. You know the days, the kind where the air is crisp and the sun is shining but it's still cold and blustery. To quote the great Marshall Crenshaw's song *T.M.D.*, "... the autumn air is filled with memories and possibilities."

You should start this soup in the morning and let it gently bubble all day until the flavors meld and the meat is tender. Pair it with a nice wintry salad, something with good acid that will cut through the depth of the stew and help you digest it. Maybe add some toasted rye bread on the side and a seasonal apple galette for dessert—or just a simple warm poached pear with crème anglaise. Then, please do me a favor and fall asleep after dinner on the couch while watching your favorite comfort movie. Mine is *American Fiction*.

Serves 6 to 8

borscht
2 tablespoons Beef Tallow (page 339; see Note)
3 pounds (1.4 kg) beef eye of round, trimmed of excess fat, cut into 2-inch (5-cm) dice
1 pound (455 g) onion, cut into ½-inch (1.3-cm) dice
8 ounces (225 g) celery stalks, cut into ½-inch (1.3-cm) dice
8 ounces (225 g) carrots, cut into ½-inch (1.3-cm) dice
2 tablespoons tomato paste (purée)
1 pound (455 g) red cabbage, shredded or finely julienned
2 cups (375 ml) red wine
1 quart (0.9 liter) beet (beetroot) juice
¼ cup (60 ml) honey (optional)
¼ cup (25 g) chopped fresh dill leaves
kosher salt

to serve
1½ cups (355 ml) Crème Fraîche (page 322) or sour cream
1 tablespoon Dijon mustard
¼ cup (60 g) prepared horseradish
kosher salt
½ ounce (14 g) or more per person caviar of your choosing

Note: You can use the raw fat trimmed from the eye of round in place of the tallow; render it in the pan, removing the solids and pouring off ¼ cup (60 ml) of the rendered fat for using in this recipe. Reserve the rest for another use.

borscht

In a wide, nonreactive pan over medium-high heat, heat 2 tablespoons of the tallow (or rendered raw fat). Add the diced beef to the hot fat with a good pinch of salt, and cook until the meat is deeply brown on each side, about 8 to 10 minutes.

Transfer the browned meat from the pan to a bowl or plate and set aside. If the pan is dry, add an additional 1 to 2 tablespoons of tallow (or rendered raw fat) to the pan, then add the onion, celery, and carrots. Cook until there's nice, even caramelization, making sure to "maintenance stir" occasionally, but not too often as the vegetables won't achieve the desired color. Add the tomato paste (purée), stir to combine, and cook, stirring, for 3 to 5 minutes.

Now, add the red cabbage and cook until it wilts. Deglaze the pan with the red wine, stirring up any fond from the pan, and reduce by half. Add the beet (beetroot) juice to the pan, along with the browned beef and any accumulated juices, and reduce the heat to medium-low. Cook until the meat is tender and the sauce no longer tastes of raw beets, around 1½ hours.

Check your seasonings, adding salt to taste and honey if needed to counteract any bitterness. Save half of the dill to sprinkle on top of the finished dish; stir the rest into the borscht.

to serve

In a mixing bowl, stir the crème fraîche, mustard, and prepared horseradish together, and add salt to taste.

Divide the borscht among warmed bowls, dollop with horseradish crème fraîche, and top with the reserved dill and the caviar.

Meatloaf & Mash

I'm just gonna throw this out there: fried shallots are insanely tasty. The amount listed here is enough for this dish. But it doesn't cover the snacking tax. Or the "I wish I had more of those" regrets. Maybe quadruple the amount. Or pentuple. That means five times. I had to look it up. You can also say quintuple, but pentuple just sounds cool. The point stands. More is more and that is better.

Serves 4

meatloaf
¼ cup (60 g) Beef Tallow (page 339)
6 ounces (180 g) leeks, cut into ¼-inch (0.6-cm) dice
4 ounces (120 g) celery stalks, cut into ¼-inch (0.6-cm) dice
4 ounces (120 g) carrots, cut into ¼-inch (0.6-cm) dice
4 ounces (120 g) cremini (chestnut) mushrooms, coarsely chopped
2½ pounds (1 kg) ground (minced) beef, 80/20 blend
8 ounces (225 g) breadcrumbs
4 ounces (60 g) Parmigiano-reggiano, grated
4 ounces (60 g) mozzarella, grated
2 large eggs
¼ cup (60 ml) whole (full-fat) milk
2 tablespoons miso
3 tablespoons tamari
1 tablespoon porcini powder
1 tablespoon grated garlic
1 tablespoon kosher salt, plus extra to taste
1 cup (240 ml) Sungold Tomato Ketchup (page 319)
chives, thinly sliced

mashed potatoes
2½ pounds (1 kg) Yukon gold potatoes, peeled and quartered
1 cup (240 ml) heavy (double) cream
1 pound (455 g) unsalted butter, cut into ½-inch (1.3-cm) dice
kosher salt

crispy shallots
4 ounces (60 g) shallots
½ cup (60 g) all-purpose (plain) flour
kosher salt
freshly ground black pepper
oil, for frying

For the bacon lardons
8 ounces (225 g) Maple Smoked Bacon (page 13), cut into ½-inch x ¼-inch (1.3-cm × 0.6-cm) strips

make the meatloaf

Preheat your oven to 300°F (150°C).

In a large skillet, heat the tallow on medium-high heat. Once it's glossy and hot, add in the leeks, celery, carrots, and mushrooms. Sauté the vegetables until they're nice and soft; color is okay, burning is bad. Remove them from the heat and cool to room temperature.

In a large mixing bowl, combine the ground beef, breadcrumbs, Parmigiana, mozzarella, eggs, milk, miso, tamari, porcini powder, garlic, and salt. Either with a large wooden spoon or (and I think this is easiest) your hands, mix the meat together really well, making sure all the ingredients are incorporated. Add the cooled sautéed vegetables and fold to combine.

Next, take out a small amount of the mix, make a small patty, and fry it up in a skillet. Once the tester patty is cooked and cooled, take a bite, we want to test out our seasonings. Here's your chance to add more (less isn't an option at this point, sorry) spice if you like. If you decide to add more spice or salt, make sure the mix is fully incorporated, and test again.

Divide the mix into 12-ounce (340-g) ovals about 2 inches (5 cm) thick and spread on a rimmed baking sheet lined with a silicone baking mat. Coat each baby meatloaf with the Sungold ketchup. Bake until you reach an internal temperature of 165°F (74°C). Remove from the oven and turn your oven to broil (grill). Coat with more ketchup if you wish, and finish on broil to caramelize, about 3 to 4 minutes.

mashed potatoes

In a large pot, cover the whole potatoes with cold water and a good pinch of salt. "Salty like the sea" is a good rule of thumb, but I have an amendment. I like to salt until it's just saltier than I would want a broth to be, just past the point of no return.

Bring the water to a boil and then simmer lightly until they are completely soft all the way through, 25 to 30 minutes. As the potatoes cook, in a small saucepan, slowly warm the cream and butter. It doesn't need to boil, but the butter should melt.

Now, drain the potatoes, and once they're cool enough to handle but still warm, peel them. Usually, the skins will come right off but feel free to use a paring knife to help any stuck bits along. Process them through a potato ricer into a large bowl and slowly incorporate the warm cream and butter until it's the texture of pudding. Writing a cookbook is hard. Now I really want mashed potatoes. Don't forget to season to taste with salt.

crispy shallots

Slice the shallots as thinly as possible on a mandoline and separate the rings with the prongs of a fork. In a bowl, toss the shallots with the flour, salt, and black pepper. Drain them in a wire basket to remove the excess flour.

In a small, heavy-bottom saucepan, heat the frying oil to 300°F (150°C). Gently add the shallots and fry until just lightly golden (they will continue to darken a bit out of the oil). Remove to paper towels to drain and season with salt.

bacon lardons

Slice the bacon slab about ¼ inch (0.6 cm) thick, then slice those into 2-inch (5-cm) strips. Place in a small skillet or saucepan and cook on medium-low heat, stirring often, until the lardons are just crisp outside and tender inside. Drain and reserve the fat for another time.

to serve

Scoop a large mound of potatoes in the center of each plate. Place a delicious meatloaf on top of the potatoes. Top the meatloaf with bacon lardons, crispy shallots, and a sprinkling of chives. Nosh.

page 291

Mr. Gray's 7-Bone Steak

I saw this steak on Instagram in 2019. Just one post. It was beautiful. A cut I had never seen, or even heard of. And the greatest, most earnest and utilitarian name: 7-Bone Steak. Without even sampling the goods, this instantly became a legend in my own mind. If I were an editor at a food magazine, I would have seen to it that thousands of words across multiple pages were devoted to this wonder steak that was sweeping the nation. Unfortunately, things don't usually go that way. The plethora of articles listing "9 Infomercial Kitchen Gadgets You Must Own" or declaring "Gummy Worm Cuisine Is Having a Moment" don't leave much room for spontaneous flashes of brilliance that may arise from a happenstance grocery store visit colliding superconductor-style with a culinary think-tank such as Momofuku Ko, the Michelin two-star restaurant where Sean Gray was executive chef.

On an ordinary day like any other—December 5, 2018, to be exact—Sean spotted a packaged cut of beef at a ShopRite in Flemington, New Jersey, labeled "beef chuck first cut chuck steak bone-in" at $4.99 per pound. Sometimes that's all it takes for inspiration to grab hold. The challenge of this steak lies in being able to cook a large cut containing over ten sections of opposing tenderness and directional grain. Although our inner monologue suggests there must be a reason why we've never heard of something, that perhaps it's a fool's errand—problem-solvers refuse to be deterred.

The 7-bone steak was available on Ko's bar menu for a stretch of time, priced to move at $100, a bargain methinks. Then it was gone, only to be remembered by a small contingent. I will leave it to you to form your own opinion on the 7-bone steak, if you can find it. But at least now you know about it. Thank you, Chef Gray, for sharing your findings with me, now us. Hopefully, after this book is published, Mr. Gray's 7-bone steak will show up on restaurant menus and become as much of a household name as ribeye or New York strip.

I have included Chef Gray's original method, which utilizes a smart oven (I use one by Rational) that your home kitchen may not have, as well as an alternate sous-vide option.

Serves 2 or more

steak
1 bone-in, first-cut beef chuck steak (2½ pounds/1 kg)
1 tablespoon (10 g) kosher salt (1 percent weight of meat)
2 to 3 cups (480 to 720 ml) Beef Tallow (page 339) or other fat (enough to cover the meat)
½ bunch thyme
5 garlic cloves, smashed, skin on

glaze
1 tablespoon (50 g) glucose
1 tablespoon plus 1½ teaspoons (22 g) creamy koji sauce (see Sources, page 350)
¾ teaspoon (4 ml) black vinegar (see Sources, page 350)
½ teaspoon (3 ml) white soy sauce (see Sources, page 350)

to serve
1 tablespoon (or more) cracked green peppercorns
flaky sea salt

make the steak

sous-vide home method

Season the steak with the kosher salt and let it sit out at room temperature for 1 hour.

In a saucepan, heat the tallow to 100°F (38°C), so it's liquid but not hot. Vacuum-seal the tempered steak with the thyme, garlic, and enough melted tallow to submerge the steak.

Set your immersion circulator to 147°F (64°C) and poach for 2½ hours. Remove the bag and let it rest at room temperature for 1 hour, then refrigerate overnight.

make the glaze

In a small bowl, mix together the glucose, koji sauce, black vinegar, and white soy.

to serve

Using your immersion circulator, re-warm the sealed steak bag in 147 °F (64 °C) water for 30 minutes.

Remove the steak from the bag, reserving the fat for another use because now you have double tallow, brush the steak all over with the glaze, and top with the cracked green peppercorns (feel free to add more).

Now, with a kitchen torch, wave the flame over the steak to torch all sides.

To carve, separate out individual pieces of meat and then slice across the grain. Finish with flaky sea salt.

smart oven/salamander method

make the steak

Preheat your smart oven to 147°F (64°C), fan speed 3.

Season the steak with the kosher salt and let it sit out at room temperature for 1 hour.

In a saucepan, heat the tallow to 100°F (38°C), so it's liquid but not hot.

Place the steak in a half hotel pan or a container that's at least 4 inches (10 cm) deep and cover with the warm tallow. Place the pan in the smart oven and cook for 2½ hours.

Pull the steak from the oven and let it rest in the fat until cooled to room temperature. Remove the steak onto a rack set in a sheet pan, then put into the refrigerator to fully chill.

make the glaze

In a small bowl, mix together the glucose, koji sauce, black vinegar, and white soy.

to serve

Remove the steak from the pan, reserving the fat for another use, brush with the glaze on all sides, then top with the cracked green peppercorns (feel free to add more).

Now, hit hard in a salamander. Hit hard is a technical term, it's in the manual.

To carve, separate out individual pieces of meat and then slice across the grain. Finish with flaky sea salt.

Lamb a la Saless

It takes me a long time to make a cookbook. *On Vegetables* took seven years, though I am improving; this one only took four years. I am emotionally attached to every recipe. That said, I do play favorites, and Lamb a la Saless is my favorite. It's entirely outside my comfort zone, created by reverse-engineering a singular bite of Baghali Polo at Raffi's Persian restaurant in Glendale, California, just minutes from my home.

This lamb's namesake and dear friend, Cameron Saless, and his husband, Matthew Allard, took Rachael and me there for a Sunday dinner, and to say Raffi's was bustling would be an understatement. After forty years of turning up my nose to dill, I now have to force myself not to include it in every single dish. By that Thursday, Rustic Canyon was serving my take on Baghali Polo: a bowl of saucy California arborio rice, heavy on the dill, dried Persian lime, and fenugreek leaves, all topped with a veil of lamb neck "carnitas." With more dill on top. Later, this would evolve into the recipe below, making the opening menu at Birdie G's and never ever leaving. Cam, thank you for sharing with me the food of your culture and gifting me its lasting inspiration.

Serves 4

beet molasses
3 cups (710 ml) fresh red beet (beetroot) juice
¼ cup (50 g) granulated sugar
¼ cup (60 ml) rice wine vinegar
1 teaspoon kosher salt

make the marinated lamb
¼ cup plus 2 tablespoons (90 ml) extra-virgin olive oil
1 tablespoon grated garlic
1 tablespoon chopped fresh rosemary leaves
1 teaspoon freshly ground black pepper
½ teaspoon rose water
4 lamb loins with fat cap attached (each about 1 pound/455 g)

saffron yogurt
1 teaspoon saffron threads
1 teaspoon kosher salt
1 cup (240 ml) plain Greek yogurt

crispy rice
2 cups (200 g) cooked long-grain rice (jasmine or basmati)
oil, for frying
1 tablespoon Persian Spice (page 308)
2 tablespoons chopped fresh dill leaves, plus extra to garnish

grilled lamb
¼ cup (50 g) Persian Spice (page 308)

to serve
lemon halves or wedges, for squeezing

make the beet molasses	In a stainless-steel pan, combine the beet (beetroot) juice, sugar, vinegar, and salt and reduce by about 80 percent. You're looking for a consistency more like maple syrup than honey. Strain through a fine-mesh sieve and cool to room temperature.
make the marinated lamb	In a large container, combine the beet molasses, olive oil, garlic, rosemary, black pepper, and rose water and mix well.
	Trim any silver skin from the bottom of the lamb loin, and even out the fat cap so it's a consistent thickness. Score the fat along the lamb crosswise ⅛ inch (0.3 cm) thick. Marinate the lamb for at least 2 days, but it gets better every day after that, up to 6 days.
make the saffron yogurt	With a mortar and pestle, grind the saffron threads to a powder. Transfer the powder to a small bowl and pour 1 tablespoon hot water over it. Let steep for 10 minutes. Add the salt, and give it a little stir. Transfer the salty saffron liquid to a bowl, mix with the yogurt, cover, and refrigerate until ready to serve.
	[...]

[...]

make the crispy rice

Allow the cooked rice to reach room temperature, about 30 minutes.

Line a rimmed baking sheet with paper or kitchen towels.

In a heavy-bottom pot, heat the frying oil to 350°F (180°C). Set a fine-mesh conical sieve into the hot oil and, working in batches, add the tempered rice to it. Cook, breaking the rice up with a wooden spoon should it stick together, until golden, 4 to 5 minutes. Simply lift up the sieve, allow it to drain slightly, then empty onto the towel-lined baking sheet. Make sure to spread out the rice to cool evenly and remain crispy.

Toss the crisped rice with the Persian spice and the fresh dill.

make the grilled lamb

Remove the lamb from the marinade and evenly coat with the Persian spice. You can let the excess marinade drip off a little, but do not dry the lamb. The marinade will char and become even more delicious.

Prepare your grill for indirect cooking. Grill the lamb, fat side down, over low heat to allow the fat to render and char up nicely; all those sugars taste great when caramelized on the grill.

Rotate the lamb to grill on each side until it reaches an internal temperature of 120°F (49°C). Let rest for 10 to 15 minutes before slicing.

to serve

Spread the crispy rice on each plate and top with the sliced lamb, a dollop of the saffron yogurt, and more chopped dill. Give each serving a squeeze of lemon.

CONDIMENTS & SAUCES	300 → 307
SPICES	308 → 311
PICKLES & FERMENTS	314 → 321
EGG & DAIRY	322 → 325
GRAINS	326 → 333
FOUNDATIONS	334 → 341

The Larder

Al's Steak Sauce

This is named for my grandfather Albert, who always poured A.1. Original Steak Sauce on his steak. Be honest, your dad or grandpa probably did, too.

Makes about 2 cups (475 ml)

½ cup (120 ml) balsamic vinegar
3 tablespoons plus 1½ teaspoons Worcestershire sauce
¼ cup (40 g) ketchup
¼ cup (40 g) Dijon mustard
1 ounce (30 g) dark raisins
¼ cup (40 g) white onion, cut into ¼-inch (0.6-cm) dice
1 tablespoon grated garlic
2 teaspoons celery seed
1 teaspoon kosher salt
½ teaspoon freshly ground black pepper
zest and juice of 1 orange

In a medium saucepan, combine all the ingredients with 5 tablespoons water and bring to a simmer with the lid on. Continue to cook at just the slightest simmer, still covered and stirring occasionally, for about 1 hour. Remove from the heat, cool slightly, then transfer to a blender and purée until smooth. Strain the sauce through a fine-mesh sieve. Cool to room temperature and refrigerate in an airtight container for up to 1 month.

Sungold Tomato Ketchup

"Real tomato ketchup, Eddie?"

Makes about 5 cups (1.2 liters)

1 tablespoon extra-virgin olive oil
1 pound (455 g) white onions, cut into ½-inch (1.6-cm) dice
¼ cup plus 1 tablespoon (45 g) grated garlic
2 ounces (60 g) fresh ginger, peeled and grated
5 teaspoons kosher salt, plus extra to taste
4 pounds (1.8 kg) Sungold tomatoes
generous ¾ cup (200 ml) sherry vinegar, plus extra to taste
¼ cup (40 g) Calabrian Chile Hybrid solids (page 304)

Place a pot over medium heat and add the olive oil; once the oil is hot (but not smoking), add the onions, garlic, ginger, and salt. Once bubbling, turn the heat to low and sweat the vegetables, stirring, until translucent, about 5 minutes.

Add the tomatoes, sherry vinegar, and chile solids and cover the pot so the tomatoes will start to burst faster. Give it a stir every 5 minutes until all the tomatoes have broken down and their juices have released. Remove the lid and continue to cook until barely any liquid remains.

Remove from the heat, cool slightly, then transfer to a blender and purée until smooth. Strain the ketchup through a fine-mesh sieve into an airtight container and then chill. Meaning the ketchup should chill. You can also chill unless you've got stuff to do. I don't want to presume.

Once completely chilled (again, the ketchup, not you), adjust the salt to your taste and add more vinegar if you prefer, not every tomato is identical. Refrigerate in an airtight container for up to 2 weeks.

Smoky Honey Mustard

I've tried smoking honey in a smoker, but I can never get it to really take on any smoky flavor. Using lapsang souchong tea changed everything. Light bulb moment.

Makes about 2 cups (475 ml)

¼ cup (60 ml) honey
1 tablespoon loose lapsang souchong tea leaves
2 tablespoons Dijon mustard
¼ cup (60 ml) sherry vinegar
½ cup (120 ml) grapeseed oil
¼ cup (60 ml) extra-virgin olive oil
⅓ cup (80 g) Apple Cider Mustard (page 318)

Bring a small pot of water to just below a simmer. Add the honey and tea leaves to a small mixing bowl, wrap tightly with plastic wrap (clingfilm), and rest on top of the pot. Let steep for 1 hour, adding more hot water to the pot if needed. Remove from the heat and strain through a fine-mesh sieve. Cool to lukewarm.

In another mixing bowl, whisk together the Dijon mustard with the sherry vinegar, then add both oils in a slow, even stream while continuing to whisk. Fold in the apple cider mustard and infused honey, and pulse with an immersion blender until creamy.

Store in an airtight container at room temperature for at least 1 week, and up to 1 month.

Yuzu Kosho Sauce

At the restaurants, we make our own yuzu kosho, but it's now easy to find in most Asian markets or online. Seek it out, and make this recipe. It's used with the Beef Carpaccio ZZ's Style (page 243), but as with most of the condiments in this chapter, it's good on practically everything.

Makes about 1 cup (240 ml)

¼ cup plus 1 tablespoon (45 g) yuzu kosho
¼ cup (60 ml) calamansi vinegar
3 tablespoons plus 1½ teaspoons extra-virgin olive oil
2 tablespoons yuzu juice

Simply shake all the ingredients in a jar, and it's ready to serve. No bowl or whisk required.

Tiki Sauce

You might notice that I usually call for tamari instead of soy sauce. The reason for this is that I have adjusted my cooking to eliminate gluten whenever possible, but you should feel free to substitute soy sauce for tamari in any recipe. The tiki sauce is an extremely versatile condiment, pairing nicely with most meats, seafood, and vegetables. Find it in the recipes for Bacon-Wrapped Oca (page 100) and Mongolian Flanken Ribs (page 252).

Makes about 4 cups (0.9 liter)

2 cups (475 ml) tamari
¾ cup (150 g) dark brown sugar
¾ cup (175 ml) honey
½ cup (120 ml) sesame oil
½ cup (120 ml) rice wine vinegar
¼ cup (60 ml) sherry vinegar
3 ounces (85 g) scallion (spring onion) whites, sliced ¼-inch (0.6-cm) thick
2 ounces (60 g) fresh ginger, peeled and grated
2 ounces (60 g) shallot, thinly sliced
3 tablespoons grated garlic
1 tablespoon Korean chili powder (gochugaru)
½ teaspoon freshly ground white pepper

Add all the ingredients to a nonreactive pan on medium-high heat and bring to a boil. Reduce the heat to a simmer and cook for 10 minutes, stirring occasionally to avoid burning or sticking.

Remove from the heat, cool slightly, then transfer to a blender and purée until smooth. Strain through a fine-mesh sieve. Cool to room temperature and refrigerate in an airtight container for up to 1 month.

Sweet Chili Sauce

If you peer over the kitchen shelves at pretty much any restaurant, you'll likely find at least one bottle of Mae Ploy Sweet Chili Sauce. Whether it's for their menu recipes or even family meal, it's there. This condiment is crucial to the Beef Tendon, Tofu, Sweet Chili & Almonds on page 244, but you'll find it works just about anywhere.

Makes about 1 cup (240 ml)

2 tablespoons Anaheim or red jalapeño chiles, seeded and minced
1 tablespoon plus 1½ teaspoons grated garlic
2 teaspoons kosher salt
1 cup (240 ml) distilled white vinegar
1 cup (200 g) granulated sugar

In a small bowl, combine the chiles, garlic, and salt and let sit at room temperature for 1 hour.

In a small pan, reduce 1¼ cups (300 ml) water with the vinegar and sugar by a little more than half. It should thicken to a slightly looser syrup consistency. Remove from the heat and stir in the chile-garlic mixture. Cool to room temperature and refrigerate in an airtight container for up to 1 month.

Scallion Jaew

Birdie G's former executive chef Matt Schaler shared this recipe for the classic spicy, sweet Thai dipping sauce with me, and he in turn learned it from chef Miles Thompson. I love when chefs share recipes and knowledge. I'm not a fan of anyone playing hide-the-ball. I was taken aback at first when I saw how freely David Kinch shared recipes, which taught all of us to do the same. To be perfectly honest, I usually have to consult my current or former team members for my own recipes.

Makes about 2 cups (475 ml)

½ cup (120 ml) fresh lime juice
¼ cup plus 1 tablespoon (75 ml) fish sauce
¼ cup (55 g) packed dark brown sugar
1 tablespoon ground ginger
1 tablespoon chili flakes
1 tablespoon finely minced fresh lemongrass (cut from near the base)
2 ounces (60 g) scallion (spring onion) or red onion, cut into fine julienne
2 ounces (60 g) shallot, finely chopped
2 ounces (60 g) fresh cilantro (coriander) leaves and stems, finely chopped

In a mixing bowl, combine all the ingredients and stir to incorporate. Refrigerate in an airtight container for several days, though the flavor will start losing its oomph after 2 days.

Calabrian Chile Hybrid

Yes, this recipe yields a lot of hybrid, but the large quantity is because both of my favorite brands of crushed Calabrian chiles come in 33.5-ounce (950-g) jars. Just halve or quarter the recipe to best suit your needs. It's good on pretty much everything and will store for quite a long time and you can even freeze half. Or, if you're like me, your wife will ask you to bring it home to give away to friends. This hybrid can be utilized in several ways: just the oil, just the solids, or both, as noted in the recipes.

Makes 3 quarts (2.8 liters)

1 × 33.5-ounce (950-g) jar crushed Calabrian chiles (chillies) in oil
2 cups (450 g) chopped garlic
2 cups (320 g) minced shallots
2 cups (475 ml) reserved oil from the Calabrian chiles jar
6 cups (1.4 liters) extra-virgin olive oil
3 tablespoons kosher salt
3 tablespoons ground fennel seed
2 tablespoons ground coriander seed
2 tablespoons sweet paprika
1 tablespoon ground yellow mustard seed

Preheat your oven to 200°F (95°C).

In a large, oven-safe vessel, combine and stir together all the ingredients, then cover with a lid or aluminum foil. Cook until the garlic and shallots are soft, 3 to 4 hours. Your house is going to smell so good.

Cool the mixture to room temperature and then transfer to a sealed container. If you're using more than one container, make sure to stir well so you fill them with an equal amount of oil and solids. Refrigerate in an airtight container for up to 3 weeks.

Nasturtium Salsa

This is a workhorse of a recipe, and it can easily be tailored to your own tastes by substituting the nasturtiums with fresh herbs, such as parsley, dill, mint, tarragon, etc. Serve this with Herb Butter Roast Chicken (page 21) or steak.

Makes about 1 cup (240 ml)

2 tablespoons shallots, minced
1 teaspoon grated garlic
½ teaspoon kosher salt, plus extra to taste
½ teaspoon chili flakes
2 tablespoons red wine vinegar
¾ cup (175 ml) olive oil
½ cup (125 g) nasturtium leaves and flowers, finely chopped, stems thinly sliced

In a mixing bowl, mix the shallots, garlic, salt, and chili flakes and allow it to sit at room temperature for 20 to 30 minutes.

Mix in the vinegar and olive oil, then adjust the seasoning with more salt to taste. The salsa will keep at this point for a few hours in the refrigerator, covered.

Wait to fold in the nasturtiums until just before serving.

Jimmy Nardello Pepper Jam

Jimmy Nardello peppers are a classic sweet red Italian frying pepper. We started seeing them more and more at the markets in California around ten years ago, during my Ubuntu days. Here, they're made into a jam that brings out their fruitiness and really lends itself to pairing with any type of roasted or grilled meat. I also love it paired with aged Cheddar, or a meta pairing with grilled Jimmy Nardello peppers... "Jimmy Nardello peppers in Their Own Jam," as pretentious restaurants such as mine would say. My mother-in-law Debbie tempers blocks of cream cheese around the holidays, then tops the softened cheese with pepper jam and surrounds it with crackers. Trust me when I tell you that this, accompanied by a dry Lambrusco, will become your next favorite party snack.

This is a quick "refrigerator" jam. Meaning it's not canned. We add pectin to thicken it quickly and so the peppers don't cook into nothingness. No need to seed the peppers, just remove the stems and slice into rounds. Much like marmalade, the thickness here should be to your liking. At Birdie G's, we slice them to about ¼ inch (0.6 cm), but there's no need to get out a ruler and be precious about it. Leave the bits of inside and seeds attached: the insides will cook away and dissolve and there aren't enough seeds to worry about.

Makes 2 quarts (1.9 liters)

6 pounds (2.7 kg) Jimmy Nardello peppers, stemmed and sliced into rounds
1 pound (455 g) granulated sugar
¼ cup (40 g) smoked paprika
1½ cups (350 ml) fresh lime juice
2 cups (360 g) apple pectin powder
¼ cup (60 ml) sherry vinegar
kosher salt

In a preserving pan, combine the peppers with the sugar, smoked paprika, and lime juice and warm over medium-high heat, stirring until the sugar dissolves. Maintaining an even medium-high temperature, allow the mixture to simmer for 20 minutes, gently stirring every few minutes and scraping down the sides of the pan.

In a small bowl, mix the pectin powder and sherry vinegar, then whisk this mixture into the simmering pepper mixture. Continue cooking, stirring so no lumps form as the jam thickens, 2 to 3 minutes more. Remove from the heat and cool to room temperature. Add a little salt to taste. Refrigerate in airtight containers for up to 1 month.

Two-Ingredient Applesauce

We're using the whole apple here: peel, stem, seeds, and core. "Everything but the sticker." Resist the urge to overcomplicate it. I can smell the wheels in your head already turning. "I could add some warm spices, maybe a little rum . . ." By all means, yes, but your only job here is to buy the nicest apples you can afford (we buy from Cirone Farms at the Santa Monica Farmers' Market) and let them cook. That's it. Get out of your own way.

Makes 1 quart (0.9 liter)

2½ pounds (1 kg) apples, coarsely chopped
1 tablespoon kosher salt

In a large mixing bowl, toss the apples with the salt. Wrap the bowl tightly with plastic wrap (clingfilm) and place atop a large pot of barely simmering water to create a double-boiler.

Cook for 1½ to 2 hours until the apples completely break down. Add more water to the pot as needed to avoid scorching.

Remove the apples from the heat and allow them to cool slightly. Work them through your food mill in batches using the fine grate. Allow to cool to room temperature and then refrigerate in an airtight container for up to 1 week.

Easy Tomato Sauce

As the title suggests, this is a fairly basic tomato sauce recipe, one that can either become your go-to or be the starting point from which you add your own nuances. It's the same recipe we use at Birdie G's for our kids' menu pasta.

Makes 2 quarts (1.9 liters)

⅓ cup (80 ml) extra-virgin olive oil
½ cup (120 g) finely diced white onion
3 tablespoons chopped garlic
¼ cup (40 g) tomato paste (purée)
1 teaspoon chili flakes
1 × 28-ounce (794-g) can crushed tomatoes
1 × 28-ounce (794-g) can water
2 teaspoons dried oregano
kosher salt

In a stainless steel or copper pan on medium-low heat, warm the olive oil and add the onion, garlic, tomato paste (purée), chili flakes, and a pinch of salt. Cook, stirring, until the garlic is super fragrant, turning the heat to low once it's bubbling. We're not looking for color here, but if it happens, it's not the end of the world. If you do burn it, throw the pan against a wall and wallow in the failure for as long as you need to move forward, then clean up the mess from your childish tantrum and begin again.

Add the crushed tomatoes, water, and oregano. Continue to cook, stirring every couple of minutes, until it reaches that ideal tomato sauce consistency, about 30 minutes. Remove the pot from the heat and cool to room temperature. Refrigerate in an airtight container for several days, perhaps up to 1 week.

Strawberry Sofrito

I am fortunate enough to have certain recipes become synonymous with my name, and this sofrito is one of the main ones. This can be attributed chiefly to it being prominently featured in the David Kinch episode of *The Mind of a Chef* and its inclusion in my first book, *On Vegetables*. While it doesn't call for many ingredients, patience and time are required to achieve the flavor that makes it more than just "good on paper." Try it instead of tomato sauce on a Margherita pizza, with roasted pork, or as a component in Sloppy Jeremy (page 251).

Makes about 4 cups (0.9 liter)

8 oz (225 g) white onion, cut into ¼-inch (0.6-cm) dice
8 oz (225 g) fennel bulb, cut into ¼-inch (0.6-cm) dice
1 cup (140 g) pine nuts (untoasted)
1 cup (240 ml) extra-virgin olive oil
1 teaspoon kosher salt, plus extra to taste
2 pounds (910 g) ripe strawberries
freshly cracked black pepper

Begin by cooking the onion, fennel, pine nuts, olive oil, and salt in a rondeau or other wide, heavy-bottom pot over low heat, stirring occasionally. The goal here is to slowly caramelize the onion and fennel evenly, while also slow-toasting the pine nuts. You should really take your time here and not rush it. This process should take around 2 to 3 hours.

Meanwhile, you can wash your strawberries. I like to let them sit in water, agitate them with my hands, and then let all of the grime fall to the bottom. Once the strawberries have been lifted from the water and left to dry, you can remove the hulls and place the strawberries in a bowl. Now give the strawberries a rough crush with your hands, like an old Italian woman making tomato sauce.

Once the onion and fennel are caramelized and the pine nuts are toasted, add the strawberries and any juice to the pot. Continue cooking over low heat for another 3 hours, or until the sofrito is dark, jammy, and savory.

Add additional salt if needed, then season with cracked black pepper. I like this with a strong dose. Remove the pot from the heat and cool completely. Refrigerate in an airtight container for up to 1 week.

Montreal Steak Rub

You'll find containers of this stuff flanking your grocer's deli case. But you know my motto: why buy it when you can spend your abundant spare time making it?

Makes about 1 cup (120 g)

4 tablespoons black peppercorns
1 tablespoon plus 1½ teaspoons coriander seed
2 tablespoons dried oregano
1 tablespoon dried thyme
1 teaspoon chili flakes
5 tablespoons onion powder
2 tablespoons garlic powder
2 tablespoons kosher salt

Coarsely grind the peppercorns, coriander seed, dried oregano and thyme, and chili flakes separately in a spice grinder, then mix well with the onion powder, garlic powder, and salt. Store in an airtight container at room temperature for up to 1 month.

United Nations Chili Mix

I am well aware that the origins of the chili powders here do not accurately represent the membership of the United Nations. I couldn't even tell you more than one of the actual countries. That said, this spice mix is quite versatile, though I am partial to using it to season a sliced ripe avocado, along with a drizzle of olive oil and a sprinkle of flaky sea salt.

Makes about 1 cup (120 g)

6 tablespoons fennel seed, ground
2 tablespoons fennel pollen
2 tablespoons Korean chili powder (gochugaru)
2 tablespoons Hungarian sweet paprika
4 teaspoons Spanish smoked paprika
4 teaspoons sweet Calabrian chili powder
4 teaspoons chili flakes

Combine all the ingredients and mix well to incorporate. Store in an airtight container at room temperature for several weeks, though the flavor will dull over time.

Persian Spice Blend

Not only perfect for the Lamb a la Saless (page 294), this Persian spice blend is wonderful on grilled meats and vegetables too.

Makes just under 1 cup (120 g)

3 tablespoons dried lime
2 tablespoons black pepper
1½ tablespoons dill seed
1½ tablespoons fenugreek leaf
1 tablespoon cumin seed
½ tablespoon green cardamom seed
½ tablespoon coriander seed
½ cup (70 g) salt

Coarsely grind all the ingredients except the salt. Once ground, stir in the salt. Store in an airtight container for up to 3 months.

Lemon Pepper Rub

At the restaurants, we cut a lot of lemons for "lemon squeezies" served alongside dishes such as grilled fish, oysters, sautéed greens, and the like. We're then left with the "core" of the lemon; much of the pith is gone, and all that remains is the middle membrane, seeds, and a bit of rind. Here, we've utilized these leftovers by fermenting, dehydrating, and blending them into a powder. It is our version of Lawry's Lemon Pepper blend. The one with the white and yellow label that most kitchens had when I was growing up in the '90s. We've added rice koji to help with fermentation. You can find it online or buy Jeremy Umansky and Rich Shih's amazing book, *Koji Alchemy,* and learn how to make your own.

Makes about 1 cup (120 g)

2 cups (240 g) lemon flesh and seeds, plus 1 tablespoon grated lemon zest (without pith)
½ cup (50 g) rice koji
5 tablespoons black peppercorns
2 tablespoons kosher salt

This rub is easy, but not quick. So plan accordingly.

In your food processor, purée all the ingredients together, scraping down the sides of the bowl and making sure all the seeds have been zipped to tiny bits.

Transfer the mixture to a quart (liter) container and cover with cheesecloth (muslin) secured with butcher's twine or a rubber band. Set the container in a dark, cool spot in your kitchen and forget about it for 4 days while the mixture ferments.

Once fermented, you can dehydrate the mixture in a dehydrator or regular oven: Spread the mixture on a dehydrator tray and dry until the paste takes on a cracker-like texture. If you're using the oven method, spread the mixture on a silicone baking mat set on a rimmed baking sheet, preheat to the lowest temperature setting, and monitor the process so your paste doesn't toast or burn.

Next, grind the dehydrated mixture to a powder in a coffee grinder reserved for spices. Store in an airtight container at room temperature for up to 3 months.

Birdie Bay Spice

Makes about 1 cup (120 g)

4 tablespoons fennel seed
4 tablespoons celery seed
1½ teaspoons black peppercorns
1 teaspoon chili flakes
3 tablespoons plus 1½ teaspoons kosher salt
3 tablespoons smoked paprika
3 tablespoons onion powder
1 tablespoon garlic powder

My big sister, Meryl, knows how much I respect Old Bay seasoning, and sometimes sends me Utz "Crab Chip" potato chips (crisps) from her home in Maryland. These chips do not contain any crab whatsoever, but owe their name to their use in traditional crab boils. Let's repeat my motto: Why buy it when you can spend your abundant spare time making it?

Finely grind the fennel seed, celery seed, black peppercorns, and chili flakes in a spice grinder, then combine with the salt, smoked paprika, onion powder, and garlic powder. Store at room temperature in an airtight container for up to 3 months.

Creole Spice

Makes about 1 cup (120 g)

3 tablespoons black peppercorns
3 tablespoons celery seed
2 tablespoons dried oregano
2 tablespoons garlic powder
2 tablespoons onion powder
2 tablespoons filé powder
1½ teaspoons cayenne powder

Used to season the pork in Blackened Pork Tenderloin with Chow-Chow (page 148) and the dredge in Creole Pig Ears & Okra (page 103), this season blend is also perfect sprinkled on grilled peppers, okra side dishes, or roast turkey legs.

Coarsely grind the peppercorns and celery seed in a spice grinder, then combine with the oregano and powders. Store in an airtight container at room temperature for up to 3 months.

Fox Spice

Makes about ½ cup (60 g)

2 tablespoons plus 1½ teaspoons black peppercorns
1 tablespoon coriander seed
1 teaspoon whole cloves
2 tablespoons ground mace
4 teaspoons ground cinnamon

This spice mix, based on Paul Bertolli's blend, is a great jumping-off point for seasoning charcuterie. I recommend starting with this formula, and as you get used to making your own charcuterie, you can play around with the quantities and ingredients.

In a sauté pan over medium heat, toast the peppercorns, coriander seed, and cloves until fragrant, 3 to 4 minutes. Let them cool, then grind finely in a spice grinder. Combine with the mace and cinnamon and store in an airtight container at room temperature for up to 3 months.

Dill Pickles

This is a relatively quick refrigerator pickle that's easy to whip up in your kitchen. You can use leftover pickle jars from the grocery store, or a bunch of airtight containers, to keep them. These are used with the Pickle Chick (page 200) or as an accoutrement on our charcuterie boards, but I mostly love them with a slice of terrine, crusty bread, and good mustard.

First, let's make a sachet of dill. I know other people let their dill be free-range here, but I don't like how it loses color once it's cooked in the brine. Sachets are easy to make with a bit of cheesecloth (muslin) and butcher's twine. Cut a double-layer square of cheesecloth and arrange all the dill in the center. Gather up the corners of the cheesecloth around the dill, twist, and tie it together at the top with the twine, leaving long ends.

In a nonreactive pot, combine 1 quart (0.9 liter) water with the vinegar, sugar, salt, onions, garlic, mustard seed, black peppercorns, chili flakes, and the dill sachet (using the long ends to tie it to the pot handle so it's easier to fish out later). Bring the mixture to a slow boil, stirring until the sugar and salt are dissolved. Remove from the heat and let cool to room temperature before removing the sachet. Chill the brine until cold in your refrigerator.

Divide the cucumbers among 8 sterilized jars, pour in the cold brine, again dividing evenly, and cover each with a cartouche (see page 35). Cover the jars and refrigerate for 7 to 10 days before using. Then they'll keep for several months.

Makes eight 1-quart (0.9-liter) jars

2 bunches dill
2 quarts (1.9 liters) distilled white vinegar
½ cup (100 g) granulated sugar
¼ cup (40 g) kosher salt
2 white onions, julienned
¼ cup (25 g) thinly sliced garlic cloves
4 tablespoons yellow mustard seed
2 tablespoons cracked black peppercorns
1 teaspoon chili flakes
5 pounds (2.3 kg) pickling cucumbers, sliced ¼-inch (0.6-cm) thick (see Note)

Note: When choosing the pickling cucumbers, sometimes referred to as Kirby cucumbers, look for medium-sized ones, 4 to 5 inches (10 to 13 cm) long.

Dill Pickle Sauce

A star component of the Pickle Chick (page 200), this condiment is a great way to utilize the used brine of the pickle recipes in this book or the remnants of the jar you bought at the store.

Makes about 2 cups (475 ml)

2 cups (475 ml) brine from Dill Pickles (page 312) or Pickled Cornichons (page 314), making sure to include the mustard seed and chili flakes
1 tablespoon plus 1½ teaspoons cornstarch (cornflour)
¼ cup (20 g) chopped dill leaves

In a small, nonreactive saucepan, bring the pickle brine to a low simmer. Meanwhile, in a small bowl, make a slurry by combining the cornstarch (cornflour) and 1 tablespoon plus 1½ teaspoons water, mixing until smooth.

While whisking, slowly add the cornstarch slurry to the brine. Simmer the mixture for about 2 minutes until the sauce thickens and any cornstarch flavor cooks out. Remove from the heat and let the sauce cool completely; at this point, the sauce can be refrigerated in an airtight container for up to 1 week. Wait to add the chopped dill when ready to serve.

Pickled Cornichons

Makes two 1-quart (0.9-liter) jars

1 pound (455 g) fresh cornichons
1 quart (0.9 liter) distilled white vinegar
¼ cup plus 2 tablespoons (60 g) kosher salt
¼ cup (50 g) granulated sugar
6 dill sprigs
2 teaspoons chili flakes
3 tablespoons yellow mustard seed
3 tablespoons cracked black pepper
6 garlic cloves, thinly sliced

Procuring fresh cornichons was once very difficult, almost impossible. Luckily, Aaron Choi from Girl & Dug Farms in San Marcos, California, was willing to start growing them. Now, we get to make our own pickled cornichons for the restaurants. Why make your own? My motto regarding this can be found on a few of the pages of this book.

Fresh cornichons come in waves. For a month or two at a time, we'll get 20 or 40 pounds (9 or 18 kg) a week, and then we're incredibly busy cleaning and pickling them. This will be followed by gaps of several months, and by the time we deplete our reserves, it's cornichon time again.

Does that make this recipe extremely inaccessible to most people? Maybe. Yes, probably. I'm sorry. But maybe you'll decide to grow fresh cornichons for pickling, too.

When fresh cornichons come in, they have a lot of fuzz on them. They sometimes have attached leaves or blossoms, which must be removed, or they'll cause the cornichons to soften while pickling (or so I was told, and I don't care to wager whether this is true). To remove the fuzz, submerge the cornichons in a large container of water and agitate them until the fuzz falls off and sinks to the bottom. Lift the cornichons from the water and dry them on paper or kitchen towels.

In a nonreactive medium saucepan, combine 2 cups (475 ml) water with the vinegar, salt, and sugar. Bring the mixture to a simmer, stirring until the salt and sugar are dissolved. Remove from the heat and let cool to room temperature.

Divide the dill sprigs between 2 sterilized jars. Then add the cornichons, followed by the chili flakes, mustard seed, black pepper, and garlic, again dividing evenly. Finally, pour in the cooled brine, making sure to fully submerge the cornichons. Cover the jars and refrigerate; they should be ready in 1 to 2 weeks, or when the cornichons have turned an olive-green color. Then they'll keep for 3 to 4 weeks.

Giardiniera

A classic and traditional recipe for spicy mixed pickled vegetables, perfect for salads, such as the Chopped Antipasto Salad (page 111), or alongside any grilled sausages.

Makes three 1-quart (0.9-liter) jars

1 pound (455 g) cauliflower, cut into small florets
1 pound (455 g) celery stalks, cut into ½-inch (1.3-cm) dice
1 pound (455 g) carrots, cut into ½-inch (1.3-cm) dice
1 pound (455 g) red bell peppers, seeded and cut into ½-inch (1.3-cm) dice
2 ounces (60 g) garlic cloves, thinly sliced
¼ cup (40 g) kosher salt
5 cups (1.3 liters) distilled white vinegar
2 tablespoons fennel seed
2 tablespoons dried oregano
1 tablespoon chili flakes
extra-virgin olive oil, to top each jar

After cutting the vegetables, weigh them to determine the exact amount of salt to use. This recipe is a guide, but you should use 5 percent of the total vegetable weight in salt.

In a large bowl, season the cauliflower, celery, carrots, bell peppers, and garlic with the salt and let them sit at room temperature for 2 hours.

Rinse the vegetables and dry them well on paper or kitchen towels, then transfer to 3 sterilized jars and fill each about three-quarters full.

In a nonreactive pot, bring the vinegar, fennel seed, dried oregano, and chili flakes to a boil. Remove from the heat and divide the hot brine among the jars, filling about ½ inch (1.3 cm) from the top to submerge the vegetables. Make sure to stir the brine as you fill the jars so the spices are evenly distributed. Top off each jar with a layer of olive oil, then seal the jars.

Let sit for 24 to 48 hours at room temperature before moving to refrigeration. The giardiniera will be ready to eat after a few days; once the jars are opened, they will keep for several weeks in the refrigerator.

Ohio Peppers, aka Pickled Hungarian Wax Peppers

When I travel to Northeast Ohio to visit my wife's family, there are two things we love to seek out and try: the first is Italian greens and the second is peppers. I'll explain. Because of the strong influence of Italian immigrants in the area, most of the restaurants make their own version of pickled Hungarian wax peppers, a variety that is spicier than a poblano but milder than a jalapeño. They're almost always sliced into rings, sometimes thin, sometimes thick. There are countless iterations. Local restaurants are judged by their pepper offerings, and certain places are even forgotten because those offerings are judged subpar.

In Southern California, we've sourced the wax peppers primarily from Beylik Family Farms as well as Aaron Choi at Girl & Dug Farm, who offered to grow them for us so we could make enough pickled peppers each summer to last until the next.

This recipe is the one my wife's family makes, usually eaten with the big corn-chip scoops (they like Fritos). I've included the measurement of a peck here because that's how the peppers are usually sold at roadside stands in Ohio. I don't recommend making less than this recipe calls for, unless you want to set yourself up for months of regret after you fly through them.

Makes about 12 cups (3 kg) sliced rings

1 peck (about 5 pounds/2.3 kg) Hungarian wax peppers
¼ cup plus 2 tablespoons (30 g) dried oregano, plus extra to taste
1 teaspoon Alum (see Note)
1 garlic head, cloves thinly sliced, plus extra to taste
¼ cup (120 g) canning salt (see Note), plus extra to taste
2 cups (450 ml) distilled white vinegar
1 quart (0.9 liter) vegetable oil or extra-virgin olive oil

Note: Alum is a preservative that helps keep fruits and vegetables crisp and firm, so please don't omit it. Unless you love soggy peppers. Canning salt is salt minus any anti-caking agents. These agents can make your brine cloudy or dark. Both of these ingredients, alum and canning salt, are readily available at most large grocery stores.

Wearing kitchen gloves, cut the top and bottom tip off each pepper. Using the handle of a kitchen spoon and working in a quick, circular motion, remove the seeds and membrane of each pepper. Simply stick the end of the spoon into the pepper and twist. Shake out the pepper guts into a separate bowl. You can leave some seeds behind depending on how hot you want your peppers; and additionally, you can set some seeds aside to adjust the heat later on.

Cut your prepared peppers into rings that are ¼ inch (0.6 cm) thick. Keep your prepared rings in a crock, glass, or plastic container. Do not use aluminum or the peppers and vinegar may react. And keep in mind, the taste may be hard to remove from a plastic container.

Next, in a large mixing bowl, combine the dried oregano, alum, garlic cloves, canning salt, vinegar, and 2 cups (450 ml) lukewarm water. Mix thoroughly until the salt is dissolved. Slowly whisk in the oil.

Pour the brine over the pepper rings and mix thoroughly. You may need to weigh the top of the peppers with a small plate to keep them submerged. (Depending on the size of your peppers and the volume of rings when cut, you may need to make extra brine to cover the peppers. If they're not fully submerged, make more.)

Cover loosely with plastic wrap (clingfilm) and store in the refrigerator. Let the peppers sit overnight, or up to several days, stirring several times a day.

Remove from the refrigerator and check the seasoning, adding more oregano, salt, garlic, or pepper seeds to your liking. Put the peppers into sterilized jars or plastic quart containers with tight-fitting lids, stirring the brine before filling each jar to keep the oil mixed through.

Make sure each jar/container is topped with ½ inch (1.3 cm) of oil. Wipe off the rim before securing the lid. The peppers will keep in your refrigerator for 1 year.

Pickled Mustard Seeds

A quick and easy accompaniment to any and all charcuterie.

Makes about 1 cup (120 g)

1 cup (100 g) yellow mustard seed
1 cup (240 ml) white wine vinegar
1 cup (200 g) sugar
1 tablespoon kosher salt

In a small saucepan, cover the mustard seed with cold water, bring to a boil, then strain through a fine-mesh sieve. Repeat this process 3 to 4 more times, or until the mustard seed are no longer bitter. Transfer the seed to a plastic container with a tight-fitting lid.

In a nonreactive saucepan, bring the vinegar, 1 cup (240 ml) water, the sugar, and salt to a boil, then pour over the mustard seed. Let cool to room temperature, cover, and refrigerate for up to 3 months.

Apple Cider Mustard

My favorite condiment for charcuterie.

Makes about 2½ quarts (2.4 liters)

2 cups (200 g) brown mustard seed
2 cups (200 g) yellow mustard seed
6 cups (1.4 liters) apple cider vinegar
1 tablespoon kosher salt
½ cup (110 g) packed brown sugar
½ cup (120 ml) beer (something not bitter)

In a large glass jar or other container, combine the brown and yellow mustard seed, vinegar, and salt. Cover with a few layers of cheesecloth (muslin), secured tightly with butcher's twine or a rubber band.

Leave it to ferment at room temperature, out of direct sunlight, for 3 days. This rather short fermentation will give your mustard a little extra zing.

Once the 3 days are up, in a small saucepan, melt the brown sugar into the beer over low heat. Working in batches, add the beer mixture and mustard seed mixture to a food processor and pulse gently until cohesive, with some of the seed broken up but others left whole.

Transfer to a sterilized jar or airtight container (or divide between smaller vessels) and refrigerate for 2 to 3 months.

Mushroom Worcestershire

This recipe sprang up from the need to utilize the peelings and scraps from a large delivery of fresh porcini mushrooms. We were so pleased with the results that we now always have some of the sauce on hand. Later, when the cooks flew through pounds of button mushrooms while practicing the Mushroom Carpaccio (page 240), it became button mushroom Worcestershire. Then, in spring: morel Worcestershire. Whatever version, I love adding it to hollandaise sauce or brushing it on a resting steak, to name just a few options. I have included ratios on page 351 so you can easily adapt the recipe based on the quantities of ingredients.

Makes about 1 quart (0.9 liter)

1 pound 4 ounces (575 g) tamari
13½ ounces (380 g) malt vinegar
10 ounces (290 g) mushroom scraps, such as stems and peelings
6¾ ounces (190 g) molasses
1¾ ounces (50 g) tamarind paste
1¼ ounces (35 g) black garlic
¾ ounces (25 g) creamy koji sauce

In a large mixing bowl or container, combine all the ingredients and pulse gently with an immersion blender just to incorporate; do not aerate or emulsify.

Transfer to sterilized jars and age for 4 to 6 weeks at room temperature. Strain the mixture through a fine-mesh sieve and refrigerate the liquid in a jar or airtight container for up to 3 months.

If you like, you can dehydrate the solids that get strained and grind them into a flavorful powder, suitable for seasoning steak, among other applications.

Sauerkraut

Makes about 6 cups (1.4 kg)

savoy cabbage, washed (outer leaves reserved for other uses such as stuffed cabbage)
cold water seasoned with kosher salt (4 percent of the cabbage's weight)

Sauerkraut was not a big part of my life growing up. It's not that I didn't like it, it's just that I only associated it with hot dogs. And I'm a purist when it comes to dogs and burgers. Once we started making our own sauerkraut at Manresa, I was instantly a card-carrying member of The Sauerkraut Fan Club. This recipe has been updated since *On Vegetables*, from fixed salt-based measurements to brine-based ratios. If you would rather stick with fixed measurements, the universal recipe to follow is 3 ounces (85 g) of salt per 5 pounds (2.3 kg) of cabbage. Enjoy fresh out of the brine, mix with shaved onions and herbs to accompany meat or fish, or braise it as the Choucroute Royale recipe (page 166) outlines.

To begin, finely chiffonade your cleaned cabbage leaves, then transfer to sterilized jars, filling no more than three-quarters full.

Pour the salted water over the cabbage so it's fully submerged, leaving about 1 inch (2.5 cm) of space below the rim. Cover tightly and store at room temperature. The cabbage will begin to ferment almost immediately, so it will be important to open the jars for a few minutes each day to allow the carbon dioxide to be released.

Make sure to practice extreme cleanliness each time you come into contact with the sauerkraut, as any unwelcome bacteria could taint the whole container. If the brine becomes cloudy and/or you notice a white residue, it's best to dispose of it.

Assuming it avoids that fate, I usually begin sampling the flavor after 2 weeks to test how its tanginess is developing. After 4 weeks, transfer the jars to the refrigerator to stop the fermentation.

Once refrigerated, the sauerkraut will keep for several months.

Aioli

This is my version of the classic French aioli—mayonnaise with garlic. Aioli literally translates to "oil" and "garlic," so saying "garlic aioli" is cringingly repetitive. Do not write "Garlic Aioli" on your menu, and make sure to spell "Mascarpone" and "Caramelized" properly while you're at it. Anyway, this recipe is a kitchen workhorse, capable of being used in so many ways, such as a dip for fries or crudités, smeared on the outside of a chicken before roasting, or brushed on fresh scallops or salmon belly and kitchen-torched. Add buttermilk and herbs, and you've got a beautiful salad dressing.

Fun fact: At the age of eight, a cruel babysitter threatened to tell my mom that I had misbehaved unless I ate a bowl of warm, microwaved mayonnaise. As a result, from that evening all the way until my senior year of high school, I refused to ingest even the most minuscule amount of anything mayonnaise related. Go fuck yourself, Maureen.

Makes about 2 cups (475 ml)

2 large egg yolks
3 to 4 garlic cloves, grated
juice of ½ lemon
2 tablespoons plus 1½ teaspoons Dijon mustard
1 cup (240 ml) extra-virgin olive oil
½ cup (120 ml) grapeseed oil
kosher salt

In your food processor, zip the egg yolks, garlic, lemon juice, and mustard to combine, scraping down the sides of the bowl as you go. With the motor still running, add your oils (the olive oil and grapeseed oil can be combined before adding), starting in the slowest of streams. As the mixture emulsifies, or comes together, you can speed up the stream until all the oil is incorporated.

I keep a little tepid water on call in case the aioli starts breaking. What a breaking aioli looks like is best described as appearing like it just won't accept any more oil. A few drops of the water will fix this. Season with salt to taste.

Transfer to an airtight container and refrigerate for up 3 to 4 days. After chilling, your aioli may seem too thick, even setting up and pulling away from the sides of the container. Good-quality olive oils will often cause this. A little bit of whisking, and perhaps adding a few drops of tepid water, will smooth things out.

Crème Fraîche

Fancy sour cream.

Makes about 2 cups (475 ml)

2 cups (480 ml) heavy (double) cream
3 tablespoons buttermilk (or crème fraîche from your previous batch)

In a container, combine the cream and buttermilk, then cover with plastic wrap (clingfilm) with a few tiny holes poked into it. Store at room temperature for 24 to 36 hours, or until nicely thickened.

Once it has achieved your desired thickness, carefully skim off the very top layer and discard. Whisk what remains to incorporate, then pour into airtight containers and refrigerate for 3 weeks.

Béchamel

The classic French white sauce, béchamel is useful in a wide variety of dishes: lasagna, moussaka, biscuits and gravy, or the Egg Salad Croque Madame on page 212. Feel free to add cracked black pepper, freshly grated nutmeg, or cheese (Gruyère and/or Parmigiano-Reggiano) to make Mornay. This is the most basic version, ready to be seasoned and added to whatever you may choose.

Makes about 2 cups (475 ml)

4 tablespoons (56 g) unsalted butter
¼ cup (30 g) all-purpose (plain) flour
2 cups (480 ml) whole (full-fat) milk
1½ teaspoons kosher salt, or extra to taste

In a large sauté pan, melt the butter on medium heat. Once the butter stops foaming (make sure not to let the butter brown), sprinkle in the flour all at once. Using your whisk, mix together the flour and butter and cook for 2 minutes. This will help to remove any lumps and lingering flour taste. Slowly add the milk, whisking to combine. Bring the mixture to a boil, stirring constantly as the sauce thickens. Pay attention to your heat; you don't want to scorch the bottom of the pot. If you do, you can try all you want to surgically remove the liquid without bringing any of the caked-on bits, but the burnt flavor cannot be removed. If it's boiling too rapidly, turn it down to a low simmer. Add salt to taste and remove from the heat.

Clarified Butter

I know I go on and on about cooking meat in its corresponding rendered fat, but there are occasions where that might be too much of a good thing. In both the Chicken Cutlets (page 230) and Chicken Kyiv (page 203) recipes, I call for clarified butter. The decadent flavor of the butter helps balance things out for a better final product.

Makes about 1 cup (240 ml)

1 cup (230 g) unsalted butter, cut into 1-inch (2.5-cm) chunks

In a small saucepan on medium-low heat, slowly melt the butter. You don't want it to burn or brown.

Remove the butter from the heat and let stand for 10 minutes. With a soup spoon or strainer, skim off the white milk solids that rise to the top. Pour into a small bowl, cover, and refrigerate until the fat solidifies.

The butter can now be popped out of the bowl, where the water will remain. Blot dry the bottom of the fat with paper towels and refrigerate in an airtight container for up to 3 weeks.

Escargot Butter

The title is deceiving; no snails are needed. The name comes from its inclusion in the classic French escargot dish that inspired my version. Let this flavorful herb butter melt on top of your hot steak or follow the recipe for Chicken Kyiv on page 203.

Makes about 2 cups (455 g)

¼ cup (60 ml) white wine, flamed off and cooled
¼ cup (30 g) chopped fresh Italian parsley leaves, plus ¼ cup (30 g) thinly sliced parsley stems
1 tablespoon Garlic Confit (page 341)
1 tablespoon grated garlic
3 shallots, minced
1 teaspoon freshly ground black pepper
1 cup (230 g) salted butter, room temperature
kosher salt

Note: We want green here, and heat is not usually a friend of green, so placing the blender base and container in the refrigerator ahead of time is not overkill.

In a blender, purée the flamed-off white wine with the parsley leaves, garlic confit, and raw garlic. Blend quickly and just long enough to make a nice purée. It doesn't need to be baby-food smooth.

In a stand mixer or by hand, fold the purée, parsley stems, shallots, and black pepper into the softened butter until well incorporated. Season to taste with salt.

Refrigerate the butter in an airtight container for up to 1 week, or freeze for a couple of months. You can also roll it into logs in plastic wrap (clingfilm), refrigerate or freeze by hanging it from a shelf, and slice into coins to melt over hot steak.

Pot Roast Butter

While the preceding recipe's title is admittedly deceiving, this one is really on the nose. The bone marrow can be substituted with any rendered animal fat, or even by the fat that may have settled at the top of your stocks.

Makes about 2 cups (455 g)

5 pounds (2.3 kg) canoe-cut marrow bones in 6-inch (15-cm) lengths (about 8 bones)
kosher salt
3 tablespoons diced carrot
3 tablespoons diced celery heart
2 tablespoons minced shallot
1 tablespoon tomato paste (purée)
¾ cup (180 ml) red wine
1 cup (230 g) salted butter, room temperature
¼ cup (60 ml) All-Purpose Meat Jus (page 336)
1 tablespoon Garlic Confit (page 341)
2 teaspoons freshly ground black pepper
1 teaspoon fresh thyme leaves
2 tablespoons fresh Italian parsley leaves, finely chopped
2 tablespoons inner celery leaves, finely chopped

A day ahead, in a brining bag or container depending on the size of your refrigerator, soak the bones in a 2 percent saltwater brine for 12 to 24 hours under refrigeration. (No judgment, my home refrigerator is pretty tiny.) This step will help extract the blood and give your marrow a clean white hue. Drain on paper or kitchen towels.

Preheat your oven to 350°F (180°C).

On a sheet pan or in a casserole dish, roast the bones for 5 to 8 minutes, or just until the marrow feels like gelatin. Remove from the oven and cool to room temperature.

In a smallish sauté pan on medium heat, add a good tablespoon of the rendered marrow fat from the sheet pan. Add the carrot, celery, shallot, and a pinch of salt, and sauté past the translucent stage—we're going for a medium level of caramelization. Add the tomato paste (purée), stir to combine, and toast it a little bit. It's okay if there's some light stickage... you want this, it's called "fond." Deglaze the pan with the wine, scraping up any fond, and reduce it by about 90 percent, or until it's the consistency of warm honey.

While the wine is reducing, either by hand or in a stand mixer or food processor, whip the butter until completely smooth.

Once the wine is reduced, add the meat jus, bring to a boil, then remove from the heat. Add the garlic confit, black pepper, and thyme leaves. Scoop the marrow from the bones, being careful to avoid any bone fragments, and add that to the pan along with any remaining rendered fat.

When the mixture has reached a lukewarm temperature, fold it into the whipped butter. Mix in the parsley and celery leaves and adjust the salt to taste.

Refrigerate in an airtight container for up to 1 week, or freeze for a couple of months. You can also roll it into logs in plastic wrap (clingfilm), refrigerate or freeze by hanging it from a shelf, and slice into coins to melt over hot steak.

Blue Cheese Butter

A classic steakhouse add-on for your steak. Enjoy it with the Apples Roasted in Bacon Fat from page 138.

Makes about 2 cups (455 g)

2 tablespoons minced shallot
2 tablespoons apple cider vinegar
1 teaspoon kosher salt, plus extra to taste
1 cup (230 g) good blue cheese (I like Point Reyes' Bay Blue)
1 cup (230 g) salted butter, room temperature
2 tablespoons finely chopped fresh Italian parsley leaves
1 teaspoon freshly ground black pepper

In a food processor or stand mixer, combine the shallot, vinegar, and salt. Add one-third of the blue cheese and all the butter and mix until completely smooth.

If using a food processor, transfer to a mixing bowl. If using a stand mixer, just dislodge the bowl and finish in that. Fold in the remaining blue cheese with the parsley and black pepper, breaking up the cheese and distributing it evenly into the butter. Adjust the seasoning with more salt.

Refrigerate the butter in an airtight container for up to 1 week, or freeze for a couple of months. You can also roll it into logs in plastic wrap (clingfilm), refrigerate or freeze by hanging it from a shelf, and slice into coins to melt over hot steak.

Garlic Bread Croutons

The Birdie G's kitchen smells so good when we're making these croutons. Hopefully, you'll experience it yourself when you make them at home. They taste like croutons from the grocery store, only better, with a great texture that melts in your mouth instead of cutting it to shreds. For extra credit, use the Pain de Mie on page 328.

Makes about 6 cups (250 g)

¾ cup (180 ml) extra-virgin olive oil
1½ ounces (45 g) Parmigiano-reggiano, finely grated
3 tablespoons grated garlic
1 teaspoon garlic powder
1½ teaspoons kosher salt
1 pound (455 g) crustless bread, cut into 1-inch (2.5-cm) cubes

Preheat your oven to 300°F (150°C).

In a small bowl, whisk together the olive oil, Parmigiano, grated garlic, garlic powder, and salt. In a large mixing bowl, add the cubed bread and pour the olive oil mixture over it, tossing gently with your hands to combine. Don't be too aggressive here, you don't want to break up the bread into crumbs.

Arrange the coated bread onto a rimmed baking sheet lined with parchment paper and bake for 10 to 15 minutes, or until the bread is crisp. I prefer no color on the croutons, just like the ones we bought in bags at the grocery store when I was a kid. Cool them to room temperature before storing; they'll hold for several days in airtight containers with silica packets.

Pain de Mie

This is fancy white bread.

Makes 1 loaf

6½ cups (795 g) all-purpose (plain) flour or bread (strong) flour, plus more for dusting
1 cup (240 ml) whole (full-fat) milk, room temperature
2 tablespoons (28 g) unsalted butter, room temperature
1 tablespoon plus 1 teaspoon kosher salt, plus a pinch for the egg wash
2 generous tablespoons granulated sugar
1 tablespoon active dry (fast-action) yeast (I like SAF)
grapeseed oil, for oiling
1 large egg

In a stand mixer with a dough hook, combine all the ingredients (except for the egg), and knead for about 15 minutes—or until it creates a somewhat smooth surface.

Once kneaded, transfer the dough to an oiled bowl or container, then cover it with plastic wrap (clingfilm) and leave it in a warm area in your kitchen to rise until it has doubled in size, about 1 hour.

Next, punch down the dough to deflate it. Lift up a corner and fold it over the top of the dough, turn the bowl 90 degrees, and repeat this process until you've done four folds. Cover the dough, and let it proof again for 1 more hour.

Now you can transfer the dough to a lightly floured work surface. Stretch the dough into a rectangular shape that is the same length as a Pullman loaf pan. Starting from the edge closest to you, roll and tuck the dough as though you were making a cinnamon roll, until you have reached the other end. You should now have a rolled loaf that is the length of the Pullman loaf pan. Oil the loaf pan, then lay the dough inside, seam side down. Cover loosely with plastic wrap (clingfilm) and let it proof in a warm area until the dough is about ½ inch (1.3 cm) past the top of the pan, about 1 hour. While proofing, preheat the oven to 350°F (180°C).

Once proofed, make an egg wash: whisk the egg with a tablespoon of water and a pinch of salt. Gently brush the egg wash over the top of the pain de mie.

Bake for around 30 to 40 minutes, until the internal temperature is between 180-190°F (82-88°C).

Once cooked, cool it in the pan on a rack for 10 minutes. After that, you can remove it from the pan and let it finish cooling on the rack. If it is sticking, carefully run a small knife between the bread and the pan to loosen it up.

Cool completely before slicing. But one warm slice with butter won't kill anyone.

Crispy Kasha

Crispy kasha, much like crispy rice, is the kind of thing you'll want on or in everything once you master making it. And mastering doesn't take much but patience. In this book, the crunchy, fried bit is used in the recipes for Pork Blood Kishka (page 82) and Grilled Lamb Heart, Spigarello, and Bagna Cauda (page 267). Any extra can be tossed into salads, sprinkled on ice cream, or maybe swapped in for the usual cereal to make a crispy kasha marshmallow treat. The possibilities are endless.

Makes about 4 cups (600 g)

1 pound (455 g) kasha (see Note)
2 tablespoons canola (rapeseed) oil

Note: I love Anson Mills Slow Roasted Buckwheat Groats.

In a wide pot, bring the kasha and 3¼ cups (770 ml) water to a simmer, stirring occasionally until all the water is absorbed. Spread the cooked kasha on a sheet pan lined with parchment paper and cool to room temperature.

Once the kasha has cooled, in a heavy-bottom pot, bring the canola (rapeseed) oil to 300°F (150°C) and line a sheet pan with paper or kitchen towels. Rest a fine-mesh sieve over the pot, with the mesh in the hot oil. This setup allows you to break up any kasha that's clumped using a wooden spoon and remove the finished kasha.

Working in batches, fry the kasha until crispy, about 2 to 3 minutes, then carefully lift out the sieve and sprinkle the fried kasha onto the prepared sheet pan to absorb the excess oil. Return the canola oil to 300°F (150°C) between batches and continue until all the kasha is fried.

Once cooled completely, the crispy kasha will last a few days in an airtight container at room temperature.

Puff Pastry

This recipe is inspired by Fran Gage's puff pastry recipe from her wonderful book, *A Sweet Quartet*. I've added notes and methods that have helped me, but the quantities are all Fran's.

And listen, I get it, making puff can be daunting. But honestly, once you make it and see it puff up and it's SO DELICIOUS, you'll be hooked. Go for it. You'll be so proud of yourself.

Makes about 2½ pounds (1 kg)

1 pound (455 g) unbleached all-purpose flour
2 teaspoons kosher salt
1 pound (455 g) unsalted butter, cold
1 tablespoon fresh lemon juice, no pulp
1 cup (240 ml) cold water

In a medium bowl, mix together the flour and salt. Cut 4 ounces (115 g) of butter into ½ inch (1.3 cm) pieces and add them to the flour mixture. Rub the flour and butter together with your fingertips, flattening the butter as you go. Work quickly so that the butter doesn't melt. The flour should look like coarse polenta when you're done.

Combine the lemon juice and water and add it to the flour/butter mixture a little at a time. Mix the dough together with your hand or a wooden spoon. It should come together fairly quickly. Lightly flour your work surface and turn the dough onto it. Knead it a few times with the heel of your palm, gathering it into a rough ball. Flatten the dough into a disk, about ½ inch (1.3 cm) thick. If the sides of the disk are still rough, flatten and smooth them with your palm. Wrap the disk in plastic wrap (clingfilm) and rest the dough in the refrigerator for 30 minutes.

Once the dough has had time to rest, remove it from the refrigerator and put it back on your lightly floured surface. If the dough disk is too hard from the refrigerator, simply bash it a few times with your rolling pin, starting at the top and working down in a straight line. Roll the circle of dough into an oval, turn it 90 degrees, and continue to roll, back and forth, until it starts to form a circle. Continue rolling and turning until it's 13 inches (33 cm) across. As you roll, allow an area in the center to be a bit thicker, about 5-6 inches (13-15 cm) across.

Now, take your remaining cold butter and, on a lightly floured surface, roll it into a disk about the same thickness and width as the thick center of your dough. Put your butter disk on top of the center of the dough and fold the edges of the dough over it.

Turn this little butter/dough package over on your lightly floured work surface so that the seam is on the bottom. Use your rolling pin to gently pound and press it to a somewhat flat circle. Now, roll the dough into a 20 × 11-inch (50 x 28-cm) rectangle. I find this easiest when you roll up and away from you.

Next, with the narrower side facing you, dust off any excess flour from the top and fold the bottom up one-third of the way. Now, fold the top down, like you're folding a letter. Top goes over bottom. Turn the dough so that the outer fold is on your left, like a book. Roll and fold the dough one more time. Here's where it gets cooking school: make 2 finger indentations on the top of the dough to remind you that you have made 2 turns. Wrap the dough back up in plastic wrap and refrigerate it for 1 hour. Remove the dough from the refrigerator and repeat the process, rolling and folding the dough 2 more times. Make 4 finger indentations in the top of the dough, wrap in plastic wrap and refrigerate for 1 more hour.

Remove the dough and roll and fold it 2 more times, for a total of 6 times, or turns. Wrap, refrigerate, and rest. After an hour it's ready to be used. It can stay wrapped in the refrigerator for up to 7 days, or put in a freezer bag and frozen for up to 3 months. If you plan on freezing the dough, only do 4 turns, freeze, and do the final 2 turns after thawing.

After the last hour of rest, it's ready to be shaped and used in your recipe.

Skillet Biscuits

For funsies.

Makes 12 biscuits

8 tablespoons (1 stick) unsalted butter, cold, plus 2 tablespoons melted and 1 tablespoon room temperature
3 cups (360 g) all-purpose (plain) flour, plus extra for dusting
1 cup (120 g) "00" flour
2 tablespoons baking powder
1 teaspoon baking soda (bicarbonate of soda)
2 teaspoons kosher salt
½ cup (110 g) Leaf Lard (page 339)
1½ cups (350 ml) high-quality buttermilk, cold
flaky sea salt

Note: In addition to a high-sided, cast-iron skillet, you'll need a biscuit cutter for this recipe. Sometimes you can buy these in sets, which is helpful for other projects, plus they'll last forever. But if you want to buy just one, or you're at a flea market and they have fun vintage ones, look for a cutter that is 2½ to 3 inches (6 to 7.5 cm) in diameter.

First, dust your stick of butter in some all-purpose (plain) flour so it's a little easier to handle. Using the butter wrapper so you don't grate your hand, grate the butter on the big holes of a box grater, then spread it out on a freezer-safe plate and freeze for 10 minutes.

Meanwhile, in a large mixing bowl, stir together both flours, baking powder, baking soda (bicarbonate of soda), and kosher salt. Add the lard. Working quickly with a fork or pastry cutter, work in the lard. It's okay if you still see dime-size chunks, just no big blobs. Put the bowl in the freezer for 10 minutes so the lard can become firm again. Lard melts quicker than butter, and we want it to melt on our terms.

Once the flour mixture is chilled, add the frozen butter shreds. Stir with a wooden spoon to incorporate, coating them in the mixture. Drizzle in the cold buttermilk and, using a fork or wooden spoon, stir it in until everything is just combined. Don't overwork it.

Turn the dough out onto a floured work surface and, with floured hands, flatten it into a square. We're going to do some quick folds: fold the top half over the bottom half, aligning the edges, and give it a pat, pat, pat. Now, turn it so that the folded side is on your left, like a book, and fold the top over the bottom again. Using your rolling pin, roll the dough to a thickness of 1 inch (2.5 cm), keeping that loose rectangle/square shape. Repeat the entire folding process one more time, and then roll the dough to a thickness of 1 inch (2.5 cm) again.

Preheat your oven to 425°F (215°C). Using the 1 tablespoon tempered butter, grease the bottom and sides of a high-sided, cast-iron skillet.

With a floured fork, poke the dough all over to create little air vents. With a biscuit cutter, cut out as many rounds of dough as possible. Do not twist the cutter when you cut, which can seal the edge and prevent a good rise in the oven. Just cut straight down. Place the dough rounds next to each other, barely touching, in your buttered skillet.

Gather the scraps, repeat the folding process, fork them, and cut out more rounds. Purists will disagree with me here; usually the scraps are just re-rolled and cut as is, but I find that treating them to another round of folding doesn't hurt.

Once all the biscuits are cut out and in the pan, brush them with the remaining 2 tablespoons of melted butter and sprinkle with flaky sea salt.

Bake in the preheated oven for 17 to 25 minutes, or until golden and risen. Remove from the oven and enjoy.

Rachael's Chicken Stock

My wife, Rachael, gets food obsessions. Something interests her, and then she reads everything she can get her hands on and tests and tests until she has something that's her own. First it was pie crusts. More recently it's been chicken stock. This recipe for chicken stock is what we now use at Birdie G's, though she's updated her version about five times since then. And we, in turn, have made the recipe our own. That's one of the best parts about food, really—collaboration and adaptation.

Yields about 4 quarts (3.75 liters)

4 pounds (1.8 kg) chicken backs
1 pound (455 g) chicken feet
2 pounds (910 g) chicken wings
12 ounces (340 g) white onions, cut into 2-inch (5-cm) pieces
½ pound (227 g) carrots, cut into 2-inch (5-cm) pieces
2 ounces (60 g) celery stalks, cut into 2-inch (5-cm) pieces
1 head garlic, halved
½ bunch thyme
4 bay leaves
3 tablespoons kosher salt
1 tablespoon black peppercorns

To a large stockpot, add the chicken backs, feet, and wings. Cover all the bones with 6 quarts (about 6 liters) cold water, leaving about 2 inches (5 cm) of headroom. Set the pot aside and let sit at room temperature for 90 minutes. I have found that this waiting period assists the clarification of the stock as it cooks.

On high heat, bring the stock to a boil, then lower the temperature to a medium simmer and skim any foam that rises to the top.

After all the foam has been skimmed, add the onions, carrots, celery, garlic, thyme, bay leaves, salt, and peppercorns. Give the pan one good stir to submerge the vegetables and chicken bones.

Reduce the heat to low and try to keep the stock at about 200°F (93°C) for 8 hours. The pot should barely simmer; every once in a while it will release a bubble or two. Alternatively, you can add the pot to a 250°F (120°C) oven overnight, letting it gently bubble away all night.

When the stock is done, it should have a thick layer of golden, rendered chicken fat on top. Strain the stock through a coarse strainer, making sure to extract as much stock as possible from the hot bones and vegetables. Reserve the bones if you'd like to prepare Dressed Chicken Bones "Isadore" (page 207).

Next, strain the stock through a fine-mesh chinois. Chill in an ice bath and refrigerate in a covered container.

For any stock you won't be using within a few days, I recommend carefully pouring it into large storage bags and laying flat in the freezer. Once each bag is frozen, they stack or file away nicely.

Beef Stock

Use this stock to braise tough cuts of beef, such as short ribs or oxtails. You can also serve this as a sipping broth, although I would recommend omitting the tomato paste (purée) if you're planning ahead.

Preheat the oven to 425°F (215°C).

Place the beef neck bones on a foil-lined sheet tray with a rack and roast until deep brown, about 1 hour.

Meanwhile, season the oxtails and chuck lightly with salt, and let sit for 30 minutes. Cut the chuck into 2-inch (5-cm) pieces.

Heat your stock pot on high heat, add the tallow and sear the oxtails and chuck on all sides until deep brown. Do this in batches if necessary.

Remove the meat and transfer it to a bowl lined with cheesecloth (muslin), then tie the cloth at the top. This step is to make it easier to serve the pulled/shredded meat to your dogs, should you wish to do so.

Add the vegetables, peppercorns, thyme, and bay leaves to the pot, and cook everything over medium heat while scraping up any fond stuck to the pot. Allow the vegetables to caramelize.

Add the tomato paste (purée), stir to combine and toast for a few minutes, but do not burn.

Add 2 cups (500 ml) of ice and scrape up any fond that forms. Reduce, and let another fond form. Scrape up the fond, add the remaining ice and the garlic, and let a third fond form. Scrape up the fond, and add 10 quarts (9.5 liters) water, oxtails, chuck, neck bones, and marrow bones. Bring everything to a boil, skim, and reduce to a suggestion of a simmer for 8 to 10 hours, skimming as you go.

Strain, cool, and refrigerate in containers or freeze in bags.

Makes 8 quarts (7.5 liters)

4 pounds (1.8 kg) beef neck bones
2 pounds (910 g) beef oxtails
2 pounds (910 g) beef chuck
¼ cup (60 ml) Beef Tallow (page 339)
2 white onions, cut into 2-inch (5-cm) pieces
1 leek, cut into 2-inch (5-cm) pieces
6 celery stalks, cut into 2-inch (5-cm) pieces
3 carrots, cut into 2-inch (5-cm) pieces
1 tablespoon black peppercorns
½ bunch thyme
2 bay leaves
¼ cup (60 g) tomato paste (purée)
4 cups (1 liter) ice cubes
1 head garlic, halved
2 pounds (910 g) marrow bones
kosher salt

Ham Hock Stock

Not just for ham and bean soup, but yes please do that. This stock is wonderful ladled over crispy toast and a poached egg, or use it to make polenta and top with grilled garlicky shrimp (prawns) and some wilted kale.

Makes about 8 quarts (7.5 liters)

6 pounds (2.75 kg) Smoked Ham Hocks (page 85)
2 onions, cut into 2-inch (5-cm) pieces
4 celery stalks, cut into 2-inch (5-cm) pieces
2 carrots, cut into 2-inch (5-cm) pieces
1 head garlic, halved
½ bunch thyme
1 tablespoon black peppercorns
2 bay leaves

In a large stock pot, combine all the ingredients with 8 quarts (7.5 liters) water. Bring to a boil on high heat, skim, and reduce to the slightest simmer for about 4 hours, or until the meat is fall-off-the-bone tender.

Remove the ham hocks, wrap each one tightly in plastic wrap (clingfilm), and cool to room temperature.

Strain the stock and cool. Pick the meat, add enough stock to completely saturate, and store in freezer-safe bags. The stock can also be stored in freezer bags.

All-Purpose Meat Jus

My version of what is commonly referred to as demi-glace—demi for short. We're fortifying our already-made stock with more caramelized beef, aromatics, and wine. The simplest application would be spooning over a steak.

Makes 2 cups (480 ml)

2 tablespoons Beef Tallow (page 339)
1 pound (455 g) raw beef scraps, cut into 1-inch (2.5-cm) pieces
1 white onion, cut into 1-inch (2.5-cm) pieces
2 celery stalks, cut into 1-inch (2.5-cm) pieces
1 carrot, cut into 1-inch (2.5-cm) pieces
1½ cups (350 ml) dry sherry
1½ cups (350 ml) red wine
4 cups (950 ml) Beef Stock (page 335) or Rachael's Chicken Stock (page 334)
2 tablespoons honey
parsley stems (optional)

In a wide pan on high heat, add the tallow, then the beef scraps, and caramelize all over. Remove the meat to a bowl lined with cheesecloth (muslin), then tie the cloth at the top.

Add the vegetables to the pan and caramelize. Deglaze with the sherry and red wine, then reduce by 80 percent. Add the stock and sachet of beef and bring to a boil. Skim, reduce the heat, whisper the word "simmer" to yourself but not out loud, and that's the temperature to cook the stock for 2 to 3 hours.

After the first 30 minutes, add the honey and parsley stems, if using.

Strain, cool, and store (refrigerated or frozen). Save the cheesecloth of spent meat for your dog.

All-Purpose Meat Brine

We are always struggling to create more storage space in the restaurants, which is why this brine has been designed to take up half of the space. Smart, right?

Bring 4 quarts (3.75 liters) water and the rest of the ingredients to a boil in a large pot. Remove from the heat, add another 4 quarts (3.75 liters) cold water, cool to room temperature, and refrigerate until ready to use.

When brining chicken, combine the brine with equal parts cold water, and fully submerge your chicken. As a guide, this brine works as a 4-hour brine on boneless, skinless chicken breasts, and an 8-hour brine on butchered half chickens. Make sure to rinse the chicken well to prevent the sugar from coloring the skin too quickly, and dry on kitchen towels or air-dry on a rack before cooking.

Makes 8 quarts (7.5 liters)

1 pound (455 g) salt
1 cup (200g) sugar
4 tablespoons black peppercorns
¼ bunch thyme
1 tablespoon dried oregano
1¼ ounces (40 g) raw garlic cloves
zest and juice of 2 lemons
1 ounce (30 g) allspice berries
½ ounce (15 g) cinnamon stick
4 bay leaves

Smoke Brine

Use this to brine pork hocks for Smoked Ham Hocks (page 85). I also use this for smoked fish, replacing the molasses with granulated sugar.

Combine all the ingredients with 4 quarts (3.75 liters) water, bring to a boil, then chill completely.

Makes 4 quarts (3.75 liters)

1½ cups (300 g) brown sugar
1½ cups (340 g) molasses
¾ cup (120 g) kosher salt

Corn Brine

I now realize that this chapter is full of misleading recipe titles. This brine: not for corn or made of corn. It's a verb. As in corned beef. Use it for the Corned Beef Tongue (page 66) and the Corned Brisket (page 73).

Combine all the ingredients with 4 quarts (3.75 liters) water, bring to a boil, cool down, and refrigerate.

Makes 4 quarts (3.75 liters)

1½ cups (240 g) kosher salt
¾ cup (160 g) brown sugar
2 tablespoons curing salt #1
1 tablespoon mustard seed
1 tablespoon black peppercorns
12 whole cloves
15 juniper berries
5 allspice berries
2 cinnamon sticks
3 bay leaves

Schmaltz & Gribenes

No, not a law firm whose phone calls you need to screen.

Schmaltz is a staple of Ashkenazi Jewish cooking, adding a depth of flavor to a number of classic dishes. You can, of course, just render chicken fat as you would other animal fats. But rendered chicken fat without onions is not schmaltz. Gribenes are the incredibly delicious fried pieces of chicken skin and onions left behind and can be enjoyed simply, spread onto rye toast. Both are used to make the Matzo Ball Soup on page 184 as flavorful as any matzo ball soup out there.

Makes about 1 quart (0.9 liter) schmaltz and 10 cups (1.3 kg) gribenes

- 4 pounds (1.8 kg) raw chicken fat
- 2 tablespoons plus 1½ teaspoons kosher salt
- 1 pound (455 g) white onions, cut into ¼-inch (0.6 cm) julienne

Mix together the chicken fat and salt in a wide pot, rondeau, or Dutch oven—you know the kind: heavy-bottomed. Pile the onions evenly on top. Cook on medium-high heat and, as the fat renders, the onions will be lowered into the hot fat bath like the culinary version of an ancient method of torture. Once the onions are well on their way into the fat, you can begin stirring as you reduce the heat to the low end of medium.

As it cooks, give it the occasional good stir so the bottom doesn't stick or—gasp!—burn.

Once the fat and onions are nice and golden, and all the fat appears to be rendered, remove from the heat and drain through a fine-mesh sieve set over a container to hold the liquid fat.

After the fat has drained, move it into a tall and narrow container. Decant the fat as much as you can from the natural stock that settles to the bottom. Anything you can't get will be easily separated once it's fully chilled.

As for the solids, these can be given a rough chop or pulsed in a food processor. Refrigerated, it will hold for 1 week. If submerged in the liquid fat, it will hold indefinitely in the refrigerator or freezer… same for the liquid fat on its own.

The decanted stock will be concentrated and flavorful, great for adding to the next batch of stock or as a secret flavor weapon for sauces, braises, or secret potions.

Beef Tallow

Tallow is a great way to add a meatier and more complex flavor profile to simple preparations such as frying potatoes or even baking. You can read more about how I like to use tallow and other rendered animal fats on page 11.

Mix the beef fat, 1½ cups (350 ml) water, the salt, and bay leaves in a wide, heavy-bottom pot on medium heat. Once the fat begins rendering and starts to bubble, reduce the heat to just the slightest bubble. After about 45 minutes to 1 hour, the fat should be soft and easily smashed with the back of a wooden spoon.

Remove from the heat and blend with a stick blender until smooth and creamy. Return to the heat and continue cooking until that creaminess is gone and the fat is clear.

Strain through a fine-mesh sieve. The liquid fat can be cooled, decanted of any sediment, and refrigerated or frozen. Any strained solids can be saved to add to the meat mixture for Chicken Scrapple (page 208).

Makes about 5 cups (1 kg)

5 pounds (2.3 kg) raw beef fat, in 1½-inch (4 cm) pieces (see Note)
3½ tablespoons kosher salt
2 bay leaves

Note: Ideally, look for leaf fat, the fat around the kidneys, or the hard fat from around the loins. Before it's rendered, this kind of fat is called suet.

Leaf Lard

Leaf lard is rendered from the fat around a pig's kidneys and is some of the best fat you can use for pastry.

Mix the leaf lard, 1½ cups (350 ml) water, the salt, and bay leaves in a wide, heavy-bottom pot on medium heat. Once the fat begins rendering and starts to bubble, reduce the heat to just the slightest bubble. After about 45 minutes to 1 hour, the fat should be soft and easily smashed with the back of a wooden spoon.

Remove from the heat and blend with a stick blender until smooth and creamy. Return to the heat and continue cooking until that creaminess is gone and the fat is clear.

Strain through a fine-mesh sieve. The liquid fat can be cooled, decanted of any sediment, and refrigerated or frozen. If any solids remain, try them on a piece of peanut butter toast.

Makes about 5 cups (1 kg)

5 pounds (2.3 kg) raw pork leaf lard, in ½-inch (1.25 cm) pieces
3½ tablespoons kosher salt
2 bay leaves

Chicken Crackling

As with anything crispy, fatty, and salty, I recommend you make more than listed here. You will want to snack on it. The smell alone will push you over the edge. It's the same with fried capers or fried shallots. You're a mere mortal, what can you do? Not try a crispy chicken skin? Not try several?! Impossible.

Makes about 1 cup (240 g)

8 ounces (225 g) chicken skins
1 teaspoon kosher salt
1 teaspoon freshly ground black pepper

Preheat your oven to 400°F (200°C).

Using a chef's knife or bench scraper, scrape off as much fat as you can from the underside of the chicken skins. Lightly season each side of the skins with salt and pepper.

There are two methods for crisping up the skins:

1: Line a half sheet pan with parchment paper or a silicone baking mat. Arrange the skins on the sheet, evenly spaced, and make sure they're flat. Bake for 10 minutes, then rotate the pan 180 degrees and cook for another 10 minutes, checking 5 minutes after you rotate. You're looking for a nice golden brown and crispness of the entire skin.

2: Alternatively, cover the chicken skins with another sheet of parchment paper and top with a half sheet pan to keep the skins flat. I like the bubbles that not flattening promotes, but I also like arming you with all the information.

Transfer the crispy skins to paper towels to soak up excess rendered fat.

Once the skins have cooled to room temperature, break them up in a mortar and pestle. The chicken crackling will hold at room temperature, in a sealed container lined with paper towels, for 1 week.

Poultry Cure

This is probably the hardest recipe in the book, requiring the stirring of dry things together. Think of this as your all-purpose cure for duck, chicken, and rabbit, full of warm spices. It is used on the Rabbit Foreleg Confit, Kriek BBQ & Pistachio Dukka (page 196).

Makes 2½ cups (350 g)

1 cup (160 g) kosher salt
1 cup (140 g) brown sugar
2 teaspoons curing salt #1
3 tablespoons Fox Spice (page 311)

Stir everything together and keep in an airtight container.

Garlic Confit

Roasted garlic, essentially.

Makes 2 cups (480 g)

1 pound (455 g) garlic cloves
4 sprigs thyme
1 teaspoon kosher salt
1 cup (240 ml) extra-virgin olive oil
1 cup (240 ml) grapeseed oil

Preheat the oven to 250°F (120°C).

Cut off the root end of the garlic cloves and remove the peel. Place the whole, peeled cloves in a pot or baking dish with a lid. Add the thyme and salt, then cover with the olive and grapeseed oils. Cover the container and place in the preheated oven for 3 to 4 hours, or until the cloves are spreadable, but not falling apart.

Remove from the oven and cool to room temperature. Transfer to storage containers and keep under refrigeration for up to 1 month.

Index

Page numbers in *italics* refer to illustrations

99 Ranch Market 221, 280

A
aioli 321
  egg salad croque madame on Texas toast 212-13, *214*
  fried pork trotter, ginger shoots & yuzu 132-4, *135*
  rosemary pork loin, avocado tonnato & capers *114*, 115
  Russian dressing 246, *247*
  soft-boiled eggs, lovage gribiche & allumette potatoes 178-9, *180*
all-purpose meat jus 336
  fermented peppercorn sauce 273, *274-5*
  oxtails with noodles 282, *283*
Allard, Matthew 294
alliums
  chicken liver & allium toast *175*, 176-7
allumette potatoes 178-9, *180*
almonds
  beef tendon, tofu, sweet chili & almond 244, *245*
  chicken cutlets with date, almond & yogurt 230-1, *232*
Al's steak sauce 300
amatriciana, long beans 142, *143*
anchovies
  grilled lamb heart, spigarello & bagna cauda *266*, 267
  rosemary pork loin, avocado tonnato & capers *114*, 115
Andouille sausage
  Manresa staff gumbo "yaya" by David Kinch 162-3, *164*
Andy's Orchard 131
antipasto salad, chopped *110*, 111
apple & black rice morcilla *80*, 81
  choucroute royale *165*, 166-7
apple cider mustard 318
  kasha cakes 198, *199*
apple cider vinegar
  apple cider mustard 318
apple pectin powder
  Jimmy Nardello pepper jam 305
apples
  apple & black rice morcilla *80*, 81
  apples roasted in bacon fat 138, *139*
  duck neck sausage, green walnuts & apples *215*, 216-17
  two-ingredient applesauce 306
artichokes
  bone marrow, miso-creamed spinach & artichoke flower 276-7, *278*
avocado tonnato 115
  rosemary pork loin, avocado tonnato & capers *114*, 115
avocados
  avocado tonnato 115
  endive Doty 108, *109*

B
bacon
  bacon-wrapped oca 100, *101*
  choucroute royale *165*, 166-7
  maple smoked bacon *12*, 13
bacon fat
  apples roasted in bacon fat 138, *139*
bagna cauda: grilled lamb heart, spigarello & bagna cauda *266*, 267
balsamic vinegar
  Al's steak sauce 300
bananas
  banana shank & banana stew with sweet potato *279*, 280-1
Bar Ama 132
barbecue sauce
  kriek barbecue sauce *195*, 196-7
  peach BBQ sauce *130*, 131
basil
  shrimp-crusted pork cutlets with Newburg sauce *153*, 154-5
Bastianich, Lidia 128
beans
  borlotti bean, sauerkraut & kielbasa stew 128, *129*
béchamel 322
  bone marrow, miso-creamed spinach & artichoke flower 276-7, *278*
  egg-in-a-basket carbonara 120, *121*
  egg salad croque madame on Texas toast 212-13, *214*
beef
  all-purpose meat jus 336
  banana shank & banana stew with sweet potato *279*, 280-1
  beef borscht, horseradish, crème fraîche & caviar *286*, 287
  beef brisket pastrami 88, *89*
  beef carpaccio ZZ's style *242*, 243
  beef pelmeni stroganoff 258-60, *261*
  beef stock 335
  butter basted steak 26-7
  corned beef brisket 72, *73*
  meatloaf & mash 288-9, *290*
  Mr. Gray's 7-bone steak *291*, 292-3
  Mongolian flanken ribs 252, *253*
  sloppy Jeremy *250*, 251
  steak tartare "Birdie G's" with mushroom carpaccio 240, *241*
beef honeycomb tripe
  tripe & chickpea gratinata 268, *269*
beef marrow bones
  bone marrow, miso-creamed spinach & artichoke flower 276-7, *278*
beef stock 335
  all-purpose meat jus 336
  beef tendon terrine *46*, 47
beef tallow 339
  Mr. Gray's 7-bone steak *291*, 292-3
  tallow-fried potato peels 238, *239*
beef tendon terrine *46*, 47
  beef tendon, tofu, sweet chili & almond 244, *245*
  steak tartare "Birdie G's" with mushroom carpaccio 240, *241*
beef tongue
  corned beef tongue 66, *67*
  corned beef tongue, cornichon & lovage *262*, 263
  creamed chipped beef tongue 264, *265*
beef tri-tip
  black sugar tri-tip *92*, 93
beer
  creamed chipped beef tongue 264, *265*
  Polska kielbasa 86, *87*
beet juice
  beef borscht, horseradish, crème fraîche & caviar *286*, 287
  beet molasses 294-7, *295*, *296*
bell peppers
  blackened pork tenderloin with chow-chow 148, *149*
  chicken paprikash with board-cut spaetzle *189*, 190-1
  chicken scrapple 208-11, *209*, *210*
  Creole pig ears & okra *102*, 103-4, *105*
  giardiniera 316
  Manresa staff gumbo "yaya" by David Kinch 162-3, *164*
Beran, Dave 222
Bertolli, Paul 9, 38, 52, 78, 311
Bestia 115
beurre poulet *227*, 228-9

Beylik Family Farms 317
Birdie Bay spice 311
biscuits, skillet 332, *333*
black rice
  apple & black rice morcilla *80*, 81
black sugar tri-tip *92*, 93
blackened pork tenderloin with chow-chow 148, *149*
blood sausages
  apple & black rice morcilla *80*, 81
  pork blood & buckwheat kishka 82, *83*
blue cheese
  blue cheese butter 326
  buffalo deviled eggs 172-3, *174*
  endive Doty 108, *109*
blutwurst 58, *59*
  blutwurst & raclette *106*, 107
bone marrow
  bone marrow, miso-creamed spinach & artichoke flower 276-7, *278*
borlotti beans
  borlotti bean, sauerkraut & kielbasa stew 128, *129*
borscht: beef borscht, horseradish, crème fraîche & caviar *286*, 287
bottarga
  salt-baked daikon, lardo & bottarga 144-7, *145*, *146*
boudin noir 82
bourbon maple syrup
  maple smoked bacon *12*, 13
Bourdain, Anthony 57
bread
  chicken liver & allium toast *175*, 176-7
  creamed chipped beef tongue 264, *265*
  egg salad croque madame on Texas toast 212-13, *214*
  garlic bread croutons 326, *327*
  pain de mie 328
  sloppy Jeremy *250*, 251
breadcrumbs
  chicken cutlets with date, almond & yogurt 230-1, *232*
  chicken Kyiv with escargot butter *202*, 203
  fried pork trotter, ginger shoots & yuzu 132-4, *135*
  meatloaf & mash 288-9, *290*
  "popcorn" sweetbreads with fermented peppercorn sauce 273, *274-5*
brines
  all-purpose meat brine 337
  corn brine 337
  smoke brine 337
brisket

beef brisket pastrami 88, 89
corned beef brisket 72, 73
corned beef steak frites 284, 285
brown butter sauce 270-1, 272
buckwheat
   pork blood & buckwheat kishka 82, 83
buffalo deviled eggs 172-3, 174
butter
   beurre poulet 227, 228-9
   blue cheese butter 326
   brown butter sauce 270-1, 272
   butter basted steak 26-7
   chicken liver parfait 43, 44-5
   clarified butter 323
   escargot butter 323
   herb butter roast chicken 20-1
   pot roast butter 324, 325
butter, clarified 323
   hot sauce hollandaise 122-3, 124
   waffled corned beef hash 248, 249
buttermilk
   crème fraîche 322
   Creole pig ears & okra 102, 103-4, 105
   johnnycakes with smoked ham hock 118, 119
   skillet biscuits 332, 333

C

cabbage
   beef borscht, horseradish, crème fraîche & caviar 286, 287
   blackened pork tenderloin with chow-chow 148, 149
   sauerkraut 320
Calabrian chile hybrid 304
   Italian sausage ravioli 125, 126-7
   olive loaf 60, 61
   red pea farinata, olive loaf & Calabrian chile 116, 117
Calabrian chili powder
   apple & black rice morcilla 80, 81
   Italian sausage 74, 75
   pork blood & buckwheat kishka 82, 83
   smoked tomato 'nduja 54, 55
   United Nations chili mix 308, 309
cannoli: chicken liver cannoli with hoshigaki & red walnut 181, 182-3
Canora, Marco 243
cape gooseberries
   Jermiah's chicken 224-5, 226
capers
   dressed chicken bones "Isadore" 206, 207
   gribiche 178-9, 180
   rosemary pork loin, avocado tonnato & capers 114, 115
caraway seeds

Merguez sausage 76, 77
carbonara, egg-in-a-basket 120, 121
carpaccio
   beef carpaccio ZZ's style 242, 243
   mushroom carpaccio 240, 241
carrots
   beef borscht, horseradish, crème fraîche & caviar 286, 287
   beef stock 335
   chicken pot pie profiteroles 186-7, 188
   corned beef brisket 72, 73
   duck tongue fried farro 220, 221
   giardiniera 316
   Jermiah's chicken 224-5, 226
   matzo ball soup 184, 185
   meatloaf & mash 288-9, 290
   oxtails with noodles 282, 283
   pig head pozole 159, 160-1
   pot roast butter 324, 325
   Rachael's chicken stock 334
cartouche 35
cauliflower
   giardiniera 316
caviar
   beef borscht, horseradish, crème fraîche & caviar 286, 287
   beef carpaccio ZZ's style 242, 243
celery
   beef borscht, horseradish, crème fraîche & caviar 286, 287
   beef stock 335
   borlotti bean, sauerkraut & kielbasa stew 128, 129
   braised rabbit legs Provençal 192-3, 194
   corned beef brisket 72, 73
   Creole pig ears & okra 102, 103-4, 105
   giardiniera 316
   matzo ball soup 184, 185
   meatloaf & mash 288-9, 290
   pig head pozole 159, 160-1
   pot roast butter 324, 325
celery seeds
   Birdie Bay spice 311
   Creole spice 311
Centeno, Josef 132
charcutière sauce 150-1, 152
cheese
   blue cheese butter 326
   blutwurst & raclette 106, 107
   bone marrow, miso-creamed spinach & artichoke flower 276-7, 278
   buffalo deviled eggs 172-3, 174
   chicken pot pie profiteroles 186-7, 188
   creamed chipped beef tongue 264, 265

endive Doty 108, 109
   garlic bread croutons 326, 327
   Italian sausage ravioli 125, 126-7
   meatloaf & mash 288-9, 290
   pressed chicken confit Parmesan 204, 205
   red pea farinata, olive loaf & Calabrian chile 116, 117
   see also ricotta
cherries
   kriek barbecue sauce 195, 196-7
   Vernors "Old School" pork collar roast 156-7, 158
cherry lambic (kriek)
   kriek barbecue sauce 195, 196-7
chicken
   chicken cutlets with date, almond & yogurt 230-1, 232
   chicken Kyiv with escargot butter 202, 203
   chicken paprikash with board-cut spaetzle 189, 190-1
   chicken pot pie profiteroles 186-7, 188
   chicken scrapple 208-11, 209, 210
   chicken stock 20
   herb butter roast chicken 20-1
   Jermiah's chicken 224-5, 226
   Joel's chicken riggies 222, 223
   lemon pepper roast chicken 227, 228-9
   Manresa staff gumbo "yaya" by David Kinch 162-3, 164
   pickle chick 200, 201
   pressed chicken confit Parmesan 204, 205
chicken bones
   dressed chicken bones "Isadore" 206, 207
chicken brine 337
chicken fat
   schmaltz and gribenes 338
chicken gizzards
   chicken scrapple 208-11, 209, 210
chicken hearts
   chicken scrapple 208-11, 209, 210
chicken liver parfait 43, 44-5
   chicken liver & allium toast 175, 176-7
   chicken liver cannoli with hoshigaki & red walnut 181, 182-3
chicken livers
   chicken liver parfait 43, 44-5
   chicken scrapple 208-11, 209, 210
   country pâté 38, 39

chicken pot pie profiteroles 186-7, 188
chicken skin
   chicken crackling 340
   schmaltz and gribenes 338
chicken stock 334
   banana shank & banana stew with sweet potato 279, 280-1
   beef pelmeni stroganoff 258-60, 261
   beurre poulet 227, 228-9
   borlotti bean, sauerkraut & kielbasa stew 128, 129
   braised rabbit legs Provençal 192-3, 194
   chicken paprikash with board-cut spaetzle 189, 190-1
   chicken pot pie profiteroles 186-7, 188
   chicken scrapple 208-11, 209, 210
   Lonnie's quail 233, 234-5
   Manresa staff gumbo "yaya" by David Kinch 162-3, 164
   matzo ball soup 184, 185
   pork chops with pan sauce 28-9
   Rachael's chicken stock 334
   shrimp-crusted pork cutlets with Newburg sauce 153, 154-5
   tripe & chickpea gratinata 268, 269
   wedding terrine 40-1, 42
chickpeas
   chopped antipasto salad 110, 111
   tripe & chickpea gratinata 268, 269
chiles (chillies)
   Calabrian chile hybrid 304
   Merguez sausage 76, 77
   pig head pozole 159, 160-1
   sweet chili sauce 303
   United Nations chili mix 308, 309
chili powder
   apple & black rice morcilla 80, 81
   Italian sausage 74, 75
   pork blood & buckwheat kishka 82, 83
   smoked tomato 'nduja 54, 55
chili sauce, sweet 303
   beef tendon, tofu, sweet chili & almond 244, 245
   black sugar tri-tip 92, 93
chips (crisps), tomato 192-3, 194
chives
   yogurt dipping sauce 198, 199
Choi, Aaron 100, 314, 317
chopped antipasto salad 110, 111
choucroute royale 165, 166-7
chow-chow, blackened pork tenderloin with 148, 149
chutney, date 230-1, 232
cilantro (coriander)

pig head pozole 159, 160-1
shrimp-crusted pork cutlets with Newburg sauce 153, 154-5
Cirone Farms 306
cloves
duck ham 64, 65
duck pastrami 90, 91
coconut aminos
beef tendon terrine 46, 47
coconut milk
banana shank & banana stew with sweet potato 279, 280-1
cognac
charcutière sauce 150-1, 152
fois gras 40-1
pickle chick 200, 201
confit
classic duck confit 22-3
garlic confit 341
pressed chicken confit Parmesan 204, 205
rabbit foreleg confit, kriek BBQ & pistachio dukkha 195, 196-7
coriander seeds
beef brisket pastrami 88, 89
Merguez sausage 76, 77
corn brine 337
beef brisket pastrami 88, 89
corned beef brisket 72, 73
corned beef tongue 66, 67
corned beef brisket 72, 73
corned beef steak frites 284, 285
Spanish tortilla but like a Reuben 246, 247
waffled corned beef hash 248, 249
corned beef tongue 66, 67
chopped antipasto salad 110, 111
choucroute royale 165, 166-7
corned beef tongue, cornichon & lovage 262, 263
creamed chipped beef tongue 264, 265
cornichons
blutwurst & raclette 106, 107
corned beef tongue, cornichon & lovage 262, 263
gribiche 178-9, 180
pickled cornichons 314, 315
pork chops with sauce charcutière 150-1, 152
cornmeal
Creole pig ears & okra 102, 103-4, 105
johnnycakes with smoked ham hock 118, 119
cotechino
choucroute royale 165, 166-7
wild ramp cotechino 78, 79
country pâté 38, 39
crackling, chicken 340
cream

apple & black rice morcilla 80, 81
chicken liver parfait 43, 44-5
chicken paprikash with board-cut spaetzle 189, 190-1
country pâté 38, 39
crème fraîche 322
fermented peppercorn sauce 273, 274-5
Lonnie's quail 233, 234-5
Spanish tortilla but like a Reuben 246, 247
cream cheese
bone marrow, miso-creamed spinach & artichoke flower 276-7, 278
buffalo deviled eggs 172-3, 174
creamed chipped beef tongue 264, 265
crème fraîche 322
beef borscht, horseradish, crème fraîche & caviar 286, 287
beef pelmeni stroganoff 258-60, 261
Creole pig ears & okra 102, 103-4, 105
Creole spice 311
blackened pork tenderloin with chow-chow 148, 149
Creole pig ears & okra 102, 103-4, 105
crispy kasha 329
croque madame: egg salad croque madame on Texas toast 212-13, 214
cucumber
chopped antipasto salad 110, 111
smashed cucumbers 256, 257
see also pickling cucumbers
cumin seeds
Merguez sausage 76, 77
cure, poultry 341

D
daikon
salt-baked daikon, lardo & bottarga 144-7, 145, 146
dates
date chutney 230-1, 232
David, Elizabeth 20, 190
De Snippe 196
Delfina 268
deviled eggs, buffalo 172-3, 174
Dijon mustard
aioli 321
Al's steak sauce 300
beef brisket pastrami 88, 89
beef carpaccio ZZ's style 242, 243
beef pelmeni stroganoff 258-60, 261
charcutière sauce 150-1, 152
corned beef steak frites 284, 285
duck pastrami 90, 91

fermented peppercorn sauce 273, 274-5
honey mustard 302
hot sauce hollandaise 122-3, 124
Jermiah's chicken 224-5, 226
pork blood kishka, hoshigaki & persimmon mustard 136, 139
rosemary pork loin 70, 71
dill
dill pickle sauce 313
dill pickles 312
dipping sauces
scallion jaew 304
yogurt dipping sauce 198, 199
Doty, Shaun 108
dressed chicken bones "Isadore" 206, 207
dressing, Russian 246, 247
duck
classic duck confit 22-3
duck ham 64, 65
duck neck sausage, green walnuts & apples 215, 216-17
duck pastrami 90, 91
seared duck breasts 24-5
duck confit 22-3
choucroute royale 165, 166-7
duck ham 64, 65
duck ham & heart skewers with grapes 218, 219
duck hearts
duck ham & heart skewers with grapes 218, 219
duck liver
fois gras 40-1
duck tongues
duck tongue fried farro 220, 221
dukkha, pistachio 195, 196-7

E
Egan, Cal 190
eggplants (aubergines)
Merguez sausage with loaded eggplant 254, 255
eggs
aioli 321
buffalo deviled eggs 172-3, 174
chicken cutlets with date, almond & yogurt 230-1, 232
chicken Kyiv with escargot butter 202, 203
chicken paprikash with board-cut spaetzle 189, 190-1
chicken pot pie profiteroles 186-7, 188
duck tongue fried farro 220, 221
egg-in-a-basket carbonara 120, 121
egg salad croque madame on Texas toast 212-13, 214
fried pork trotter, ginger shoots & yuzu 132-4, 135

hangtown brei 122-3, 124
hot sauce hollandaise 122-3, 124
Italian sausage ravioli 125, 126-7
johnnycakes with smoked ham hock 118, 119
matzo ball soup 184, 185
'nduja & saffron pizzelle sandwiches 96, 97
pickle chick 200, 201
"popcorn" sweetbreads with fermented peppercorn sauce 273, 274-5
salt-baked daikon, lardo & bottarga 144-7, 145, 146
soft-boiled eggs, lovage gribiche & allumette potatoes 178-9, 180
Spanish tortilla but like a Reuben 246, 247
endives
endive Doty 108, 109
equipment 14-18
sausage making and stuffing 30
terrine making 32
escargot butter 323
chicken Kyiv with escargot butter 202, 203

F
farinata
red pea farinata, olive loaf & Calabrian chile 116, 117
farro
duck tongue fried farro 220, 221
The Fat Duck 170
fava (broad) beans
rabbit mortadella, fava beans, pistachio & mint 170, 171
fennel
braised rabbit legs Provençal 192-3, 194
strawberry sofrito 307
fennel pollen
griddled potatoes with fennel pollen & lemon 140, 141
'nduja & saffron pizzelle sandwiches 96, 97
United Nations chili mix 308, 309
fennel seeds
Birdie Bay spice 311
Calabrian chile hybrid 304
Italian sausage 74, 75
Italian sausage ravioli 125, 126-7
smoked tomato 'nduja 54, 55
United Nations chili mix 308, 309
fermented peppercorn sauce 273, 274-5
Florence, Tyler 208
flower petals
whipped lardo with flowers 98, 99
foie gras 40-1
wedding terrine 40-1, 42

fox spice 311
   apple & black rice morcilla 80, *81*
   duck ham *64*, 65
   pork blood & buckwheat kishka 82, *83*
   poultry cure 341
Fra-Mani 9
Frasca Food & Wine 78
Freddy Smalls 172
French breakfast radishes
   blutwurst & raclette *106*, 107
   whipped lardo with flowers *98*, *99*
frites, corned beef steak *284*, 285

G
garlic
   all-purpose meat brine 337
   aioli 321
   beef stock 335
   braised rabbit legs Provençal 192-3, *194*
   brown butter sauce 270-1, *272*
   Calabrian chile hybrid 304
   chicken scrapple 208-11, *209*, *210*
   fried pork trotter, ginger shoots & yuzu 132-4, *135*
   garlic bread croutons 326, *327*
   garlic-mint yogurt 256, *257*
   giardiniera 316
   gremolata 282, *283*
   ham hock stock 336
   Italian sausage 74, *75*
   long beans amatriciana 142, *143*
   Manresa staff gumbo "yaya" by David Kinch 162-3, *164*
   Merguez sausage *76*, 77
   Mr. Gray's 7-bone steak *291*, 292-3
   Ohio City Provision's lamb shawarma 62, *63*
   Ohio peppers 317
   pancetta cotto *68*, 69
   peach BBQ sauce *130*, 131
   pickled cornichons 314, *315*
   Polska kielbasa 86, *87*
   Rachael's chicken stock 334
   whipped lardo with flowers *98*, *99*
garlic bread croutons 326, *327*
   grilled lamb heart, spigarello & bagna cauda *266*, 267
garlic confit 341
   escargot butter 323
giardiniera 316
ginger
   beef tendon terrine *46*, 47
   date chutney 230-1, *232*
   peach BBQ sauce *130*, 131
   Sungold tomato ketchup 300
   tiki sauce 303
ginger shoots

fried pork trotter, ginger shoots & yuzu 132-4, *135*
Girl & Dug Farm 100, 314, 317
Golden Empress 252
goose liver
   fois gras 40-1
gougères: chicken pot pie profiteroles 186-7, *188*
grapes
   duck ham & heart skewers with grapes 218, *219*
gravy: choucroute royale *165*, 166-7
Gray, Sean 292
gremolata 282, *283*
gribenes 338
   chicken pot pie profiteroles 186-7, *188*
   chicken scrapple 208-11, *209*, *210*
   kasha cakes 198, *199*
gribiche, lovage 178-9, *180*
grill pan 17
Gruyère cheese
   chicken pot pie profiteroles 186-7, *188*
guajillo chiles
   Merguez sausage *76*, 77
guanciale *51*, 52-3
   choucroute royale *165*, 166-7
   country pâté 38, *39*
   egg-in-a-basket carbonara 120, *121*
   long beans amatriciana 142, *143*
gumbo: Manresa staff gumbo "yaya" by David Kinch 162-3, *164*
Gyro Wrap Café 62, 256

H
H Mart 221
ham
   duck ham *64*, 65
   smoked ham hocks *84*, 85
   ham hock stock 336
   borlotti bean, sauerkraut & kielbasa stew 128, *129*
   charcutière sauce 150-1, *152*
   chicken scrapple 208-11, *209*, *210*
   Creole pig ears & okra *102*, 103-4, *105*
   pig head pozole *159*, 160-1
hangtown brei 122-3, *124*
Hazan, Marcella 20
hog bladder
   smoked tomato 'nduja 54, *55*
hog casings
   blutwurst 58, *59*
   Italian sausage 74, *75*
   olive loaf *60*, 61
   rabbit & myrtle berry mortadella *56*, 57
hollandaise, hot sauce 122-3, *124*
hominy
   pig head pozole *159*, 160-1
honey
   honey mustard 302
   tiki sauce 303
horseradish

beef borscht, horseradish, crème fraîche & caviar 286, *287*
hoshigaki
   chicken liver cannoli with hoshigaki & red walnut *181*, 182-3
   pork blood kishka, hoshigaki & persimmon mustard *136*, 139
hot sauce hollandaise 122-3, *124*
Hungarian paprika
   Merguez sausage *76*, 77
   Polska kielbasa 86, *87*
   pork blood & buckwheat kishka 82, *83*
   United Nations chili mix 308, *309*
Hungarian wax peppers
   Ohio peppers 317
hurka 82

I
Italian sausage 74, *75*
   Italian sausage ravioli *125*, 126-7

J
jalapeño chiles
   pig head pozole *159*, 160-1
   sweet chili sauce 303
   jam, Jimmy Nardello pepper 305
Jeremiah's chicken 224-5, *226*, 228
Jimmy Nardello pepper jam 305
Jocko's 270
Joel's chicken riggies 222, *223*
johnnycakes with smoked ham hock *118*, 119
juniper berries
   pancetta cotto *68*, 69

K
kale
   chopped antipasto salad *110*, 111
kasha
   crispy kasha 329
   grilled lamb heart, spigarello & bagna cauda *266*, 267
   kasha cakes 198, *199*
   pork blood & buckwheat kishka 82, *83*
Katz, Isadore 206, *207*
ketchup, Sungold tomato 300
kielbasa
   borlotti bean, sauerkraut & kielbasa stew 128, *129*
   choucroute royale *165*, 166-7
Kinch, David 162, 304, 307
kishka
   pork blood & buckwheat kishka 82, *83*
   pork blood kishka, hoshigaki & persimmon mustard *136*, 139
Korean chili powder (gochugaru)

Polska kielbasa 86, *87*
pork blood & buckwheat kishka 82, *83*
United Nations chili mix 308, *309*
Korsh, Eric 178
Kostow, Christopher 258
kriek barbecue sauce: rabbit foreleg confit, kriek BBQ & pistachio dukkha *195*, 196-7
Kyiv: chicken Kyiv with escargot butter *202*, 203

L
Lacsamana, Jeremiah 224
Lahlou, Chef Mourad 77
lamb
   lamb a la saless 294-7, *295*, *296*
   lamb shawarma platter 256, *257*
   Merguez sausage *76*, 77
   Merguez sausage with loaded eggplant *254*, 255
   Ohio City Provision's lamb shawarma 62, *63*
lamb casings
   Merguez sausage *76*, 77
lamb hearts
   grilled lamb heart, spigarello & bagna cauda *266*, 267
lamb kidney fat
   Ohio City Provision's lamb shawarma 62, *63*
Lambert, Adam 62, 256
lardo 48-9, *50*, 52
   blutwurst 58, *59*
   olive loaf *60*, 61
   rabbit & myrtle berry mortadella *56*, 57
   salt-baked daikon, lardo & bottarga 144-7, *145*, *146*
   whipped lardo with flowers *98*, *99*
Lata, Michael 108
leaf lard 339
   Creole pig ears & okra *102*, 103-4, *105*
   griddled potatoes with fennel pollen & lemon *140*, 141
   Polska kielbasa 86, *87*
   whipped lardo with flowers *98*, *99*
Lee, Phong 252
leeks
   meatloaf & mash 288-9, *290*
lemon pepper rub 310
   lemon pepper roast chicken *227*, 228-9
lemons
   all-purpose meat brine 337
   fried lemons *227*, 228-9
   gremolata 282, *283*
   griddled potatoes with fennel pollen & lemon *140*, 141
   lemon pepper rub 310

whipped lardo with flowers 98, 99
lettuce
  chopped antipasto salad 110, 111
Liberty Ducks 65
lime juice
  Jimmy Nardello pepper jam 305
  scallion jaew 304
limes
  Jermiah's chicken 224-5, 226
livers, chicken
  chicken liver parfait 43, 44-5
  chicken scrapple 208-11, 209, 210
  country pâté 38, 39
livers, duck
  fois gras 40-1
livers, goose
  fois gras 40-1
long beans
  long beans amatriciana 142, 143
Lonnie's quail 233, 234-5
lovage
  corned beef tongue, cornichon & lovage 262, 263
  gribiche 178-9, 180
  soft-boiled eggs, lovage gribiche & allumette potatoes 178-9, 180

M
mace
  fox spice 311
McGee, Harold 170
Mackinnon-Patterson, Chef Lachlan 78
madeira
  chicken liver parfait 43, 44-5
  country pâté 38, 39
makrut lime leaves
  banana shank & banana stew with sweet potato 279, 280-1
  beef tendon terrine 46, 47
Manresa 9, 81, 103, 132, 162, 170, 270, 320
Manresa staff gumbo "yaya" by David Kinch 162-3, 164
maple smoked bacon 12, 13
  bacon-wrapped oca 100, 101
  choucroute royale 165, 166-7
maple syrup
  maple smoked bacon 12, 13
marrow bones
  pot roast butter 324, 325
matzo ball mix
  matzo ball soup 184, 185
  pork blood & buckwheat kishka 82, 83
matzo brei 122-3, 124
matzo meal
  hangtown brei 122-3, 124
meat jus, all-purpose 336
  fermented peppercorn sauce 273, 274-5

oxtails with noodles 282, 283
meatloaf & mash 288-9, 290
melon
  pancetta-wrapped melon with scallion jaew 112, 113
Menashe, Ori 115
Merguez sausage 76, 77
  Merguez sausage with loaded eggplant 254, 255
milk
  béchamel 322
  creamed chipped beef tongue 264, 265
milk, powdered
  Polska kielbasa 86, 87
mint
  garlic-mint yogurt 256, 257
  rabbit mortadella, fava beans, pistachio & mint 170, 171
  shrimp-crusted pork cutlets with Newburg sauce 153, 154-5
miso
  bone marrow, miso-creamed spinach & artichoke flower 276-7, 278
  matzo ball soup 184, 185
  Mr. Gray's 7-bone steak 291, 292-3
Mistral 192
Momofuku Ko 292
Mongolian flanken ribs 252, 253
Montreal steak rub 308
  black sugar tri-tip 92, 93
morcilla 82
  apple & black rice morcilla 80, 81
  choucroute royale 165, 166-7
morels
  morel and truffle stuffing 233, 234-5
mortadella, rabbit & myrtle berry 56, 57
  chopped antipasto salad 110, 111
  rabbit mortadella, fava beans, pistachio & mint 170, 171
Mouradian lamb sausage 77
Mumbo Jumbo 108
mushrooms
  beef pelmeni stroganoff 258-60, 261
  meatloaf & mash 288-9, 290
  morel and truffle stuffing 233, 234-5
  mushroom carpaccio 240, 241
  mushroom Worcestershire 319
  oxtails with noodles 282, 283
mustard
  aioli 321
  Al's steak sauce 300
  beef brisket pastrami 88, 89
  beef carpaccio ZZ's style 242, 243

beef pelmeni stroganoff 258-60, 261
blutwurst & raclette 106, 107
charcutière sauce 150-1, 152
corned beef steak frites 284, 285
duck pastrami 90, 91
fermented peppercorn sauce 273, 274-5
honey mustard 302
hot sauce hollandaise 122-3, 124
Jermiah's chicken 224-5, 226
kasha cakes 198, 199
pork blood kishka, hoshigaki & persimmon mustard 136, 139
rosemary pork loin 70, 71
mustard seeds
  apple cider mustard 318
  blackened pork tenderloin with chow-chow 148, 149
  dill pickles 312
  duck ham 64, 65
  Jermiah's chicken 224-5, 226
  pickled cornichons 314, 315
  pickled mustard seeds 318
  Polska kielbasa 86, 87
myoga
  fried pork trotter, ginger shoots & yuzu 132-4, 135
myrtle berries
  rabbit & myrtle berry mortadella 56, 57

N
nasturtium salsa 305
'nduja
  'nduja & saffron pizzelle sandwiches 96, 97
  smoked tomato 'nduja 54, 55
New Zealand yams
  bacon-wrapped oca 100, 101
Newburg sauce 153, 154-5
noodles
  oxtails with noodles 282, 283

O
oca
  bacon-wrapped oca 100, 101
Ohio City Provisions 62
Ohio City Provision's lamb shawarma 62, 63
  lamb shawarma platter 256, 257
Ohio peppers 317
  chopped antipasto salad 110, 111
  Merguez sausage with loaded eggplant 254, 255
Okinawan black sugar
  black sugar tri-tip 92, 93
okra
  Creole pig ears & okra 102, 103-4, 105
olive loaf
  chopped antipasto salad 110, 111

red pea farinata, olive loaf & Calabrian chile 116, 117
olive oil
  aioli 321
  Calabrian chile hybrid 304
olives
  braised rabbit legs Provençal 192-3, 194
  chopped antipasto salad 110, 111
  olive loaf 60, 61
onions
  apple & black rice morcilla 80, 81
  beef borscht, horseradish, crème fraîche & caviar 286, 287
  braised rabbit legs Provençal 192-3, 194
  chicken liver & allium toast 175, 176-7
  chicken paprikash with board-cut spaetzle 189, 190-1
  corned beef brisket 72, 73
  long beans amatriciana 142, 143
  Manresa staff gumbo "yaya" by David Kinch 162-3, 164
  Ohio City Provision's lamb shawarma 62, 63
  pig head pozole 159, 160-1
  Polska kielbasa 86, 87
  pork blood & buckwheat kishka 82, 83
  Rachael's chicken stock 334
  schmaltz and gribenes 338
  strawberry sofrito 307
  Sungold tomato ketchup 300
oregano
  guanciale 51, 52-3
  Ohio City Provision's lamb shawarma 62, 63
Orsa & Winston 132
oxtails
  beef stock 335
  oxtails with noodles 282, 283
oysters
  beef carpaccio ZZ's style 242, 243
  hangtown brei 122-3, 124

P
pain de mie 328
  chicken liver & allium toast 175, 176-7
  creamed chipped beef tongue 264, 265
  egg-in-a-basket carbonara 120, 121
  egg salad croque madame on Texas toast 212-13, 214
  sloppy Jeremy 250, 251
pan sauce, pork chops with 28-9
pancetta cotto 68, 69
  blutwurst 58, 59
  chopped antipasto salad 110, 111
  endive Doty 108, 109

hangtown brei 122-3, *124*
pancetta-wrapped melon with scallion jaew 112, *113*
panko breadcrumbs
  chicken cutlets with date, almond & yogurt 230-1, *232*
  chicken Kyiv with escargot butter *202*, 203
  fried pork trotter, ginger shoots & yuzu 132-4, *135*
  "popcorn" sweetbreads with fermented peppercorn sauce *273*, 274-5
paprika
  apple & black rice morcilla *80*, 81
  Birdie Bay spice 311
  chicken paprikash with board-cut spaetzle *189*, 190-1
  Jimmy Nardello pepper jam 305
  Merguez sausage *76*, 77
  Polska kielbasa 86, *87*
  pork blood & buckwheat kishka 82, *83*
  United Nations chili mix 308, *309*
paprikash: chicken paprikash with board-cut spaetzle *189*, 190-1
parfait, chicken liver *43*, 44-5
Parmesan
  pressed chicken confit Parmesan *204*, 205
parmigiano-reggiano cheese
  garlic bread croutons 326, *327*
  Italian sausage ravioli *125*, 126-7
  red pea farinata, olive loaf & Calabrian chile 116, *117*
parsley
  apple & black rice morcilla *80*, 81
  gremolata *282*, 283
  pork blood & buckwheat kishka 82, *83*
Pasjoli 222
pasta
  beef pelmeni stroganoff 258-60, *261*
  Italian sausage ravioli *125*, 126-7
  Joel's chicken riggies 222, *223*
pastrami
  beef brisket pastrami *88*, 89
  duck pastrami 90, *91*
pastries: chicken liver cannoli with hoshigaki & red walnut *181*, 182-3
pastry
  puff pastry 330
pâté, country 38, *39*
peaches
  peach BBQ sauce *130*, 131
peas
  egg-in-a-basket carbonara 120, *121*

pelmeni: beef pelmeni stroganoff 258-60, *261*
peppercorns
  all-purpose meat brine 337
  beef brisket pastrami *88*, 89
  Creole spice 311
  dill pickles 312
  duck ham *64*, 65
  fermented peppercorn sauce *273*, 274-5
  fox spice 311
  guanciale *51*, 52-3
  Italian sausage 74, *75*
  lemon pepper rub 310
  Montreal steak rub 308
  Ohio City Provision's lamb shawarma 62, *63*
  pancetta cotto *68*, 69
  pickled cornichons 314, *315*
  wild ramp cotechino 78, *79*
peppers
  blackened pork tenderloin with chow-chow 148, *149*
  chicken paprikash with board-cut spaetzle *189*, 190-1
  chicken scrapple 208-11, *209*, *210*
  Creole pig ears & okra *102*, 103-4, *105*
  giardiniera 316
  Jimmy Nardello pepper jam 305
  Manresa staff gumbo "yaya" by David Kinch 162-3, *164*
  Merguez sausage with loaded eggplant *254*, 255
  Ohio peppers 317
  pig head pozole *159*, 160-1
Persian cucumbers
  smashed cucumbers 256, *257*
persimmon hoshigaki
  chicken liver cannoli with hoshigaki & red walnut *181*, 182-3
  pork blood kishka, hoshigaki & persimmon mustard *136*, 139
pickle chick 200, *201*
pickled cornichons 314, *315*
  corned beef tongue, cornichon & lovage *262*, 263
pickled mustard seeds 318
  Jermiah's chicken 224-5, *226*
pickles
  dill pickles 312
  giardiniera 316
  pickled cornichons 314, *315*
  pickled Hungarian wax peppers 317
  pickled mustard seeds 318
pickling cucumbers
  dill pickles 312
pie crust, leaf lard 329
pig ears
  Creole pig ears & okra *102*, 103-4, *105*
pig heads

pig head pozole *159*, 160-1
pine nuts
  endive Doty 108, *109*
  strawberry sofrito 307
pineapple
  Jermiah's chicken 224-5, *226*
  Vernors "Old School" pork collar roast 156-7, *158*
pistachios
  pistachio dukkha *195*, 196-7
  rabbit & myrtle berry mortadella *56*, 57
  rabbit mortadella, fava beans, pistachio & mint 170, *171*
pizzelle irons 96
pizzelle sandwiches, 'nduja & saffron 96, *97*
poblano peppers
  pig head pozole *159*, 160-1
polenta
  chicken scrapple 208-11, *209*, *210*
Polish sausage 86, *87*
Polska kielbasa 86, *87*
  borlotti bean, sauerkraut & kielbasa stew 128, *129*
  choucroute royale 165, 166-7
  "popcorn" sweetbreads with fermented peppercorn sauce *273*, 274-5
pork 94-167
  apples roasted in bacon fat 138, *139*
  bacon-wrapped oca 100, *101*
  blackened pork tenderloin with chow-chow 148, *149*
  blutwurst 58, *59*
  blutwurst & raclette 106, *107*
  borlotti bean, sauerkraut & kielbasa stew 128, *129*
  chopped antipasto salad *110*, 111
  choucroute royale 165, 166-7
  country pâté 38, *39*
  Creole pig ears & okra *102*, 103-4, *105*
  egg-in-a-basket carbonara 120, *121*
  endive Doty 108, *109*
  fried pork trotter, ginger shoots & yuzu 132-4, *135*
  griddled potatoes with fennel pollen & lemon *140*, 141
  hangtown brei 122-3, *124*
  Italian sausage 74, *75*
  Italian sausage ravioli *125*, 126-7
  johnnycakes with smoked ham hock *118*, 119
  long beans amatriciana 142, *143*
  Manresa staff gumbo "yaya" by David Kinch 162-3, *164*
  maple smoked bacon *12*, 13
  'nduja & saffron pizzelle sandwiches 96, *97*
  olive loaf *60*, 61
  pancetta cotto *68*, 69

pancetta-wrapped melon with scallion jaew 112, *113*
pig head pozole *159*, 160-1
Polska kielbasa 86, *87*
pork blood & buckwheat kishka 82, *83*
pork blood kishka, hosigaki & persimmon mustard 136, *137*
pork chops with pan sauce 28-9
pork chops with sauce charcutière 150-1, *152*
red pea farinata, olive loaf & Calabrian chile 116, *117*
rosemary pork loin 70, *71*
rosemary pork loin, avocado tonnato & capers *114*, 115
salt-baked daikon, lardo & bottarga 144-7, *145*, *146*
shrimp-crusted pork cutlets with Newburg sauce *153*, 154-5
smoked tomato 'nduja 54, *55*
spareribs with peach BBQ *130*, 131
Vernors "Old School" pork collar roast 156-7, *158*
wedding terrine 40-1, *42*
whipped lardo with flowers *98*, 99
wild ramp cotechino 78, *79*
pork blood
  apple & black rice morcilla *80*, 81
  blutwurst 58, *59*
  pork blood & buckwheat kishka 82, *83*
pork blood & buckwheat kishka 82, *83*
  pork blood kishka, hoshigaki & persimmon mustard *136*, 139
pork casings
  apple & black rice morcilla *80*, 81
  Polska kielbasa 86, *87*
  wild ramp cotechino 78, *79*
pork fatback
  apple & black rice morcilla *80*, 81
  blutwurst 58, *59*
  duck neck sausage, green walnuts & apples *215*, 216-17
  lardo 48-9, *50*
  olive loaf *60*, 61
  pork blood & buckwheat kishka 82, *83*
  rabbit & myrtle berry mortadella *56*, 57
  wedding terrine 40-1, *42*
  wild ramp cotechino 78, *79*
pork hocks
  smoked ham hocks *84*, 85
pork jowl/cheeks
  guanciale *51*, 52-3
pork leaf lard 339
pork skin
  wild ramp cotechino 78, *79*
pork trotters

fried pork trotter, ginger
    shoots & yuzu 132-4, *135*
port
    chicken liver parfait *43*,
        44-5
pot roast butter 324, *325*
potato flakes
    pickle chick 200, *201*
potato peels
    tallow-fried potato peels
        238, *239*
potatoes
    blutwurst & raclette *106*,
        107
    choucroute royale *165*, 166-7
    frites *284*, 285
    griddled potatoes with
        fennel pollen & lemon
        140, 141
    mashed potatoes 288-9, *290*
    soft-boiled eggs, lovage
        gribiche & allumette
        potatoes 178-9, *180*
    Spanish tortilla but like a
        Reuben *246*, 247
    waffled corned beef hash
        248, *249*
poultry cure 341
    classic duck confit 22-3
pozole, pig head *159*, 160-1
prawns
    beef carpaccio ZZ's style
        242, 243
pressed chicken confit
    Parmesan 204, *205*
profiteroles, chicken pot pie
    186-7, *188*
provolone
    chopped antipasto salad
        110, 111
    puff pastry 330
    choucroute royale *165*, 166-7

Q
quail, Lonnie's *233*, 234-5
Quatrano, Anne 108

R
rabbit
    braised rabbit legs
        Provençal 192-3, *194*
    rabbit & myrtle berry
        mortadella *56*, 57
    rabbit foreleg confit, kriek
        BBQ & pistachio dukkha
        195, 196-7
    rabbit mortadella, fava
        beans, pistachio & mint
        170, *171*
rabbit & myrtle berry
    mortadella *56*, 57
rabbit mortadella, fava
    beans, pistachio & mint
    170, *171*
Rachael's chicken stock 334
    banana shank & banana
        stew with sweet potato
        279, 280-1
    beef pelmeni stroganoff
        258-60, *261*
    beurre poulet *227*, 228-9

braised rabbit legs
    Provençal 192-3, *194*
chicken pot pie profiteroles
    186-7, *188*
chicken scrapple 208-11,
    209, *210*
Lonnie's quail *233*, 234-5
Manresa staff gumbo "yaya"
    by David Kinch 162-3, *164*
matzo ball soup 184, *185*
tripe & chickpea gratinata
    268, *269*
wedding terrine 40-1, *42*
raclette cheese
    blutwurst & raclette *106*,
        107
radicchio
    chopped antipasto salad
        110, 111
radishes
    blutwurst & raclette *106*,
        107
    whipped lardo with flowers
        98, 99
Raffi's 294
ramps
    wild ramp cotechino 78, *79*
ravioli, Italian sausage *125*,
    126-7
Reading 107
red pea flour
    red pea farinata, olive loaf &
        Calabrian chile 116, *117*
red wine
    all-purpose meat jus 336
    beef borscht, horseradish,
        crème fraîche & caviar
        286, *287*
    chicken liver & allium toast
        175, 176-7
    oxtails with noodles 282,
        283
The Reluctant Trading
    Experiment 274
Restaurant Gordon Ramsay
    170
rice
    apple & black rice morcilla
        80, 81
    crispy rice 294-7, *295*, *296*
    rice bran oil 17
rice flour
    pickle chick 200, *201*
ricotta cheese
    Italian sausage ravioli *125*,
        126-7
Riesling
    choucroute royale *165*, 166-7
rigatoni
    Joel's chicken riggies 222,
        223
Rodgers, Judy 20, 160
rosemary
    apples roasted in bacon fat
        138, *139*
    lardo 48-9, *50*
    rosemary pork loin 70, *71*
rosemary pork loin 70, *71*
    chopped antipasto salad
        110, 111
    egg salad croque madame on
        Texas toast 212-13, *214*

rosemary pork loin, avocado
    tonnato & capers *114*, 115
Rotisserie & Wine 208
Rubicon 268
rub, Montreal steak 308
Russell, David O. 234
Russian dressing *246*, 247
Rustic Canyon 222, 224, 294

S
saffron
    'nduja & saffron pizzelle
        sandwiches 96, *97*
    saffron yogurt 294-7, *295*,
        296
sage
    chicken scrapple 208-11,
        209, *210*
St. John 170
salad, chopped antipasto *110*,
    111
Saless, Cameron 294
salsa, nasturtium 305
salt-baked daikon, lardo &
    bottarga 144-7, *145*, *146*
sanguinaccio 82
Santa Monica Farmer's
    Market 131
sauces
    aioli 321
    Al's steak sauce 300
    béchamel 322
    brown butter sauce 270-1,
        272
    charcutière sauce 150-1, *152*
    dill pickle sauce 313
    easy tomato sauce 306
    fermented peppercorn sauce
        273, 274-5
    hot sauce hollandaise 122-3,
        124
    kriek barbecue sauce *195*,
        196-7
    Newburg sauce *153*, 154-5
    pan sauce 28-9
    peach BBQ sauce *130*, 131
    scallion jaew 304
    Sungold tomato ketchup
        300
    tiki sauce 303
    tropical sauce 224-5, *226*
    truffle sauce *233*, 234-5
    two-ingredient applesauce
        306
    yogurt dipping sauce 198,
        199
    yuzu kosho sauce 302
sauerkraut 320
    borlotti bean, sauerkraut &
        kielbasa stew 128, *129*
    choucroute royale *165*, 166-7
    kasha cakes 198, *199*
    Spanish tortilla but like a
        Reuben *246*, 247
sausage stuffers 30
sausages
    duck neck sausage, green
        walnuts & apples *215*,
        216-17
    Italian sausage 74, *75*
    Italian sausage ravioli *125*,
        126-7

making and stuffing 30-1
Manresa staff gumbo "yaya"
    by David Kinch 162-3, *164*
Merguez sausage *76*, 77
Merguez sausage with
    loaded eggplant *254*, 255
Polska kielbasa 86, *87*
see also blood sausages
scallion jaew 304
    pancetta-wrapped melon
        with scallion jaew 112, *113*
scallions (spring onions)
    beef tendon terrine *46*, 47
    hangtown brei 122-3, *124*
    Mongolian flanken ribs 252,
        253
    scallion jaew 304
Schaler, Matt 228, 304
schmaltz 338
    chicken paprikash with
        board-cut spaetzle *189*,
        190-1
    rabbit foreleg confit *195*,
        196-7
scrapple, chicken 208-11, *209*,
    210
shallots
    Calabrian chile hybrid 304
    charcutière sauce 150-1, *152*
    crispy shallots *175*, 176-7
    nasturtium salsa 305
shawarma
    lamb shawarma platter 256,
        257
    Ohio City Provision's lamb
        shawarma 62, *63*
sherry
    all-purpose meat jus 336
    Joel's chicken riggies 222,
        223
Shih, Rich 310
shrimp
    Manresa staff gumbo "yaya"
        by David Kinch 162-3, *164*
    shrimp-crusted pork cutlets
        with Newburg sauce *153*,
        154-5
skewers: duck ham & heart
    skewers with grapes 218,
    219
skillet biscuits 332, *333*
sloppy Jeremy *250*, 251
smashed cucumbers 256, *257*
smoke brine 337
    smoked ham hocks 84, *85*
smoked ham hocks 84, *85*
    ham hock stock 336
    johnnycakes with smoked
        ham hock 118, *119*
smoked honey mustard 302
    blutwurst & raclette *106*,
        107
smoked paprika
    Birdie Bay spice 311
    Jimmy Nardello pepper jam
        305
smoked sun-dried tomatoes
    smoked tomato 'nduja 54, *55*
smoked tomato 'nduja 54, *55*
    'nduja & saffron pizzelle
        sandwiches 96, *97*
smoky honey mustard 302

sofrito, strawberry 307
Sonoma Café 148
soups
    beef borscht, horseradish, crème fraîche & caviar 286, *287*
    matzo ball soup 184, *185*
sour cherries
    kriek barbecue sauce *195*, 196–7
Spadafore, Joel 222
spaetzle, board-cut *189*, 190–1
Spanish smoked paprika
    United Nations chili mix 308, *309*
Spanish tortilla but like a Reuben *246*, 247
spareribs with peach BBQ *130*, 131
spice mixes
    Birdie Bay spice 311
    Creole spice 311
    fox spice 311
spigarello
    grilled lamb heart, spigarello & bagna cauda *266*, 267
spinach
    bone marrow, miso-creamed spinach & artichoke flower 276–7, *278*
    Lonnie's quail *233*, 234–5
Spring Brook Farm 107
steak
    Al's steak sauce 300
    butter basted steak 26–7
    Mr. Gray's 7-bone steak *291*, 292–3
    Montreal steak rub 308
    steak tartare "Birdie G's" with mushroom carpaccio 240, *241*
stews
    banana shank & banana stew with sweet potato *279*, 280–1
    borlotti bean, sauerkraut & kielbasa stew 128, *129*
    oxtails with noodles 282, *283*
stock
    beef stock 335
    beef tendon terrine *46*, 47
    beurre poulet *227*, 228–9
    braised rabbit legs Provençal 192–3, *194*
    chicken pot pie profiteroles 186–7, *188*
    chicken scrapple 208–11, *209*, *210*
    chicken stock 20
    ham hock stock 336
    matzo ball soup 184, *185*
    pork chops with pan sauce 28–9
    Rachael's chicken stock 334
    wedding terrine 40–1, *42*
Stoll, Craig 268
Stouffer 264
strawberries
    strawberry sofrito 307

stroganoff, beef pelmeni 258–60, *261*
Stuckey, Bobby 78
stuffing, morel and truffle *233*, 234–5
Sullivan, CJ 228
sundae 82
Sungold tomato ketchup 300
sweet chili sauce 303
    beef tendon, tofu, sweet chili & almond 244, *245*
    black sugar tri-tip *92*, 93
sweet paprika
    chicken paprikash with board-cut spaetzle *189*, 190–1
sweet potatoes
    banana shank & banana stew with sweet potato *279*, 280–1
sweetbreads
    "popcorn" sweetbreads with fermented peppercorn sauce *273*, 274–5
    sweetbreads a la Jocko's 270–1, *272*

T
tallow
    beef tallow 339
    tallow-fried potato peels 238, *239*
tamari
    beef tendon terrine *46*, 47
    black sugar tri-tip *92*, 93
    mushroom Worcestershire 319
    tiki sauce 303
tartare: steak tartare "Birdie G's" with mushroom carpaccio 240, *241*
terrines 32–3
    beef tendon terrine *46*, 47
    country pâté 38, *39*
    wedding terrine 40–1, *42*
Texas toast, egg salad croque madame on 212–13, *214*
Thompson, Miles 304
thyme
    apple & black rice morcilla *80*, 81
    braised rabbit legs Provençal 192–3, *194*
    pork blood & buckwheat kishka 82, *83*
    pork chops with pan sauce 28–9
    seared duck breasts 24–5
tiki sauce 303
    bacon-wrapped oca 100, *101*
    Mongolian flanken ribs 252, *253*
toast
    chicken liver & allium toast *175*, 176–7
    egg salad croque madame on Texas toast 212–13, *214*
tofu
    beef tendon, tofu, sweet chili & almond 244, *245*
    tomato sauce 306

Italian sausage ravioli *125*, 126–7
Joel's chicken riggies 222, *223*
tomatoes
    braised rabbit legs Provençal 192–3, *194*
    easy tomato sauce 306
    long beans amatriciana 142, *143*
    Sungold tomato ketchup 300
    tomato chips (crisps) 192–3, *194*
    tripe & chickpea gratinata 268, *269*
tomatoes, green (unripe)
    blackened pork tenderloin with chow-chow 148, *149*
tomatoes, sun-dried
    smoked tomato 'nduja 54, *55*
tonnato, avocado 115
torques 34
tortillas: Spanish tortilla but like a Reuben *246*, 247
Touhy, Michael 108
Trader Vic's 100
TransparentSea Farm 154
tri-tip
    black sugar tri-tip *92*, 93
tripe
    tripe & chickpea gratinata 268, *269*
tropical sauce 224–5, *226*
truffles
    morel and truffle stuffing *233*, 234–5
    truffle sauce *233*, 234–5
    wedding terrine 40–1, *42*
Tuscan kale
    chopped antipasto salad *110*, 111
two-ingredient applesauce 306

U
Ubuntu 9, 247
Umansky, Jeremy 310
uni tongues
    beef carpaccio ZZ's style *242*, 243
United Nations chili mix 308, *309*

V
veal sweetbreads
    "popcorn" sweetbreads with fermented peppercorn sauce *273*, 274–5
    sweetbreads a la Jocko's 270–1, *272*
vermouth
    Lonnie's quail *233*, 234–5
Vernors "Old School" pork collar roast 156–7, *158*
vinegar
    blackened pork tenderloin with chow-chow 148, *149*
    corned beef tongue 66, *67*
    dill pickles 312
    giardiniera 316
    mushroom Worcestershire 319

Ohio peppers 317
    pickled cornichons 314, *315*
    pickled mustard seeds 318

W
waffled corned beef hash 248, *249*
walnuts
    chicken liver cannoli with hoshigaki & red walnut *181*, 182–3
    duck neck sausage, green walnuts & apples *215*, 216–17
Waxman, Jonathan 20
wedding terrine 40–1, *42*
whey
    chicken scrapple 208–11, *209*, *210*
whipped lardo with flowers 98, *99*
white wine
    banana shank & banana stew with sweet potato *279*, 280–1
    beef pelmeni stroganoff 258–60, *261*
    bone marrow, miso-creamed spinach & artichoke flower 276–7, *278*
    braised rabbit legs Provençal 192–3, *194*
    chicken paprikash with board-cut spaetzle *189*, 190–1
    "popcorn" sweetbreads with fermented peppercorn sauce *273*, 274–5
wild ramp cotechino 78, *79*
Worcestershire, mushroom 319

Y
yogurt
    chicken cutlets with date, almond & yogurt 230–1, *232*
    garlic-mint yogurt 256, *257*
    Merguez sausage with loaded eggplant *254*, 255
    saffron yogurt 294–7, *295*, *296*
    yogurt dipping sauce 198, *199*
yuba (tofu skin)
    beef tendon, tofu, sweet chili & almond 244, *245*
yuzu
    fried pork trotter, ginger shoots & yuzu 132–4, *135*
    yuzu kosho sauce 302

Z
Zuni 160
ZZ's Clam Bar 243

Sources

Andy's Orchard
www.andysorchard.com
Fresh fruits

Anson Mills
www.ansonmills.com
Farro
Hominy
Polenta

BDDW
www.bddw.com
Furniture, Art & Objects

Chefs Press
www.chefspress.com
Steel Cooking Weights

Craft Butchers' Pantry
www.butcherspantry.com
Bactoferm
Twine
Sausage Pricker
Meat Grinders/Stuffers
Casings

Frog Hollow Farm
www.froghollow.com
Banana Vinegar

Girl & Dug
www.girlndug.com
Fresh Cornichons
Specialty Vegetables

Hawkins New York
www.hawkinsnewyork.com
Netherton Foundry Spun Iron Cookware

Heath Ceramics
www.heathceramics.com
Dinnerware & Décor

La Boite Spices
www.laboiteny.com
Smoked Cinnamon
Spices
Spice Blends

The Japanese Pantry
www.thejapanesepantry.com
Creamy Koji
Black Vinegar
White Soy

JB Prince
www.jbprince.com
Pullman Molds

Liberty Ducks
www.libertyducks.com
Organic Duck Products

Made In
www.madeincookware.com
Stainless Steel & Cast-Iron Cookware (Rondeaus)

The Matzo Project
www.matzoproject.com
Matzo
Matzo Meal
Matzo Ball Mix

Meiji Tofu
www.meijitofu.com
Kumidashi Tofu

Rancho Gordo
www.ranchogordo.com
Beans
Prepared Hominy

Reluctant Trading
www.reluctanttrading.com
Salted Pepperberries
Spices

Sheldon Ceramics
www.sheldonceramics.com
Dinnerware & Décor

Smithey Ironworks
www.smithey.com
Cast-Iron & Carbon Steel Cookware

Staub
www.staub-cookware.com
Terrine Molds
Dutch Ovens

Tehachapi Grain Project
www.tehachapigrainproject.org
Eight Row Flint Corn Polenta

Victorinox
www.victorinox.com
Poultry Shears

Ratios

Country Pâté (page 38)
Pork shoulder 100%
Pork jowl 66%
Chicken livers 52%
Egg 22%
Madeira 17%
Cream 17%
Shallot 9%
Guanciale 25%
Parsley 2%
Kosher salt 4%
Curing salt #1 1%
Black pepper 1%
Dextrose .5%
Thyme .5%
Fox spice .5%

Wedding Terrine (page 40)
Foie gras
Fattened duck/goose liver 100%
Cognac 13%
Kosher salt 1.75%
Granulated sugar .5%
Curing salt #1 1%
White pepper 1%
Terrine
Pork shoulder 100%
Pork fatback 25%
Stock 50%
Kosher salt 1.75%
Curing salt #1 .33%
Rosemary .5%
Black winter truffles 10%

Lardo (page 48)
Pork fatback 100%
Granulated sugar 4%
Kosher salt 3%
Rosemary 1.5%
Curing salt #2 .5%
Black peppercorns .5%

Guanciale (page 52)
Pork jowl 100%
Granulated sugar 4%
Kosher salt 3%
Black peppercorns 1%
Curing salt #2 .5%
Dried oregano .5%

Smoked Tomato 'Nduja (page 54)
Pork belly 100%
Sweet Calabrian chili powder 6.5%
Smoked sun-dried tomatoes 5%
Hot Calabrian chili powder 3.5%
Kosher salt 3%
Granulated sugar 2%
Fennel seed 1.75%
Curing salt #2 .5%

Ohio City Provision's Lamb Shawarma (page 62)
Lamb shoulder 100%
Lamb kidney fat 25%
White onion 27%
Garlic 1%
Olive oil .5%
Kosher salt 2%
Black pepper 1%
Dried oregano .75%

Pancetta Cotto (page 69)
Pork belly 100%
Kosher salt 2.5%
Pepper 1%
Juniper 1%
Brown sugar 1%
Curing salt #1 .25%
Nutmeg .25%

Mushroom Worcestershire (page 319)
Tamari 100%
Malt vinegar 66%
Mushroom scraps 50%
Molasses 33%
Tamarind paste 9%
Black garlic 5%
Koji sauce 4%

About the Authors

Jeremy Fox worked at restaurants across the US and Europe, including Rubicon in San Francisco, and staging at De Snippe in Belgium, then at Restaurant Gordon Ramsay and Fergus Henderson's iconic nose-to-tail restaurant, St. John, in London. While in California, he opened Ubuntu and was voted a "Best New Chef" by Food & Wine, plus awarded the first Michelin star for a vegetarian restaurant. A three-year break followed, chronicled in the global bestseller, *On Vegetables*, and he is now chef/owner of Rustic Canyon and Birdie G's in Santa Monica.

Rachael Sheridan is married to Jeremy Fox and is a writer and actress.

Acknowledgments

I would like to acknowledge the following people...

Jim Sullivan: You really fought for this and I'm glad you did. Loved working with you. Let's do it again.

Emily Takoudes: Thank you for giving me a chance for round 2. Phaidon for life, or as long as you're there.

Rachel Malig: You're a saint for having to deal with me.

The teams of Birdie G's & Rustic Canyon: I am so grateful for you all covering me while this was being made.

My parents: Thank you for actually pushing me into cooking long before it was fashionable or respectable.

Rachael Sheridan: The world's best co-author. This book would not exist without you, on many levels. I love you forever.

Birdie Fox: Mom & Dad made another thing! And we love you to infinity plus one more any number you say.

Phaidon Press Limited
2 Cooperage Yard
London E15 2QR

Phaidon Press Inc.
111 Broadway
New York, NY 10006

Phaidon SARL
55, rue Traversière
75012 Paris

phaidon.com

First published 2025
©2025 Phaidon Press Limited

ISBN 978 1 83729 086 4
ISBN 978 1 83729 118 2 (signed edition)

A CIP catalogue record for this book is available from the British Library and the Library of Congress.

All rights reserved. No part of this publication may be reproduced, stored in a retrieval system or transmitted, in any form or by any means, electronic, mechanical, photocopying, recording or otherwise, without the written permission of Phaidon Press Limited.

Commissioning Editor: Emily Takoudes
Project Editor: Rachel Malig
Designer: Lacasta Design
Production Controller: Gary Hayes
Photography: Jim Sullivan

Printed in China

The publisher would like to thank Evelyn Battaglia, Vanessa Bird, João Mota, Ellie Smith, Tracey Smith, and Kathy Steer for their contributions to the book.

Quote on page 191 from *When Harry Met Sally*; quote on page 300 from *National Lampoon's Vacation*.

Recipe Notes

Individual vegetables and fruits, such as onions and apples, are assumed to be medium, unless otherwise specified.

Exercise a high level of caution when following recipes involving any potentially hazardous activity, including the use of high temperatures, open flames and when deep-frying. In particular, when deep-frying add food carefully to avoid splashing, wear long sleeves, and never leave the pan unattended.

Cooking times are for guidance only. If using a fan (convection) oven, follow the manufacturer's instructions concerning the oven temperatures.

All herbs, shoots, flowers, and leaves should be picked fresh from a clean source. Do exercise caution when foraging for ingredients, which should only be eaten if an expert has deemed them safe to eat. In particular, do not gather wild mushrooms yourself before seeking the advice of an expert who has confirmed their suitability for human consumption. As some species of mushrooms have been known to cause allergic reaction and illness, do take extra care when cooking and eating mushrooms and do seek immediate medical help if you experience a reaction after preparing or eating them.

Exercise caution when making fermented products, ensuring all equipment is spotlessly clean, and seek expert advice if in any doubt.

When no quantity is specified, for example of oils, salts, and herbs used for finishing dishes, quantities are discretionary and flexible

All spoon and cup measurements are level, unless otherwise stated. 1 teaspoon = 5 ml; 1 tablespoon = 15 ml. Australian standard tablespoons are 20 ml, so Australian readers are advised to use 3 teaspoons in place of 1 tablespoon when measuring small quantities.

Cup, metric, and imperial measurements are used in this book. Follow one set of measurements throughout, not a mixture, as they are not interchangeable.